My Years in Nanking

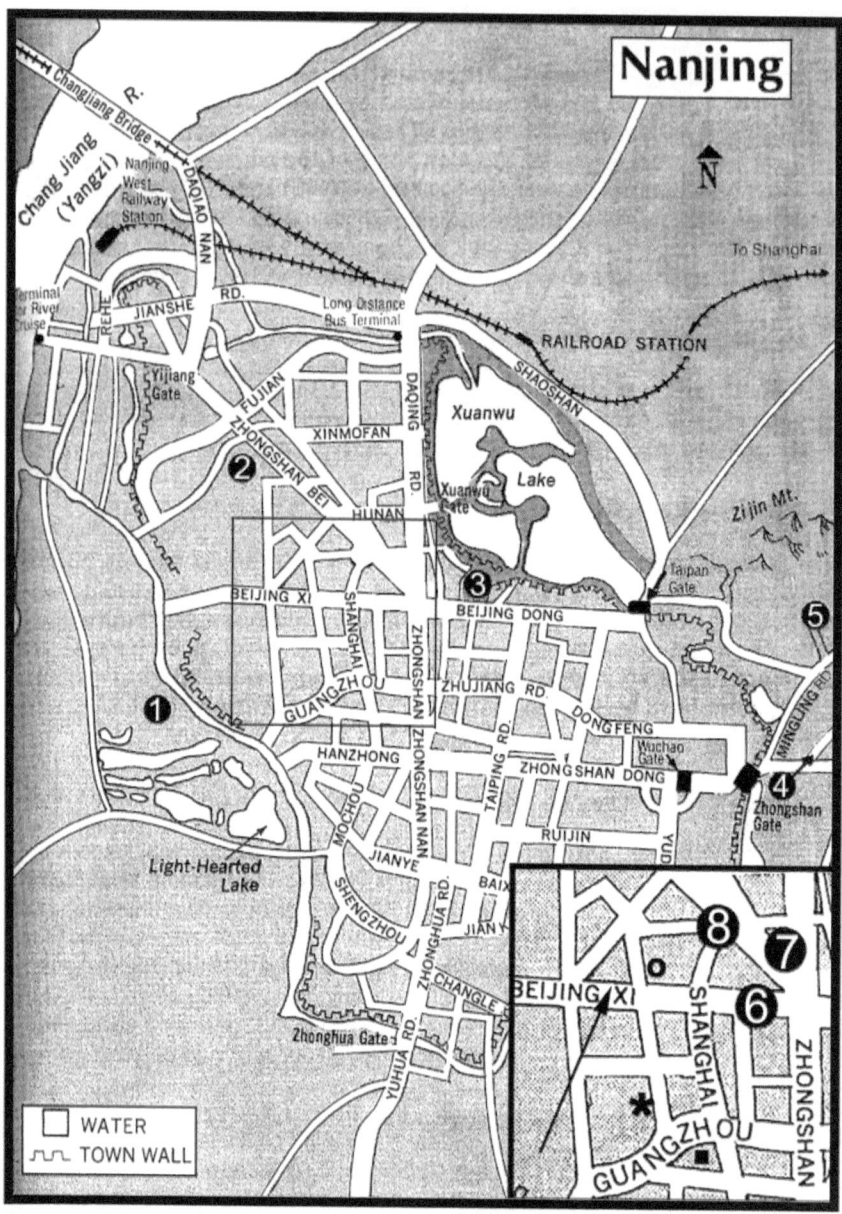

Map of Nanjing. *1,* Nanking-Massacre Memorial Park; *2,* Former U.S. Officers Club; *3,* Academia Sinica Nanjing Institute of Geology and Palaeontology; *4,* Sun Yat-sen Tomb; *5,* Tann Mu (tomb of the Republlic of China's 1st Prime Minister Tann Yen-kai). *INSET: 1937-38 Nanking Safety Zone.* **O**, Safety Zone Headquarters; **Arrow,** "White House," the mayor's residence, 38 Peiping Rd (now renamed Beijing Xi Rd); ✱, Ginling Women College; ■, the Author's home at Wutai San; *6,* Drum Tower; *7,* Bell Tower; *8,* Nanking University.

My Years in Nanking

Reminiscences of Inyeening Shen

Inyeening Shen

Jane Shen Schopf, Editor

iUniverse, Inc.
New York   Bloomington

My Years in Nanking
Reminiscences of Inyeening Shen

Copyright © 2009 Jane Shen Schopf

iUniverse books may be ordered through booksellers or by contacting:

iUniverse
1663 Liberty Drive
Bloomington, IN 47403
www.iuniverse.com
1-800-Authors (1-800-288-4677)

ISBN: 978-1-4401-2256-9 (pbk)
ISBN: 978-1-4401-2258-3 (cloth)
ISBN: 978-1-4401-2257-6 (ebk)

Printed in the United States of America

iUniverse rev. date: 6/17/09

In, Y. (1935, 1st ed; 1938, 2nd ed) Diary from
Europe, Zhong-hua Publ., Shanghai, China

In, Y. (1971) A Journey of Seventy Days, vol I & II, Biographical
Literary Publ. (Zhuengji Wenxue), Taipei, Taiwan, 327 pp.

Shen, I. (1985) Shen Inyeening Autobiography, Biographical
Literary (Zhuangji Wenxue), Taipei, Taiwan, 373 pp.

CONTENTS

This volume by author Inyeening Shen was completed in 1954 in Bangkok, Thailand. For a great many years she was reluctant to have these reminiscences published, for fear that her criticism of the corruption pervading the Chinese Nationalist Government would offend the high officials involved. Now ready, the world can learn her views about a pivotal time in the history of her country.

Remarkably talented and an accomplished artist, Inyeening Shen authored books, essays and poetry, became a university professor of Chinese literature, and for her writing was awarded an honorary Doctorate degree. This book is her only work written in English, a personal account of her experiences as the First Lady of China's capital of Nanking from 1946 to 1948. Included here is her "Auto-Bio-Poetry," a beautiful poem recounting the first 42 years of her life that she had been encouraged to write by a leading educator/philosopher/diplomat of modern China, her close family friend Dr. Hu Shih.

To place this work in context, this section records the status of China in 1946 when Inyeening Shen's reminiscences begin—including the role her husband played in the May 4th Student Movement of 1919 that excited the China public before the onset of the Sino-Japanese war, and an account of the 1937-38 Nanking Massacre that set the stage for her arrival as the wife of the Mayor of the city, the nation's new capital. Summarized also are the effects on China of the 1945 Yalta Agreement that brought a close to WWII, a pact regarded by the Chinese as a "great betrayal."

The year was 1946 when China reclaimed Nanking as its capital from the occupying Japanese at the end of the Sino-Japanese war. Nanking had been devastated by the rape and massacre of its citizens. A new feeling of sweet peace filled the city as Nanking's newly installed mayor, Dr. Shen Yi, the author's husband, assumed his post and his family joined him from Shanghai.

By 1948, inflation was rampant. The so-called "rice mob," everyday staples for the people of Nanking, were in short supply; the city's graineries were at a standstill; and Mayor Shen was engulfed by the crisis. Here related are touching and intimate exchanges between the author and her husband, the mayor, about the ongoing turmoil, and a heartfelt account of her "nine-ox-two-tiger" effort ("jiu-niu er-hu") to build, from scratch, their dream house, Villa Sheaffer, on Wutai San.

With Mao Ze-dong's Red Army surging toward its city walls, the fall of Nanking was imminent. The capital was in triple darkness—civil war, winter, and continuous electrical outage. Despite being urged by American-born communist-sympathizers to switch allegiance to Mao's side, in late-December 1948 Mayor Shen resigned. A senior military officer from the Generalissimo's staff took his place. Borrowing words from the Tang poet Li Bai about the city she had come to love, the author laments: "Thou that hast seen six kingdoms pass away [and] called down the dreams of sunset into stone." To her, departure from Nanking was yet another passage in her life.

PROLOGUE

---------- *The map of Nanjing used as the* Frontispiece *of this book provides a view of the city today and shows the location of many of the sites noted in the text.*

A Photographic Atlas *of people, places and events noted in the text is included in the middle section of the book* (Plates 1-10).

Where it has seemed necessary, background remarks and footnotes are provided to clarify and document the text (also see, References).

For Transliterations *current phonetics are provided and the traditional pinyin system is kept in the chapter proper that fits the period of this memoir.*

An Index *section is included at the end.* ----------

My Years in Nanking, Reminiscences of Inyeening Shen is my mother's captivatingly personal and vivid account of tumultuous times in China's not-too-distant past. It records events in the capital city of Nanjing from 1946 through the end of December 1948, after the Nationalist Government had returned to Nanjing from its war capital, Chongqing. These two years encompassed the final days of the reign of the Republic of China on the mainland, a period when my father, Dr. Shen Yi, served as Mayor of Nanjing and Mao Ze-dong's Red Army was relentlessly surging forward. The capital fell to the Communists in the spring of 1949 as the Nationalist Government retreated to Taiwan (*Life Magazine,* 1949; Bodde, 1967; Hsü, 1975).

In 1982, while Mom was packing for a move from California to Maryland, she pulled out a neatly tied package from a wooden chest and thrust it into my arms. This bundle, with its lingering camphor fragrance, was wrapped in pale lavender paper bearing the name of department store in Bangkok, Thailand. On the reverse side of this wrapping she had penned, in large blue letters, "My Two Years in Nanking" (her original title, recast here as *My Years in Nanking, Reminiscences of Inyeening Shen*).

The package from Mom contained her neatly written pages on lined paper bound together with strings by my ever-methodical father. The memoir had been finished in 1954 in Bangkok, after our family had moved there in 1949, and had been stored in a conference folder that bore a seal of the United Nations Economic Commission for Asia and the Far East from my dad's U.N.-ECAFE office. Pencil-written notes and pages on loose sheets, as yet unincorporated, were tucked into a flap of the folder. Mom had published books, essays, and poems in Chinese, but this memoir was her only work in English. She uttered a sigh when she unpacked her manuscript, then quietly asked,

"Would you read my writing and see if this can be published?"

I was pleased that Mom was finally ready to reveal her memoir to me, her family, and the world. Years before, whenever we asked her about publishing this work she would say, "It is not yet time." I am sure her reason was that Dad was still in government service and that she was concerned that her opinions might upset his colleagues and the family of his boss, Generalissimo Chiang Kai-shek (Plate 1; Boorman and Howard, 1967; Boorman and Cheng, 1970).

In late October 2003, the death in New York City of Mme. Chiang Kai-shek (at age 105), the last of the major figures of World War II, was front-page news (Meisler, 1995; Woo, 2003). With Mme. Chiang's passing, I decided that the time had finally come for Mom's Nanjing reminiscences to be prepared for publication. "Madame" (accented on the last syllable, as my mother always intoned when speaking of Mme. Soong Mayling Chiang) and the Madame's family were the very people Mom most feared to offend. Following the death of Mme. Chiang, the only prominent survivor of the Soong clan would be her elderly niece, daughter of her oldest sister, Soong Eiling Kung (Lin, 2000).

It is easy to understand Mom's reluctance to reveal publicly her feelings about the Soongs, an exceedingly powerful and evidently quite ruthless familial tribe. According to the noted investigative reporter Sterling Seagrave (1985), for example, "Unwholesome interest in the Soongs, or less than a religious attitude toward the Chiangs in particular, was enough to jeopardize a journalist's livelihood. Many careers were destroyed and reputations ruined." Seagrave added further, "it was customary for anyone who criticizes the Soong clan to find himself branded a communist sympathizer. The Soongs were so powerful that they could punish anyone who was indiscreet."

Indeed, throughout the mid- to late-1900s the Soongs and their friends and allies of the "China Lobby" cast a steely net that stretched even to the United States. Publishing magnates Henry and Clare Luce, and General Claire Lee Chennault and his wife Anna (Plate 1), of "Flying Tigers" fame, were staunch and powerful allies of the Nationalists (Seagrave, 1985; Lin, 2000), as were many others— journalist Joseph Alsop, diplomat William Bullitt, President Franklin Roosevelt's close aide Tommy Corcoran, and such influential "China Hands" as Congressman Walter Judd (R-MN), Senators William Knowland (R-CA) and Joseph McCarthy (R-WI; Kahn, 1976). Given such powerful backing, the Chiang government was free to wield an iron fist, to work its will on the Chinese people.

As you will find, my Mom's description of her reminscens is vivid, moving and firm, as she ushers her readers into an arena of poignant scenes and her inner thoughts. In places where I became puzzled as I worked over her script, I consulted the autobiographies written by each of my parents (Shen-I, 1985; Shen-Y, 1985). In the two following sections that precede Mom's account, I provide an introduction *About the Author* and a *Historic Foreword* that leads up to the time when this memoir was written.

Chapters. In her memoir, Mom chronicles her struggles as a socially shy but privileged and confidant housewife enmeshed in an alien world in which she often felt ill at ease (*Chapters 3, 4, 7*). A thoughtful and serious person, most comfortable with matters of substance, she was both interested in and knowledgeable about Dad's work, not only in his capacity as mayor of the nation's capital (*Chapter 10*) but in his professional activities as a hydraulic engineer and expert on China's major river systems. In *Chapter 2* she writes about the initial planning for the Yangtze-Gorge Dam, a design for which was first proposed in 1946 by U.S. Bureau of Reclamation engineer Dr. John L. Savage (Plate 1; Fleming, 1946; Kristof, 1993; Tempest, 1995) who, some years later, became guardian "Uncle Jack" to my sister Hwa-hwa and me when we first entered college in the United States.

Dr. Savage, the U.S. high-dam designer was invited to China by my dad on behalf of Chiang Kai-shek's government to discuss Savage's proposed design (Shen, 1974) a project that only now, many decades later, is coming to fruition. Close to completion (Lin et al., 1998; *Reuters*, 2002; Verhovek, 2003), the massive Three Gorges Dam— some 135 meters high and acclaimed to be among China's "top ten" advances in science and technology (*China S&T Newsletter*, 2004) will create—not only the world's largest inland ship channel but the world's greatest hydroelectric power plant, surpassing by threefold the previous record holder, Grand Coulee Dam in the state of Washington (Kristof, 1993).

Among Mom's many roles as First Lady of the Nationalist capital, she had the task of creating aesthetically attractive surroundings for official mayoral functions at our home, the "White House" (*Chapter 3*), so nicknamed by diplomats because of its color, official status, and rounded end-wall (Plate 3). When we first arrived, this house and its surrounding grounds, situated in the "Safety Zone" established during the 1937 Nanking Massacre of the Sino-Japanese war (*Frontispiece*; Chang, 1997; Rabe, 1998), were in disrepair, thoroughly dilapidated. Mom and the many workers she "commanded" as the Mayor's wife, soon put the place in order (*Chapters 3, 4*).

Though Mom dealt easily with the White House residence and its aesthetics, she was not so adept with Mme. Chiang and the Soongs. Official protocol demanded that she have social and professional interactions with the First Lady of China, Mme. Chiang Kai-shek (Plate 6; *Chapters 5, 9*). As she recounts in her memoir, Mom was deeply distressed by the corruption and humiliation that the Soong family had brought to the nation and to the common people ("*lao bai-xing*," see *Transliterations*). President Harry Truman, in his plain speaking-style, referred to the Soong sisters and their relatives as a "den of thieves," asserting that at a very minimum "they stole seven hundred and fifty million dollars out of the thirty-five billion that we sent to Chiang" (Miller, 1984).

In spite of Mom's dismay and the resentment she harbored toward many in Chiang Kai-shek's government, officials she knew to have acquired a habit of redirecting public funds to their own benefit ("*jia-*

gong ji-si"), she nevertheless was fiercely loyal to the Nationalists and held an unwavering disdain for the Communists and their Soviet-inspired upheaval of her country.

In *Chapter 6* Mom provides an intimate glimpse of herself—her upbringing and education by a traditional Buddhist mother; her rebellion against a strident British schoolmarm who had punished her for mistakes in the recitation of scripture; and her open resistance to an arranged marriage that her mother sought to impose on her when she was a girl of just 14. Mom's account of the experiences that led her to embrace Christianity, and of her baptism as a full-grown adult, are vivid and deeply personal.

In *Chapter 7*, *"Friends of Wine and Meat"* (a Chinese equivalent of the English phrase, "fair weather friends"), Mom recounts her discomfort with, and even disdain for some of the foreign dignitaries and their wives whom she encountered, but she speaks warmly of others whom she numbered among her friends. And she also records private meetings between Dad and envoys from the United States: China lobbyist and former U.S. Ambassador to the Soviet Union, William C. Bullitt; President Harry Truman's personal envoy, Lt. General Albert C. Wedemeyer; and the last U.S. Ambassador to the Republic of China on the mainland, John Leighton Stuart, with whom she struck a firm friendship (*Chapter 8*).

Mom's stint as Head of the Nanking Women Work Committee for the civil-war relief effort (*Chapter 9*), a program established under the auspices of Chairman Chiang Kai-shek's New Life Movement and patterned after FDR's New Deal, presented one of the most difficult challenges she had ever faced. When she first journeyed to Nanking in 1947, the faces of China's poverty-stricken farmers and refugees, viewed from the windows of the opulent rail car in which she was riding, had left a deep mark of sorrow and remorse on her conscience (*Chapter 1*).

Though Mom had not the slightest experience in running a governmental organization, she was strongly affected by the inequity she witnessed en route to Nanking. As Head of the Women Work Committee (a position that she did not seek, having been appointed only because she was the wife of Nanking's mayor) she embraced her task with deligence. Soon thereafter, she bravely launched a fund drive to support the Committee's efforts. Despite the fact that her Committee had virtually no tangible assets, by dint of courage and her sheer perseverance she managed to borrow a large sum from a local bank which the Committee used to clothe and feed refugees in the Nanking region. In this horrendous time, she rose to meet the challenge (Plate 10, *Chapter 9*).

Rising still, she single handedly, with Dads' blessing and assist of course, built from scratch a house of their very own, *Villa Sheaffer* on *Wutai San* (Plate 9; *Frontispiece; Chapter 10*).

In the final chapter, "*Farewell Nanking, Fare Well*" (*Chapter 11*) Mom paints a touchingly nostalgic picture of her departure from the capital, a home she had come to love inspite of her many difficulties, the many tests of her human spirit. At the end of her memoir, she appends a poem written by the Tang poet Li Bai which artfully describes her sentiments about the passing of the Nationalist "Dynasty" to which she was so strongly committed. (As much as the Author and her husband loved and longed for their homeland, after their departure from Nanking in 1948 and from China in 1949, neither of them set foot on the China mainland again.)

Chinese Language. Mom's two-page long "*Auto-Bio-Poetry*" (appended at the end of *About the Author*) highlights the first half of her life before and after her time in Nanjing, a poem she wrote at the encouragement of Dr. Hu Shih, an influential educator, philosopher and diplomat, and a long-time friend of my parents who was an official witness at their wedding (Plate 1). This poem serves as a preface to her autobiography (Shen-I, 1985). Years ago, Mom and I would sit face-to-face and recite this poem aloud, she from total recall. Because it was written in classical Chinese, not in the standard plain talk ("*bai-hua*") of today, I made notes on the meanings of the various words and phrases (e.g., "*hua-mei ren*," a phrase meaning husband; "*mu jian bei*," mother met her back, meaning that mother had died). I am deeply moved that Mom and I had such times together, she teaching me the basics of Chinese classical language.

In China, the "tyranny of classics"—the traditional Chinese language that few now have an opportunity to learn—was cast away in the 1920s when the Western-educated but classics-trained Dr. Hu Shih (1891-1962; Plate 1) and his colleagues advocated the use of the more accessible *bai-hua* plain talk. (A *bai-hua* poem translated into English, "*On the Lake*" by Hu Shih, is included at the beginning of *Chapter 2*). Hu's *bai-hua* ushered in the conventions of the Chinese language used today (Hsü, 1975; Fairbank, 1983; Fu, 1984; Roberts, 1999; Elman, 2001). Nevertheless, Hu insisted that the transition to modernity of the Chinese language would not have come so smoothly had it not been aided by the long evolution of Chinese literature (Hu, 1969). In his view, plain talk began to ferment in written Chinese as early as 1800 years ago.

Dr. Hu Shih trained as a scholar of the Chinese classics, he credits two Westerners with his advocacy of *bai-hua*, Thomas Henry Huxley and John Dewey: "The former taught us to doubt when there is inadequate support ... the latter taught us to formulate hypothesis that awaits substantiation" (Hu, 1962). Hu's ideas about the progress of the Chinese language are in accord with Darwin's views of biological evolution (views trumpeted by Huxley, a subject with which Hu was thoroughly acquainted). Hu Shih concluded that rather than representing a devolution of classical Chinese, *bai-hua* is just as beautiful as the classics and is a product of the natural, logical evolution of spoken and written Chinese (Hu, 1962).

Transliterations. Many of the transliterated terms in this memoir are common phrases used by common people. Some are proverbial, so-called ready-made sayings ("*chenyu*") that owe their origin to quotations, lines in a poem, proverbs, puns, and so forth in the Chinese classics (Smith, 1965; *Chenyu* Story, 1980; Zhang, 2000).

According to Chinese scholar Arthur Smith (1965), such "economic" ready-made phrases are "the fruits of the longest experiences expressed in the fewest words ... a generalization condensed into a nutshell ... which goes at once to the mark." Even without the following of a finishing verse or phrase, the meaning of such "arrowy brevity," as Smith (1965) terms it, can be immediately understood. The lack of "kicker," the finale to similar phrases in English, is common in Chinese. As noted by Cranmer-Byng (1928), years ago, "A favorite feature of [such Chinese] verses is the stop short ... only the words stop, while the sense goes on." In times past, such classic phrases were readily understood, both by the well-educated and the common people alike, expressions repeated routinely by storytellers in popular teahouses, particularly in rural villages. Even today, many Chinese use such phrases in daily conversation. The definitions of such transliterated terms and phrases (and, for some, their historical sources) are included in the section on *Transliterations*.

Acknowledgements. Finally, on behalf of my Mom, I want to express my heartfelt gratitude to the many people who helped with this work. First and foremost, I want to thank my rock-solid Dad, Shen Yi, Mom's untiring and loving helpmate. To complete this memoir, I am grateful also to Dad for his Christmas present of 1976 of two volumes of the then newly published "*Ci Hai*" (*Encyclopedia of Phrases*) that have enabled me to learn the meanings and origins of classical Chinese phrases here included in *Transliterations*.

In Bangkok, the loosely bound pages of the memoir were penciled in red by Avis Belt, a Yale music-graduate and our family's English and piano tutor who, with her Thai architect husband, lived next door at Dan Udom. A modest person and a friend of our family, Avis suggested only minor changes. Before this, in Nanjing, Mom enlisted a young engineer, Gu Wen-su to read her work. Gu, a graduate of Shanghai's St. John University and a good friend of my parents and us children, was well versed in English. He spent many Sunday afternoons working with Mom on her writing and, afterward, playing sports with us kids.

Jean Factor Stone (Plate 1), wife and life-long editor of the works of her American biographical novelist husband, Irving Stone (1903-1989; Plate 1), read an earlier version of the reminiscences in 1991. I am grateful for her friendship, her wisdom and her help. Though claiming to be "unable to face a blank page"—as Irving did on a daily basis—Jean was wonderfully gifted at critiquing and organizing the pages of others (including each of Irving's many books). As Jean read Mom's manuscript, she "blued" the pages, suggesting changes in blue-penciled script (a tradition with Irving), and she then read the blued areas aloud with me, by her side, in her Beverly Hills living room (another tradition). After reading the entire manuscript, Jean noted the following on a yellow sheet of paper: "It is good material… can make a publishable book, a good one! But it will take a full effort … What would science or literature be worth without antecedents? … I spent eight solid hours today on your script without taking any time off for lunch … Love, Jean."

Thanks to Jean Stone's suggestions, I become sensitized to relevant passages in books and newspapers on China from the period of Mom's work. Jean noted: "Never do you say what the corruption [of the Nationalists] is except hitting the Soong women" (see, *Chapter 5*). She then handed me a book from her home library, "*The Soong Sisters*" (by Emily Hahn, 1941). This helped me to understand my Mom's reluctance to publish her story, since it was retribution from the Soongs that my mother feared quite deeply (also see, Seagrave, 1985). The diligence and thoroughness of research carried out by the Stones for each of their fifty-some masterful biographical novels (*Lust for Life, Clarence Darrow for the Defense, The Passions of the Mind, The Origin*, and many more, several having been made into blockbuster movies) greatly impressed me as I began preparing Mom's work for publication.

Jean Stone was much taken by Mom's courage, adventure and insight, to her mind a confluence of values and personality of which she strongly approved that was even more bolstered when she noted in the first chapter of the memoir that Mom first journeyed from Shanghai to Nanking on February 27, 1947—February 27th being Jean's birthday.

I thank also Professor Vera Simone (California State University, Fullerton) for having made available to me the various older publications listed in *References* that provide a flavor of China through the eyes of American, British, Chinese and Japanese authors of the time. And I am grateful to Sonya Huang Lee, my schoolmate of the Nanking Ginling Middle School, who sent me material on John L. Savage, the "high dam" Yangtze-Gorge designer. Others, also, deserve my thanks: Cousin Victor Keh, helped by giving me a pocket-sized Chinese pinyin dictionary (*Xin Hua Zidian*, 1982), providing precise modern-day transliterations; my cousin-in-law, Wu Qi and Ginling classmate, Jean Chen, sent me a collection of Chinese books and newspaper clippings on the Three Gorges Dam and Nanking Massacre during the Sino-

Japanese war; and Professor Vladimir Keillis-Borok, a distinguished UCLA geophysicist, gave me suggestions that were absolutely on-the-mark.

Finally, I am grateful to my husband, Professor J. William Schopf, whom I affectionately call "*Lao Xiong*" (elder brother), an award-winning author/editor who at every step of the way has helped immeasurably in my editing of Mom's book.

Most of all, I thank my mother for giving me the privilege of rekindling in me her stories, and the history and endearing memories from her wonderfully rich and adventuresome life.

—J. Shen Schopf, Editor, July 2008, Big Bear City, CA—

ABOUT THE AUTHOR

—Foreword to In Yeening's 1971 volume "Journey of Seventy Days"—

By Author's husband, Shen Yi, translated by J. Shen Schopf, Editor

Journey of Seventy Days *is the second travelogue written by my wife* ("nei ren"), *Yeening. The earlier work,* "Diary from Europe" *(1935, Tsong-hwa Publishing, Shanghai) published—some thirty years ago—recounts our first long journey together, in 1934, which was also our first joint travel abroad. Our first stop on that trip was in Germany where I had a two-fold mission, to attend the 7th International Roads Congress and to participate in a series of experimental field-tests that had been designed by my former doctoral thesis advisor, Herr Professor Dr. Hubert Engels, to investigate aspects of China's planned Yellow River project. Following our time in Germany, we traveled Italy, the Soviet Union, Czechoslovakia, England, France, Switzerland and, for shorter intervals, to The Netherlands, Poland, and the Baltic States.*

Throughout this trip, which took us nearly half a year, Yeening faithfully kept a diary. Shortly after our return my good friend Pan Gong-zhan "caught wind" of the Yeening's trove. A close colleague of mine in the Shanghai Municipal Government, Gong-zhan "Xiong" ("Brother" Gong-zhan) was Chief of the Bureau of Municipal Affairs and Editor-in-Chief of the Morning News, *one of the city's major newspapers. He soon arranged for Yeening's diary to be published as a multipart serial in his newspaper, the manuscripts of which Yeening then collated into a published volume. Her book seems to have been very well received; my friend Tao Sen-yang, for example, has mentioned to me on more than one occasion that his decision to pursue an advanced degree in Germany was stimulated largely by my wife's writings. Though Tao's praise may be a bit overblown, it is nevertheless true that many readers greeted Yeening's diary with considerable enthusiasm[1].*

Now, some thirty years after the publication of her diary, Yeening has prepared yet another major travelogue, "Journey of Seventy Days" *[that recounts her travels through Europe, America, and parts of East*

Asia]. The completion of this volume brings to mind fond memories of my old acquaintance Mr. Zhao Jun-hao, now deceased, who was founding publisher of Free Dialogue ("Zi-you Tan"), the magazine in which this travelogue first appeared.

For many years, beginning in 1960 when our family moved to Taiwan [from Bangkok], Publisher Zhao of the Free Dialogue repeatedly asked me for manuscripts. One day, when he brought up the subject yet again, I was at last able to counter, "Mr. Zhao, I marvel at your "ben-ling" (facility) in at least being able to capture my wife, who has contributed her Journey of Seventy Days to your magazine." Now, after having her travelogue serialized over a period of some two years in issue after issue of Mr. Zhao's Free Dialogue, Yeening has faithfully completed her "Journey." I am deeply pleased to see her manuscript, in its entirety, being published in the Biographical Literary ("Zhuanji Wenxue") New Literature and History series.

In her student-days, Yeening used numerous pen-names to send articles to various journals and newspapers. The love of writing is second nature to her. She has sometimes lamented not being as able to express herself in conversation as easily as she would like. But as soon as she picks up a pen, not only do her words flow like running water over a precipice, she becomes totally and gleefully "inebriated" ("tao-zui") as though she were part of another world ("tian-di"). Such moments are among her happiest. She has great tenacity for thoroughness, time and again reading and re-reading every word, writing and re-writing every sentence.

There can be no doubt that Yeening is a writer gifted with an admirably unique style. In her travelogue, she not only recounts vividly the events of her journey, but she brings forth her sentiment to a scene, her moment of joy or of sorrow, and she is not shy about expressing her personal views on subjects beyond the immediacy of the journey. Her patriotism for her country, and her grievances about how the nation has sometimes failed, are shown on many of her pages. With her great skill and delicate pen she can transform dry events into animated vibrant scenes. And her writing is heart-felt and often poignant as her emotion pours forth, yielding many a tear-smudged page. As I read her work, I quietly noted all this and much more, with admiration and wonderment.

Yeening's credit of my help for her book embarrasses me. Admittedly, I did help in editing some of her writing and copying it onto clean pages, but I completely lack her facility for the use of throbbing words and her ease in the conveyance of resounding sentiments. On the contrary, it is I who must credit Yeening for her helpful attempts to enliven the dryness of my own writing. In short, through our mutual encouragement and love we have treaded our moments of writing together, one of the happiest experiences of our marriage.

Shen Yi, October 17th, 1970, Rio de Janeiro, Brazil

Footnote:
        [1]A popularity of Author's "Diary from Europe" that led to the volume being reprinted in 1938; see References.

Inyeening Shen began writing this memoir more than half a century ago. "*Inyeening*," a combination of "*In*," my mother's maiden name, and "*Yeening*," means "*Echoes-of-Crystalline-Virtuosity*," a name that fits her well, composed of three very complicated characters that in Chinese calligraphy require a total of 55 strokes (Plate 2). Mom began writing this narrative in Nanjing and completed it in Thailand, where our family had moved in 1949 when my dad (Shen Yi) was appointed Chief of the Bureau of Flood Control and Water Resources Development of U.N.-ECAFE, the United Nations Economic Commission for Asia and the Far East (Dag Hammarskjöld Library, 2008).

Upon arrival in Bangkok, Mom quickly settled into the new environment and, while the events chronicled in her manuscript were still fresh in her mind's eye, she plunged into polishing her memoir. Absorbed in her work, she was totally oblivious to the enthusiasm with which we children greeted the grand festivities surrounding the imminent wedding of the King of Siam, Bhumibol Adulyadej (Plate 3).

At the time when Mom began her reminiscences of Nanking in 1946 she was not quite 40. She had a long slender figure (a reflection of her one-quarter Manchu heritage), a beautiful face, and a full head of jet-black hair that she combed upward from her nape (Plate 2). With her delicate features and a skin of porcelain fineness and clarity, she was considered a beauty (*"mei-nu"*; Plate 3), a true Hangzhou lassie (*"gu-niang"*) from a beautiful city known for its beautiful women. Exceptionally talented, she was strong, perceptive, able, and had a deep and easy confidence. True to her name, she possessed an impeccable sense for aesthetics.

Upbringing. Coming from a family that was "musty" with books (*"su-xian ren-jia"*), Mom was initially home-schooled by her mother and then by private tutors in classes held within the family compound. These tutored sessions were attended also by her siblings and cousins (Plate 3) from the clan of five families that lived together under the roof of their beloved grandpa, Qing Administrator-Scholar Ying Bao-shi.

Mom was raised in a feudal family. The attitude was that a girl of a good home (*"da-jia gui-xiu"*) deserved a good husband, not a stressful education. For a proper wife, having a "mindless" demeanor was something of a virtue (*"nu-zi wu-cai bian-shi de"*). And in the world of Mom's youth, wariness of non-Chinese culture was the norm, as had been reflected some years earlier, for example, by the Boxer Rebellion (see, *Historic Foreword*). Western ways were of little consequence and Western education was viewed as vacuous and far from rigorous. Mom's mother (Plate 4) was convinced that no harm would come from sending her little girl to Western schools where she would be kept out of mischief and her mind would not be overly taxed. Her mother placed her first in British schools, in Hangzhou and Shanghai, followed by a high school operated by Christian missionaries.

After her graduation from the Christian academy in Shanghai, Mom's mother prohibited her from further schooling. So, resourceful as she was, Mom secretly began to write articles and essays for publication in newspapers and magazines, under assumed names. Her aim was to earn enough money for a college education. Though her writings together with a few part-time jobs fetched enough money to cover the first two years of college expenses (Shen-I, 1985), her wish to be a university-graduate was never fulfilled.

Though a mother of seven (Plate 3), had Mom been given the

choice she would certainly have preferred not to raise a family. She was the product of an earlier time—when a woman's ambition was suppressed by tradition—an entrenched culture that molded her being and constrained the course of her life.

Marriage. In the final chapter of Dad's autobiography, "*Golden Anniversary: A Remembrance*" (Shen-Y, 1985), he describes his first meeting with Mom. He knew her hometown well and had heard wonderful stories about the beauty of the local maidens. His friends joked that some day he might take a Hangzhou lassie for his wife.

The joking became reality. One autumn evening in 1927, Dad met his "*dui-xiang*" (love-mate), Ms. In, at a party in Shanghai. Their meeting having been arranged by mutual friends Zhao Shu-yong and his wife who were acting as go-betweens "*mei ren.*" The dinner party was small, but the guest list was impressive: the Mayor of Shanghai, General Huang Fu (Dad's brother in-law, a ritual "blood-brother" of Nationalist Commander Chiang Kai-shek); Dad's elder sister (Shen Yi-yun; Plate 2), wife of Huang Fu; and the Chief Councilor to Commander Chiang Kai-shek and Shanghai Mayor-to-be Chang Ch'un and his wife (Plate 1).

Mom knew nothing of the arranged meeting. Dad was nervous with anticipation. Immediately, he was much impressed by her understated but stylish outfit that accentuated her fine figure and flawless complexion. Though he had no chance to exchange conversation with this comely young woman, he felt the satisfaction of stealing an occasional glance. Later, at an informal gathering for the viewing of a night-blooming *Cereus*, Dad was smitten. Attracted by this young lady's beauty and unassuming demeanor, he soon became fixated.

(In Mom's autobiography [Shen-I, 1985], she writes about her own first impressions of Dad, a handsome eligible young bachelor who was Chief of Shanghai's Public Works, whom she and her schoolmates had admired from his photographs in newspapers [Plate 5]. After her first meeting with Dad, Mom was giddy with excitement about his good looks, his scholarly seriousness, and his quiet smiles full of sentiment.)

Soon after the "go-between" party, Dad's elder sister, Mrs. Huang, paid a formal visit to Mom's rather well-to-do parents, Mr. and Mrs.

Ying De-wu (Plate 4). Mrs. Ying became teary when she learned about Dad's childhood, of him having been orphaned at the age of fourteen[1], and she was impressed by his rise to prominence from an educated but exceedingly poor family[2] (Plate 2). She and her husband were much taken by Dad's personal achievements—the Ph.D. degree he had earned some two years earlier in Germany and the status he had already attained in the city government as Chief of Shanghai's Bureau of Public Works. Without hesitation, they agreed to the marriage.

On the very next day (October 27, 1927) after Mrs. Huang's visit, Dad came to call on the Yings. (Years later, Mom re-enacted to us children how Dad presented himself to her parents during this visit. Bowing deeply, he repeatedly stepped back and uttered many heartfelt words of gratitude. He then turned and shook hands with his official go-betweens, Mr. and Mrs. Zhao. Then, finally, with a warm smile he extended his hands to Mom, his newly betrothed, and happily declared, "Let us share our congratulations—*gong-xi, gong-xi*"). A courtship of daily letter exchanges soon followed (Shen-I, 1985), and Mom and Dad were married the following spring, on February 12, 1928 (Plate 4).

Husband. To understand my mom and the reminiscences she records here one must also understand my dad, her Jun-yi (Dad's familial name). Dad's training was in hydraulic engineering (Boorman and Cheng, 1970), and throughout his career he focused his interests on two major rivers in China, the Huang He (Yellow River) and the Zhang Jiang (Long River, known also as the Yangtze).

Advanced Studies. Studies of the two waterways Huang He and Zhang Jiang formed the basis of Dad's doctoral thesis, "*Der Flussbau in China*" (Water Works in China), work accomplished in Dresden, Germany that was supported by a scholarship from the Chinese Ministry of Communications where Dad had held his first job as an office clerk.

Upon arrival in Dresden in 1921, Dad learned to his dismay that university regulations prohibited the award of the Ph.D. degree to students from China unless they first enrolled for another four years in a German university. Undeterred, he pursued his studies with diligence. In fact, he was so determined to succeed in his studies that he purchased and wore a wedding band in order to discourage the distractions presented by the local fräulein. He completed his dissertation in less than four years (Boorman and Cheng, 1970). His mentor, Herr Professor Doctor Hubert Engels, a revered hydraulic authority in Europe, was wonderfully pleased.

Dad informed Herr Engels of the "forbidden rules" of additional schooling-requirement on the Chinese students, of which the professor had had no prior knowledge. Engels was furious. Taking personally this injustice, the professor, together with colleague Prof. Marx Foerster, pleaded with the university authorities on behalf of his charge. Following numerous discussions, the matter was relayed to the Saxony Ministry of Education. After due consideration the Dresden Technischen Hochschule relented and granted an exception, on July15th 1925 awarding Dad, Shen Yi, the degree of Doctor of Philosophy in hydraulic engineering (Shen-Y, 1985). Dad was the only Chinese student, among nine enrolled, who obtained a doctoral degree during this period.

Public Works. Upon returning from abroad, Dad was appointed Chief of the Bureau of Public Works in the Municipal Government of Shanghai where he devoted ten years to the development of greater Shanghai. During this period (1927-37), his Bureau was responsible for overseeing the construction of streets, boulevards, bridges and buildings in preparation for the development of the New Civic Center in the northeastern region of the city (*Chapter 6*). Once completed, the Civic Center was touted by China's Central Government as a shining example of achievement of the goals of the "New-Life Movement" formulated by Chairman Chiang Kai-shek (Wakeman, 1995).

During the war years of 1941-1945, with the able assistance of two former schoolmates of Shanghai Tong-ji University (Plate 2), Dad devoted his attention to developing the northwest hinterland where he served as Chief of the Bureau for the Development of Gansu Water Resources, Forestry and Animal Husbandry, in Lanzhou (Boorman and Cheng, 1970; Shen-Y, 1985).

City Governments. At the end of WWII Dad was first appointed mayor of the port city Dalian (*Chapter 6*) and later the Nationalist capital, Nanking (this reminiscence).

United Nations. In 1949, when the war with Communists interrupted Dad's expertise on the waterworks of China, he accepted appointment to the United Nations, based in Bangkok (*Chapter 11*). In his capacity as Head of U.N's Economic Commission of Asia and the Far East Bureau of Flood Control and Water Resources Development, in 1951, he initiated the Mekong River Project (Wightman, 1963; Jenkins, 1968; Boorman and Cheng, 1970; Shen-Y, 1985; Hori, 2000).

Mekong River Project. This project, designed by Dr. Shen Yi, was to improve the linked waterways of Cambodia, Laos, Thailand and Vietnam, where the Mekong River traverses[3]. Dad enlisted the assistance of experts from Britain, China, France, India, and Thailand (Shen-Y, 1985). Together, they made countless field studies throughout Asia and the Far East (Plate 5; Shen-Y, 1985; Hori, 2000). In an invited address to the Third International Congress of the Association of Asia and West Pacific Economic Reconstruction on the Development of the Mekong River Project, Dad ended his speech saying that it was his *"fond hope that by nurturing a collaborative interest in this shared waterway, common benefits would be reaped and peaceful coexistence might come to pass"* (Shen-Y, 1985).

After an 11-year effort at ECAFE, supported by eleven U.N. member-nations Dad's Mekong River Project came to fruition, establishing a solid footing that to this day continues its firm success (Wightman, 1963; MRC reports, 2003, 2006). Economist Wightman (1963) viewed the Project as "a notable feather in the cap for the Secretariat [U.N.-ECAFE]." In 1960, Dad was happy to hand over care of the project to his friend and colleague Dr. P.T. Tan, a Chinese expert whom he had brought to ECAFE (Jenkins, 1968; Shen-I, 1985). Now, some fifty years later, the project continues still, overseen by the Mekong River Commission (MRC) and funded by the World Bank and a 19-nation partnership (Hori, 2000; MRC Annual Report, 2003, 2006; http:www.mrcmekong.org).

My dad, Dr. Shen Yi, husband of the author of this memoir and—

Father of the Mekong River Project (Boorman and Cheng, 1970) would be—smiling broadly its lasting success.

Nationalist Government. Although to Dad it was a great honor to contribute to the work of the United Nations, he was ill at ease with endless criticism of his Nationalist Chinese Government, by this time established on Taiwan. Being deeply patriotic, he felt that no one had a right to judge his country unless he himself had made an effort to serve on its behalf (*"guo-jia xing-wang pifu you-ze"*). With four of his children having graduated from or entered college, leaving only two more to go, and his financial burdens thus lightened, he felt at ease when he resigned from his senior post at the U.N.

Having only a few years to go at the U.N. Dad could have waited until his retirement age and received a handsome pension, but in 1960, hoping to help his government, he moved his family to Taiwan. In that same year, U.N. Secretary-General Dag Hammarskjöld[4] presented him a formal letter of commendation for his contributions (Plate 6), having in mind particularly the Mekong River Project that Dad had initiated during his tenure and that Hammarskjöld had so approvingly endorsed (Boorman and Cheng, 1970).

Communications and Transport. Upon arrival in Taiwan, Dad became Minister of Communications, heading the same organization in which he held his first job as an office clerk many decades before. In addition to his ministerial duties, he served as a government representative to numerous international conferences (Plate 5; Boorman and Cheng, 1970).

Presidential Advisor and Diplomat. After serving his government for some eight years, Dad's patriotic enthusiasm had faded to frustration[5]. For a short while in 1967 he served as Presidential Advisor to Chiang Kai-shek (Plate 1; Boorman and Cheng, 1970), but soon thereafter he left Taiwan to assume the position of Ambassador to Brazil (Plate 5), a post he held with distinction from 1968 to 1971.

University. Finally, at age 70, Dad retired from public service, easing the transition to full retirement by becoming a Visiting Professor in 1971 at the Technischen Hochschule zu München (now, München

Technical University), where he happily lectured on rivers, dams and international cooperation, subjects dear to his heart.

On September 1, 1980, two years after my parents' 50th Wedding Anniversary (Plate 4) and a month short of Dad's 79th birthday, he succumbed to cancer.

Homemaking. Though Dad did his level-best to back Mom however he could (as we children discovered whenever we tried to play one parent against the other), she rarely needed his help. In fact, at home Mom was very much the leader. She was a remarkably accomplished person and homemaker, even under our unusual living conditions.

As a child, Mom had been taught by her mother how to embroider, sew, knit, mend, and cook—all traits of a good housewife. She tailored and knitted all our clothes (Plate 4); trained the staff and cooks how to prepare and present elaborate banquet dinners; and she showed the household-help how to set a proper banquet table, complete with meticulously crafted floral arrangements. I am sure that Mom never imagined that several of the kitchen staff she trained would one day rise to become acclaimed chefs in Shanghai, Tokyo, Bangkok, and Rio de Janeiro (Shen-Y, 1985).

Having appreciation for the art and aesthetics, Mom designed and supervised house-constructions (Plate 7, *Chico Villa;* Plate 9, *Sheaffer Villa, Chapter 10*); decorated and landscaped our family residence (*Chapter 3*); managed a large household staff (*Chapter 4*); hosted visiting dignitaries at innumerable formal dinners; produced home-grown food for our family; taught the art of sewing and gave piano lessons to her children (Plate 4); provided support and understanding to her overtaxed husband—and even performed Peking-opera entertainment for one of Dad's scientific meetings (Plate 4)—while at the same time, for the sake of her husband's position, she took up chairmanship of the Nanking Women Work Committee, and headed a major relief effort that provided education, food, clothing, blankets and healthcare to countless refugees in the war-torn Nanking area (Plate 10, *Chapter 9*). Plainly put, she was instilled in work etheics and had been gifted with a pair of able hands, "*qiao-shou.*"

War Years. During the war with Japan in the 1940s, Lanzhou was a haven safe from air raids and bombs. Our family spent a peaceful and happy time there during WWII (Plate 7). Mom's skill at making do with Dad's meager government pay had been honed by years of practice. Early on, when our family lived in Lanzhou, Mom perfected ingenious ways to adapt simple and inexpensive local goods ("*tu-chan*") to create a beautiful home.

In the remote hinterland, Lanzhou was far removed from Western influence. Outhouses and buildings made of bricks of straw-and-mud were the norm. Nevertheless, Mom, together with her resourceful brother Ying Jin-san (Plate 3), showed the local workers how to construct a Western-style terrazzo bathtub, toilet, and washbowl which she had installed in our home. And Lanzhou itself, "lying between the snow-capped mountains of Tibet and the Gobi Desert of Mongolia … an historic stopping place for the camel caravans that plied the old East-West Silk Route" (Kahn, 1976), was for our family a tranquil and pleasant outpost. In a poem to her sister Duan (Plate 3), rendered here in English translation, Mom describes her first impressions of the hinterland:

> *Lush green, south fragrance, I've known as home,*
> *New land bare earth, desolately alone.*
> *"Li"* upon li, I traveled to north and west,*
> *Over hills and fields I glance, but where do I find rest?*
> *—A slight breeze whips up a battle of dusts,*
> *Small rains churn down puddles of mud—*
> *In defeat I sigh, yet happiness chimes,*
> *Sweet pears and crispy dates aplenty at harvest time!*

A *li, a Chinese unit of distance, is equivalent to about half a kilometer.

In rural Lanzhou Mom's love for gardening and the raising of fowl (*Chapters 3, 4*) made a great impression on us children. We attentively watched as she carefully penciled on eggs the dates when they'd been laid. When a hen no longer paced about, a sign that it was ready for egg-sitting, Mom made a nest indoors and filled it with straw where she settled the "hen-in-waiting" on a nest of about ten eggs. Soon, we children became skilled in "walking" such hens, taking them out for a daily feeding. On the preordained day of hatching (21 days for chicks, 28 for ducklings), the whole household buzzed with excitement. One by one the hatchlings began to peck at one end of their enclosed chambers, bit by bit tearing open the shell to thrust forth their tiny wet bodies. The most exciting moment came when Mom took up the "*chickwifery*" of eggs that had failed to hatch on time.

Mom began her "midwife" chore by washing her hands and readying a few warm salt-soaked towels. She then made a crack at the large end of each silent egg, and located the beak of a little chick within. After a few moments, a black beady eye would peer out from the shell and, looking up at the huge alien creature above, the tiny bird would recoil and squeak with surprise. We children stomped and cheered. Mom then placed the egg and its not-yet-fully-emerged chick in a basket under a lamp and covered it with salted towels. Occasionally she would help the little wet body emerge by peeling back the shell a little at a time, a process that could take hours. During such excitement, we children sat around the lamp watching with wide-eyed amazement, often keeping vigil into the wee hours of the night.

(These lessons, imprinted on me so many years ago, later proved useful when I raised ducklings myself in Downers Grove a suburb of Chicago and copied Mom's role for my own "*duckwifery*"). I imagine that Mom had learned these magical tricks from her bird-loving father[6], my grandpa (Plate 4).

Accomplishments. Mom's second nature in literature led her to writing poetry, essays and books[7]. In her *Auto-Bio-Poetry* (Shen-I, 1985) an autobiographical poem appended at the end of this section that recounts the first four decades of her life, she gives a glimpse of her upbringing as a well-bred cloistered young woman. Like most Chinese women of the time she lacked a college education, yet in today's world she would have been a professional, no doubt a writer or painter, for even in her youth she showed a striking ability for stirring writing and fluid artistry (Plate 2). A much-admired author, she was adventuresome, independent, and outspoken (see, *Chapters 4, 5, 9;* In, 1935).

Indeed, in Mom's travel journal, *Journey of Seventy Days* (In, 1971), she was not the least timid in expressing her views as to the impropriety of "test tube" babies and the incursion of science into human reproduction (matters even today, in an age of stem-cell research, that are hotly debated). Serious and thoughtful, her journal also vividly recounts her tour of the nuclear reactor facility at Argonne National Laboratory near Chicago and the details she learned about the crucial moment when Enrico Fermi and his Manhattan Project group achieved the self-sustaining nuclear reaction that ushered in the atomic age.

In 1954 and after seeing each of her four elder daughters entered college, Mom decided to cash-in on a promise for her continued education that Dad had made before their marriage (Shen-Y, 1985). While Dad stayed behind, she and the two youngest children came to the United States[8] where Mom enrolled in the English Department of the University of Oregon. All of us children were terrifically impressed by her pluck and her obvious thirst for knowledge. Finally, after so many years, Mom had become a "Betty Coed" (Plate 2)! I well remember that in Bangkok and during these college days she kept a little book in which she diligently jotted down various particularly interesting English words and phrases that she had not heard before (such as, "at sea," "ill at ease," "running riot," "studied disorder" and many others) some of which she later inserted, where appropriate, into her memoir.

Despite Mom's desires for higher education, her life continued to be filled with family obligations and social duties and she was not able to complete her college degree. This "deficiency," a lack that she felt deeply, was more than made up for in later years when she was appointed Professor of Chinese Literature at the Chinese Istitute of Culture in Taipei and received from that institute an honorary degree of Doctor of Philosophy (Plate 2). My sisters, brother and I were thrilled, telling her that an honorary doctorate means far more than a standard one. The titles that have been bestowed on Mom—Professor, Dr., Author, Essayist and Poet—are all richly deserved.

Mom also pursued the art of Chinese brush painting under the tutelage of the famous Chinese Grandmaster Chang Ta-ch'ien (Boorman and Howard, 1967). Mom's painting, *White Sacred Lotus* (Plate 2), was highly lauded by the Grandmaster who admiringly autographed the painting and penned the phrase " *The essence of scholarship is purity.*"

Grandmaster Chang, Mom's art teacher, was known throughout China, noted particularly for his hundreds of copies of the Dun-huang Cave Paintings[9] (Sun, 1992), many commissioned as early as the Tang Dynasty (618-907 AD) by rich merchants as tributes to Lord Buddha to insure their safe journey along vast stretches of the East-West Silk Route. During an exhibition of his paintings in Paris, Chang met the Grandmaster of the Western world, Pablo Picasso. Picasso invited him to his villa in southern France. After this "East-West" encounter, it is said that Chang's "creative talent broke free and soared" (Sullivan, 1999). But even as Chang's fame spread to the West, the time Mom now devoted to painting began to wan.

Mom's plight is aptly captured by an old Chinese adage about choosing between two highly coveted banquet delicacies, bear paws or shark's fin (*"xiong-zhang huo yu-chi"*). She reluctantly placed aside one of her great loves, her brushes, and chose the other, her pen.

Later Years. Though we children never really knew Mom's age, we were told that she was born in the "Year of the Sheep[10]". In China, farm animals such as sheep, horses, roosters and boars are symbolic signs of the year of one's birth; for example, 2008 is the Year of the Rat; 2009, the Year of the Ox. According to Chinese lore, Sheep is not a preferred sign for girls—so Mom simply changed the year of her birth to that of the Horse. (Later, after she had given birth to two "sheep" of her own and spurred by the notion that a family having three sheep was said to be especially peaceful and prosperous, *"san-yang kai-tai,"* she changed her birth year back to that of the sheep.)

In 1990, at (what I believe to be) the age of 82, Mom broke both hips and had difficulty walking. She now needed constant attention, so we moved her into a board-and-care home in Los Angeles. Two years later, she was diagnosed as having suffered a spate of so-called ministrokes. Her physician, Dr. Wang, promptly prescribed baby aspirin.

Soon, however, Mom's memory became faulty as she began to erase layer upon layer of faces and events from her past. Though she could then not remember the names of her 10 grandchildren (Plates 4, 7), she was still able to recite with gusto the poems she had written some 50 years earlier. And she entertained us at family dinners by reciting verses taught her by her mother (Plate 4) that in her youth she had memorized from the classic volume "*Tang-si San-bai Shou*"(*300 Poems of Tang*).

Settling into a new surrounding, Mom amused herself by reading repeatedly, cover to cover, her dog-eared copies of the autobiographies that she and Dad had written (Shen-I, 1985; Shen-Y, 1985). She remained sensitive and feisty, and she cried sorrowfully when she read her own narratives about her favorite grandfather, Ying Bao-shi[11] (1821-1890), a high official and scholar during the Qing Dynasty who had died before she was born. She was particularly fond of the passages she had written about her grandpa's heart-felt friendship with his trusted colleague Zeng Guo-fan (1811-1872; Fu 1984), a scholar and senior military and provincial official (Shen-I, 1985; Elman 2001). But, reading still from her own narrative, she became outraged at the injustice and jealousy inflicted upon grandpa Ying by another famous Qing statesman, Li Hong-zhang (1823-1901; Fu, 1984; Shen-I, 1985; Roberts, 1999; Elman 2001).

Mom preferred solitude when she was young. At the boarding house, she reverted to this solitary lifestyle, often opting not to leave her room even for meals in the dining commons. She preferred to see no one but her children. Her one-room world was a large, modern, pastel-colored chamber filled daily with fresh flowers and having a view of a handsome tree and its fluttering green foliage just beyond her windows. Whenever we children inquired about her day-to-day life, she would reply, "I've been writing." (She hadn't, of course, but writing had been her love and her life, and she wanted us to know that she was still able.)

Mom always had an explosive temper, having been spoiled by her father (Plate 4) when she was a little girl. One day in 1992 it came to the fore, when she had a tiff with a difficult neighbor. Returning from a stroll in the hallway, she had become confused as to which room was her own. She settled into the room next door, where she soon became upset by the unfamiliar surroundings. The real occupant returned and less than friendly words were exchanged. The neighbor was right. Mom was wrong. We now had to find her a new home. Fortunately, within a few days we found an even more aesthetically pleasing facility, Bentley

House in West Los Angeles. Unlike the large board-and-care home where she had lodged before, this home had only five elderly residents, each provided with her/his own bed and bathroom.

At first, Mom still preferred to stay in her room, but I was glad to see that within only a few weeks she became sociable, congenial and obviously more happy (Plate 7) in these new surroundings. She seemed to have reverted to the docile manners her mother had taught her as a child. Endearingly she called Ron, the owner of the facility, "Papa," and everyone in the house liked her. She took her meals in the dining room with her housemates, and chatted and watched television with them, and she even let the caregivers help her with her daily bath. Mom was happy. One of her housemates, Ruben, commented to me about how fortunate we children were to have such a cultured mother, and another, Morris (Plate 7), became especially fond of Mom—they sat side-by-side, sometimes holding hands, as she would share with him her lunch and dinner.

Except for her faulty memory, Mom was healthy in all respects until her death. She had a wonderful life, passing on December 29, 1999.

When I first began to help Mom with this manuscript, we worked happily together side by side. Now, as I finish this section of her book and find that I have to refer to her in the past tense, I am reminded all too sadly that my mother is no more.

Auto-Bio-Poetry

"Sha-long Xing" (Journey in a Netted Cage[12], from Childhood to 42nd Birthday)

(Shen-I, 1985; translation by J. Shen Schopf, Editor)

[Arrival in Siam]

Why this travel I know not, traded Xi-hu[13] for Bangkok?
A steamy city of stifling clime, day into night toiled body and mind.

No bamboo shades or lotus breeze, but floating
melon and broken rhizome teased.
On slanting sunbeams a thousand memories
swayed, bygone is just a yesterday.

[Early Childhood - Grandpa's Hangzhou Homestead]

Shi Yuan[11] thirty years ago, high towers, books full, who's now to behold?
Deep gardens prismatic flowers, long halls
and playgrounds children's hour.
Goldfish fondled in Yaoyue Ting[14], bird fights in front of Anya Tang[14].
In Saode Fen Xiang[14] classes began, by Douhua
Shuyu[14] embroidery sapient.
In Shediao Guan[14] ancestral volumes piled, tall
scrolls of thousands neatly filed.
Xiang-xue Lu[14] with snow and cherry bloom', in
Lufei Hongsou[14] Grandpa's papers loomed.
Double-Eyed Well[14] in a deep citrus grove, by
foothill watched Father[9] let birds go.
Up River Ting[14] steeply soar', a nestled flock
awakened by wind chimes' roar.
Twin Orm' twin brace Sheying Guan[14], pine,
plum and bamboo cuddly entwine.
Welcoming New Year with joyous hoots, again
and again gongs, lanterns and flutes.
By Nan Xuan windows sat boys and girls,
books and history teachers drilled.
"Lung-lung" recitation boomed across the court,
children savored all that was taught.
By school end moon beam already high, sweet
Elaeag' permeated Shouxuan Tai[14].

[From Hangzhou to Shanghai]

Peaceful months and years fled by, prosperity
and poverty in candle flames flied.
Resounding drumbeats quivered sky and earth
helpless generals wept their men in dirt.
Chaos joined from summer to winter, loomed
then wanned Shi Yuan's color.
Flowers bloom flowers fade have no scheme, the
sickened river turned to a red stream.

Cloud-piercing towers and horses and cart', but
why so many blue-eyes in Western garb?
Recalling Grandpa's hometown deed', peace
spread schools built, for those who need.
Great Hall[15] built by grateful citizens, each spring
and fall of solemn remembrance.
Number-two brother ignorant of history, mused
by its common name mystery.

[Schooling, Marriage, Sino Japanese War]

Too young to know ancestral feats, yet loved
the pages of their historic deeds.
Parent[16] taught girls to surpass boys, a lone
kernel[17] un-husked a family's joy.
At seven, books, classics, and rhymes begot, forever
indebted to the mother who taught.
Entered Jinshi Yuan[18] at age fourteen, graduated
Muer Tang[18] by double ten.
Wondrous suitors a maiden sought, up from the crowd a scholar brought.
Admiration bonded hearts embraced, notes
exchanged, and promise made.
At Twenty-and-one came repeated prods, as
spring returned a nuptial nod.
Winsome mate likens a sibling bond, elbow-to-elbow we strode on.
Warm sun fragrant on spring breeze rolled, years
and months of springtime dazzlingly unfold.
Angelic youth knew no sorrow, rapture, then, pain, soon followed.
First son brought bliss in a perfect year, a
flowering Cereus[19] soon disappear'.
On blushed bloom Mother met her back, Japanese
invasion, an autumn attack.
Grief upon sorrow came close to hand, enemy brutality pillaged the land.
Eight long years, a bitter war, cold peace fell and calm soon tore.

[Civil War]

Home again years of ten, roiling waters showed no pity on gray tress ran.
Watching children in a long line came, bemoaned
our "green spring[20]" not again.
Prosperous landscapes hurried by, torturous
robbers heaved earth and sky.

Red flames glowed and red blood flowed,
innocent lambs piled high and cold.
Sun-moon dimmed as goblins hovered, beauty capsized on hills and river.

[Bangkok]

Gone from home another winter and spring,
faint hope fades on homecoming.
A wandering swallow has lost her nest
everywhere's home nowhere finds rest.
Coco' breeze and 'nana palms though tranquil, a floating cloud
aimlessly drifts in a futile woe.
Yet shadows freshen on a new grass green,
rainbow dances on a sunset scene.
Home gate arched on a small bridge-path,
a cozy studio beautifully lathed.
Three-sided screens and savory air, a room built upon a loving affair[21].
Birds rest silent in warm soft breeze, in writing
in painting the hot air ease'.
With hope these lines may see the world, at DaFeng[22]
savor the paintbrush swirl.
Happiness bounces from earth to sky a smile lifts clouds of weary pride.
Plenty of riches have come my way, ancestral
gifts, silken clothes, and food in jade[23].

[Husband]

Heart-to-heart with painter-of-the-brows, clean and
tall he stood, above the worldly crowds.
Shanghai municipal in ten years built[24], at
Gansu[25] another four years fulfilled.
Dams[26] and waterways in Northwest-land, thirst
quenched for men, animals and plant'.
In peace anointed Head of Capital new[27], a big
scene changed after years of two.
Tossed own interests to serve the World[28], on
four-river bends[29] success unfurled.
Mekong waters full and flow, a project accomplished All Eyes glow[30].
Trips on trips, both east and west, boundaries
dissolved conflicts found rest.
With United effort ambition capped, sweet dews on grasses richly tapped.
In bitter, in sweet, on each the other leaned,

children found joy in books they gleaned.
Ambition fades as bodies aged, yet happily
hand-in-hand thoroughly engaged.
Lovely hues adorn the crest of autumn, to East[31]
bereft, an arching chrysanthemum[32].

Footnotes:

[1]In near-desolation, the author's husband, Shen Yi, watched with envy during the various school-breaks when his schoolmates returned home, while he remained behind. Being exceedingly poor, in the winters he ate cold dumplings for lunch, warmed under his arms. Such hardships instilled in him a determination to excel.

In 1916, at the age of 15, Shen Yi was admitted, with a full scholarship, to Shanghai's German-run Tong-Ji University of Medicine and Engineering (Deutsche Medizin und Ingenieurschule; Plate 2), from which he graduated at the age of 19. Three years later he traveled to Dresden, Germany for advanced studies (Plate 5), where at the age of 25 he obtained his doctorate degree in hydraulic engineering from the Dresden Technischen Hochschule (Boorman and Cheng, 1970; Shen-Y, 1985).

[2]In 1901 at the age of 32, Shen Bing-jun (1869-1915; Plate 2)—father of the author's husband, Shen Yi—achieved, by passing a Qing Dynasty regional examination, the title of Exalted Scholar, "Ju-ren" (Fu, 1984; Shen-Y, 1985; Elman, 2001). Later, in 1914, he was Lead Editor of the first Chinese New Dictionary ("Xin Zidian"), published in Shanghai (Shen-Y, 1985).

Shen Yi's mother, Keh Jin-chen (1875-1915; Plate 2), was a selfless, progressive, generous, and adventurous woman of exceptional scholarship (Shen-Y, 1985). As Shen Yi phrased it, "When others give, others still have. When Mother gives, she keeps none."

[3]In 2009 the editor and her youngest sister, Lan-lan, during a trip to the northern tip of Thailand, personally witnessed the muddy Mekong River at the Golden Triangle, bordering Thailand, Laos and Burma Their dad, Dr. Shen Yi, "Father of the Mekong River Project" initiated this river work more than half a century ago, in 1951, under the auspieces of the UN-ECAFE (Burma not being part of the U.N. project).

[4]According to a Gallup Poll of the time, when Dag Hammarskjöld (Plate 5) was Secretary General, the United Nations was favored by some 60% of Americans, the "Golden Age" of the U.N. When on the tenth anniversary

of its founding, in 1955, Hammarskjöld's picture graced the cover of the October issue of Time Magazine.

[5]In the Epilogue of the author's autobiography (Shen-I, 1985), she indicates that her husband, Shen Yi, had written a section for his autobiography (Shen-Y, 1985) that he withheld from publication. Author's children learned later that this section recorded the "backroom story" of his departure from the Ministry and his appointment as Advisor to President Chiang Kai-shek (Boorman and Cheng, 1970). During Yi's eight years in the Ministry, he had become increasingly displeased with the in-fighting and jealousy among Chiang's top aides, and although President Chiang held him in especially high regard he relinquished his post of Presidential Advisor to avoid these un-pleasantries. Directly thereafter, in 1968, Shen Yi assumed the position of Ambassador of the Republic of China to Brazil (Plate 5; Boorman and Cheng, 1970).

[6]The author's father, Ying De-wu (1884-1969; Plate 4), the youngest of five sons, was a colorful person, an outdoorsman and lover of adventurous sports. A skilled motor-cyclist whose daring rivaled that of today's skate-boarders, he was locally famous for being able to mount his bike with a run and a jump, and then at high speed race up the vertical city wall and quickly back down to the starting point, ending upright and motionless. A flyer of huge kites emblazoned with intricate designs—a long meandering centipede with its swaying segmented body being one of his grandchildren's favorites—he also raised homing-pigeons and birds which he taught to talk, to sing new songs, and to fight (Shen-I, 1985).

[7]The author's major works include *Diary from Europe, Journey of Seventy Days, Shen Inyeening Autobiography*, and volumous essays in Biographical Literary (see, References).

[8]During her college days at the University of Oregon (while her husband, Yi, remained in Bangkok), the author rented a lovely little house on 2062 Orchard Street in Eugene. For a year or so this house became the home for her U.S. family, where she spent a summer and in which her family celebrated a Thanksgiving and a Christmas holiday. At the University (Plate 2), she was delighted to become a schoolmate of her eldest daughter, Hwa-hwa.

[9]The Dun-huang Cave paintings in Gansu Province, covering 45,000 square meters of wall-space in 492 caves, date from as early as the Tang Dynasty (618-907 AD) and are said to include the world's largest collection of Buddhist artwork (Sun, 1992).

[10]The Chinese "Zodiacs," similar to but somewhat different from the Greek zodiacal signs, are representations of twelve animals, ordered in the twelve-year cycle of the Chinese lunar calendar. The sequence starts with the Year of the Rat, followed by the Years of the Ox, Tiger, Rabbit, Dragon, Snake, Horse, Sheep, Monkey, Rooster, Dog and Boar. The Western calendar year 2009 is the Lunar year 4707, Year of the Ox.

[11]"Shi Yuan," Garden of Tranquility or Shi Garden (Shi being the name of the author's grandfather), is the Hangzhou homestead of Grandpa Ying Bao-shi.

[12]"Netted Cage" refers to the author's studio, designed and built by her husband, Shen Yi, at their home on Sathan Road in Bangkok, a comfortable and breezy setting where she could write and paint (Plate 4; Shen-I, 1985).

[13]Xi-hu is West Lake in Hangzhou. Sudi (Plate 9), the beautiful dyke at West Lake and a favorite year-round tourist spot, was built during the Song Dynasty (960-1280) and named after the poet Su Dong-po. Hangzhou was the author's hometown.

[14]The names of many of the smaller buildings at the Shi Yuan homestead end with "guan, lu, tai, tang, ting, or yuan," characters that identify them as being a hall, hut, tower or garden. For example, Yaoyue Ting (Tower of Invitation-to-the-Moon) was an open structure beneath which was a goldfish pond spanned by an arching bridge that connected it to a lotus-filled lake. In Xian-xue Lu (Hut of Fragrant Snow), the author's grandfather entertained noted poets.

The names of some of the buildings at Shi Yuan that lack such identifying characters are humorous, for example, Lufei Hongsou (Fat-green Skinny-red) and the name of the building that housed the author's immediate family, Saode fenxiang (Floor-swept Incense-burnt). Many ghost stories were told about the mysterious Double-Eyed Well ("Shuang-yan Jing") which was said to be haunted. The author was born in one of the larger structures in the compound, Douhua Shuyu (Pea-blossoms Gentle-rain), a name engraved on the personal chop she used to stamp several of her brush paintings (Shen-I, 1985).

[15]The Great Hall of "Ying-gong Shi" (Temple of the Venerable Mr. Ying) was built in honor of the author's grandfather, Ying Bao-shi (1821-1890), on the campus of the former Dragon Gate Academy ("Longmen Shu-yuan") in Shanghai. A highly respected scholar, in 1844 Grandpa Ying was awarded the prestigious title Ju-ren (Exalted Scholar).

Author's grandpa Ying Bao-shi was also a noted military commander, said to have led his men into battle amidst the roar of "kill, kill, kill" as his frightened mother, who from the safety of a boat followed the battle on a nearby shore for seven days and nights, without food or sleep, as she prayed relentlessly to Lord Buddha for her son's safe return. He and his mother relied on each other throughout their lives ("xiang-yi wei-ming") and Grandpa Ying's filial piety was famous throughout his hometown (Shen-I, 1985).

[16]The author's mother, Jin Xing-fang (1879-1937; Plate 4), was a Hangzhou beauty, her parents' "shou-shang ming zhu" (lustrous pearl on the palm), and highly educated in the classics (Shen-I, 1985).

[17]Lone "un-husked kernel" (in a bed of rice) refers to the author being the only girl among many boys in the family school.

[18]Jinshi Yuan, known also as Zhongxi or McTyeire and built on the former homestead of a Jin family, was a Western school for girls in Shanghai attended by the author (and, earlier, by Mme. Chiang Kai-shek; Hahn, 1941). Muer Tang, also in Shanghai, was a Christian missionary academy of higher learning for women (Shen-I, 1985).

[19]The large showy flowers of the night-blooming Cereus (a genus of cactus) emerge in the evening and last for only a few hours. Their fleeting beauty symbolizes the precious short life ("tan-hua yi xian") of Author's first-born child, Yee-zi (Plate 3), named by use of one character from each parent (Yee, from the author's name, Yeening; and Zi, her husband's familial name).

[20]Green spring ("qing-chun") symbolizes youth.

[21]The study area (the "Netted Cage" of the poem's title) built for Author in Bangkok by husband Yi.

[22]"Dafeng Tang" (Hall of Grand Style) is the name of the art studio of the author's teacher, Grandmaster Artist Chang Ta-ch'ien (Plate 2; Boorman and Howard, 1967). Chang and Pablo Picasso were described by art historian M. Sullivan (1999) as "Two luminaries [having] much in common … star-quality, highly skilled, energetic and productive, both mischievous."

[23]"Food in jade" denotes a feast befitting royalty.

[24]From 1927 to 1937, the author's husband, Shen Yi, Chief of the Bureau of Public Works of the Shanghai Municipal Government, developed the New Civic Center (Boorman and Cheng, 1970; Shen, 1970; Wakeman, 1995).

[25]From 1940 to 1945, the author's husband served as Chief of the Gansu Provincial Bureau of the Northwestern Regional Development of Water Resources, Forestry and Animal Husbandry at Lanzhou (Boorman and Cheng, 1970; Shen, 1970).

[26]More than a dozen dams were constructed during Shen Yi's tenure in Gansu (Shen-Y, 1985). Most notable among these was the large (36-m-high) earthen dam of the Yuan-yang Reservoir, situated on the west bank of the Yellow River in the upper reaches of Mt. Chi-lian and providing irrigation for some 16,000 acres of fertile farmland (Shen-Y, 1985; Plate 7).

In 2003, in Gansu, a 60th Anniversary of the construction of the still-operating Yuan-yang Reservoir was celebrated by the provincial government and attended by the author's daughter Chuan-chuan, engineers and grateful farmers (Plate 7). Shen Yi would have been proud and pleased; as he noted at the time when the reservoir was being designed and built, "Our goal is to serve the people; in other words, the love that is passed on will remain with the people" (Shen-Y, 1985).

The two prime engineers of the Yuan-yang Reservoir who collaborated with Shen Yi in its construction were Yuan Su-xing and Lin Tung-yen (Shen-Y, 1985). As construction began, Engineer Yuan and his family of six sold their belongings so that they would have sufficient funds to live under the harsh conditions at Mt Ji-lian. Deeply touched by Yuan s heroic efforts, Chairman Chiang Kai-shek awarded him special commendation and presented him a heavy fur-lined leather coat and a pair of fur-lined leather trousers (Shen-Y, 1985).

In later years, Yuan-yang Reservoir Chief Engineer Lin Tung-yen moved to the United States where he became Professor of Engineering at the University of California, Berkeley and was the principal designer of the 300-foot-long arch that supports the ceiling of San Francisco's Moscone Conference Center (LA Times, Obituary, 2003).

[27]"Capital new" refers to Nanjing, established as the capital of China after WWII where Author's husband Shen Yi served as Mayor for two years, from 1946 to 1948. Nanjing fell to the Communists in the spring of 1949.

[28]The phrase "Serve the World" refers to Shen Yi's contributions as Father of the Mekong River Project at the United Nations ECAFE (Boorman and Cheng, 1970; Shen-Y, 1985).

[29]"Four-river bends" is in reference to the lower Mekong River

Basin which traverses the four Asian countries of Khmer, Lao PDR, Thailand, and Vietnam (Shen-Y, 1985; Hori, 2000; MRC, 2003, 2006). In its upper reaches, in Yunnan, China, the Mekong River is known as the Lancang River (Timeline China 1925-1995)

[30]"All Eyes glowed" refers to the glowing reaction of the United Nations to the solid foundation of the Mekong River Project put in place during Shen Yi's tenure at the U.N.-ECAFE (see, U.N. Secretary General Dag Hammarskjöld's letter of commendation, Plate 6; Boorman and Cheng, 1970; Shen-Y, 1985; Hori, 2000; Wightman, 1963).

[31]"East" refers to the location of the author's hometown, Hangzhou, to the east of Bangkok (where this poem was written).

[32]"Arching chrysanthemum" describes the author's longing for home.

HISTORIC FOREWORD

Nanjing (Nanking). Nanjing (literally, "Southern Capital") was the capital city of many Chinese dynasties, beginning as early as 476 BC and continuing intermittently over the following 2000 years. From its strategic location on the Yangtze River (*Frontispiece*), the city has served as the command-post for many emperors, not least among them Qin-shi Huang-di (Qin Dynasty 221-206 BC), China's first great leader who is credited with linking together pre-existing battlements to construct China's Great Wall and for uniting diverse Chinese peoples under his rule.

During the Tang Dynasty (618-907 AD), the "Golden Age" of China's history, high culture flourished in Nanjing, and during the Ming Dynasty (1368-1644 AD) the city's industries of shipbuilding, metal production, timber and pottery rose to prominence (Summerfield, 1992). Nanjing also became a center for higher learning. "*Fuzi Miao*," Nanjing's old town (where the Nanjing City Hall was located in 1946-48), was once the principal site for the scholarly examination of prospective governmental appointees. In the 1870s, toward the end of the Qing Dynasty, the city declined in stature.

Qing Dynasty (1644-1911 AD, the last dynasty of China). During the latter part of the Qing Dynasty, China, the Middle Kingdom ("*Zhong Guo*"), suffered numerous setbacks at the hands of foreigners. Britain defeated China in the Opium War of 1839-1842, and in the treaty, China ceded the Hong Kong Peninsula to England (Hsü, 1975; Fu, 1984; *Chapter 7*). In disgust, the Chinese people revolted and came to regard outsiders as so-called foreign devils ("*yang gui-zi*"). In the last decade of the 1800s, the Boxer Rebellion united the Chinese against Westerners, Western religion, and Western ways.

In retaliation to the Boxer Rebellion, an army of eight nations, "*Ba-guo Lian-jun*"—Austria, Belgium, Britain, France, Japan, Germany, Russia, and United States—advanced on the crumbling Qing regime (Tuchman, 1972; Hsü, 1975; Fu, 1984). In 1901, China was forced to pay monetary tribute to the victors and to cede to them specified territories (Fu, 1984). Shanghai, the city of the author's childhood and early schooling (*About the Author*), was one such region, subdivided by the foreigners into a number of smaller regions, each under the autonomous control of one of the Western powers. The Chinese were deeply humiliated by the foreign control of their lands, with signs posted in the British concession on the Shanghai park greens along the Huang-pu River that read: "No dogs or Chinese allowed."

Among the eight conquering powers, the United States was said to be the only country that waived the punitive payments and the acquisition of major Chinese lands. Instead, the U.S. returned a substantial sum of money to the Qing government, specifying that the funds were to be used to establish in Beijing (Peking) what is now Tsinghua University (Fu, 1984; Roberts, 1999) and to send abroad Chinese students (such as Dr. Hu Shih, shown in Plate 1, who through this program carried out his advanced studies in the United States). Beginning with these transactions, American influence on Chinese ideals and culture gradually began to take hold as China moved to become a modern nation (Fu, 1984).

The Republic. Following China's defeat by the Western powers and the concessions that resulted, the formerly impenetrable door of China burst open and Western culture began to permeate en masse. At the beginning of the 1900s, the two-and-a-half centuries of rule by the corrupt and by now much weakened Qing Dynasty was cast aside by the revolution led by Dr. Sun Yat-sen. In 1911, Sun founded the Republic of China and, later, the Kuomintang (Nationalist) Party.

Upon the death of Sun Yat-sen in 1925, Chiang Kai-shek (1886-1975; Plate 1), a military officer trained in Japan, came to power (Hsü, 1975; Fu, 1984; Lin, 2000). Two years later, on 18 April 1927, the city of Nanjing was designated the first capital of the Nationalist Government (*Ci Hai*, 1976), a position of prominence it held for the next 10 years, falling to the invading Japanese in 1937. Chiang's reign was to last for 47 years, from 1928 until his death, in Taiwan, on April 5, 1975 (Boorman and Howard, 1967; Hsü, 1975; Roberts, 1999).

Sino-Japanese War. Dating from Japan's defeat of China in 1895, the Japanese government had begun to covet the rich soil and resources of Manchuria in China's northeast, a region specified in 1912 by Japanese expansionists as the "next logical target for conquest" (Hsü, 1975). Soon thereafter, unrest among Chinese students about their government's friendliness toward Japan began to simmer in Peiping (Beijing), coming to a boil in Shanghai on May 4, 1919. The Chinese nation responded.

May Fourth Movement. At the age of 17, my father, Shen Yi (the author's husband), was one of the youngest student leaders of the uprising in Shanghai where he was a student at Tong-Ji University (Plate 2; Shen-Y, 1985). Day after day, morning into night, students from many schools, each represented by banners and signs, formed a phalanx of orderly marchers. Outfitted in white uniforms emblazoned on front and back with the slogan "Strict Observance of Order" ("*Yan Shou Ci-xu*"), printed in Chinese and English, as they roared in unison and paraded through the Shanghai streets amidst rousing cheers.

Some of those involved in the May-Fourth student movement, as in Dad's case, gave provocative speeches urging the boycotting of all things Japanese. Shopkeepers, in force, boarded-up their storefronts and showered the young marchers with fresh fruits, tea and (when necessary) medication, and loaned them wooden stools to use as platforms for oration. Like a pack of everyday street vendors, the idealistic students rang bells to gather an audience and Dad, among others, was selected to speak (a training that no doubt helped him in later years to become a forceful plainspoken public speaker, known for his strong voice and concise clear message). Each of the students was hopeful that he or she might be arrested, thereby becoming the focus of an increased public awareness of their cause. The protests, marches and speeches went on for an entire week.

Thinking back on those heady days of May Fourth (five four, 5-4) Movement, Dad later was embarrassed by his naiveté, but the enthusiasm ("*re xue*") of China's heated young blood was deeply moving. This "show of force," known as the May Fourth Movement ("*Wu Si Yundong*"), soon became the impetus for the founding of the Youth Society of China ("*Shao-nian Zhong-guo Xue-hui*") led by professors from "*Peita*" (Peking University), among them Dr. Hu Shih (Plate 1; Shen-Y, 1985). Dad, being an orphan and having no real home, could not have been more enthusiastic about forging camaraderie and exchanging ideas with this serious learned group of young patriots (Shen-Y, 1985). The publications of the Youth Society (an organization known commonly as *Zhong Shao Hui*) were avidly sought by the educated youth, and a number of its charter members, including Mao Ze-dong (a student of Hu Shih; Hu, 1967), went on to shape the nation.

Despite the Youth Society's brilliant beginnings, however, the success of the association was to prove short-lived, undermined by its strict requirements for membership and the weight of competing idealisms (communism, nationalism, the Three People's Principles, etc; Shen-Y, 1985).

Although in retrospect, the Youth Society is perhaps best viewed as the forerunner of what later came to be known as the "New Cultural Movement" (Hsü, 1975), it and its predecessor, the May Fourth Movement, were pivotal in providing a springboard for later success in the careers of numerous young students (Shen-Y, 1985), in the case of Mao Ze-dong—the founding of the People's Republic of China. Mao later claimed, perhaps with hyperbole, that the 1919 "5-4 Movement formed part of Lenin's world revolution" (Hsü, 1975).

Nine-One-Eight (918). Some 12 years later, an event that today may seem to have been a relatively minor incident—the explosion of a Japanese bomb on the Southern Manchurian Railway outside the town of Mukden (Shenyang) in Liaoning Province (*Ci Hai*, 1976)—"sowed the seeds of World War II" (Hsü, 1975). This bombing event, occurred on September 18, 1931 (and commonly known as 918, "*Jiu-Yi-Ba*") enraged the Chinese public. In "self-defense," the Chinese army retaliated.

Marco-Polo Bridge Incident. On the 7th of July 1937 an all-out Sino-Japanese War erupted when in Beijing fighting broke out at the Marco Polo Bridge ("*Qi-qi Lugou Qiao Shi-bian*," the so-called 7-7 Lugo Qiao Incident; see, *Chapter 6*). Tuchman (1972) vividly describes a scene from that fateful night, the prelude to the full-scale invasion of Japanese forces, "a soft moon hovered over the ancient city of Beijing" as Tuchman and her friends from the American Embassy quietly boated on Beihai Lake, then, suddenly, "reality glided by in another boat, carrying a group of Japanese officers." The invading Japanese adopted the policy of the "three alls—kill all, burn all, destroy all" (Roberts, 1999; Zhu, 2002).

Nanking Massacre. As chronicled by Chinese, Japanese and Western historians (Tuchman, 1972; Hsü, 1975; Johnson, 1983; Xu, 1994; Chang, 1997; Rabe, 1998; Asuma, 1999; Zhu, 2002), the streets of Nanking ran red with blood as one of the greatest large-scale massacres in the history of the modern world took place when the capital of Nanking fell to the Japanese on 13 December, 1937. Our future home, the mayor's residence, was located within the "Safety Zone" that been established by an International Committee, but the neighboring areas of the city were savaged by the bloodbath (Chang, 1997; Rabe, 1998).

Gruesome images of the Japanese massacre were captured on film and are recorded in Iris Chang's book *"The Rape of Nanking"* (1997). The caption of one such image reads: *"Blindfolded and propped on two sticks, this poor man served as the living target for a Japanese officer's sword practice."* Another describes *"The* [severed] *head of a Chinese soldier placed on a barbed-wire barricade ... with a cigarette butt inserted between his lips as a joke"* (Chang, 1997; see also, Xu, 1994).

A photograph reminiscent of the infamous icon of the Vietnam War[1] (taken by *Associated Press* photographer Eddie Adams that shows a grimacing young fellow being shot at point blank range) has a man naked to the waist, an expression of grim resolve across his face, kneeling before a Japanese soldier as he awaits to be beheaded by a dagger across the back of his neck. The caption reads: *"The Japanese turned murder into sport. Note the smiles on the Japanese in the background"* (Chang, 1997).

Similar scenes of butchery of humans are included in Xu's *"Massacre of Nanjing"* (1994), Rabe's diary (1998), and Zhu's pictorial history (2002), and a picture taken by Japanese photographer M. Moriyasu documents the final fate of the city's people: *"Corpses of Nanking citizens were dragged to the banks of Yangtze and thrown into the river"* (Chang, 1997). John Rabe (1998) includes a photograph of Japanese soldiers standing above a pile of charred corpses and burnt wood with the explanation: "*The Japanese army attempted to destroy the evidence of the slaughter by wholesale burning of bodies.*"

Other pictures of massacre are just as vivid—young men in civilian clothes herded like cattle for slaughter; women en masse, raped, tortured, and mutilated and prisoner buried-alive (Xu, 1994; Chang, 1997; Rabe, 1998; Zhu, 2002). One snapshot shows a helpless naked woman with her legs outspread: "*The Japanese bound this young woman to a chair for repeated attack*" (Chang, 1997). Another has a long dagger stuck in the widely spread private parts of a woman with her head and upper torso fully covered (Chang, 1997).

These atrocities in Nanjing recall scenes from a film made in Nanking on 13 December, 1937 by Rev. John G. Magee, of the American Church Mission, that show a girl of 16, who "*after being raped by 2-3 men ... was stabbed afterwards, and a cane was rammed into her vagina*" (document 16, Rabe, 1998; Zhu, 2002). Six decades later, in October of 2000, Magee's film, smuggled out of China under Japanese occupation, was shown in the U.S. on the Discovery Channel with narration by the Reverend's son.

A particularly gripping Nanking Massacre scene in another documentary film ("*Nanking*," made in 2007) shows a mother who had been stabbed by a bayonet, but who upon hearing her infant cry then suckles and comforts the child as the woman collapses and dies. This documentary, dedicated to Author Iris Chang and viewed by millions worldwide (Welkos, 2008), won the editing award at the 2007 Sundance Film Festival and was nominated by the Writers Guild of America for the best documentary screenplay award.

Despite reluctance of the Japanese government to admit the reality of the Nanking atrocities (Wallace and Ueno, 2008), the massacre did, in fact, occur, recorded even by Japanese eyewitnesses (e.g., Asuma, 1999). As British journalist Paul Johnson (1983) put it, "Men, women, and children ... were hunted like rabbits. Everyone seen to move was shot."

To the Chinese, perhaps the one hero of this terrifying rape of Nanking was John Rabe, a representative of the German Siemens Company, who to them was regarded the "Oskar Schindler" of the

Sino-Japanese war (Chang, 1997). A thoroughly decent man, moved by compassion and moral outrage, Rabe was even more than a Schindler (Mills, 1999). Yet in spite of his heartfelt efforts to safeguard some 250,000 citizens of the occupied capital, within a scant 40 days hundreds of thousands of Nanjing's people—perhaps as many as 350,000—are reported to have been slaughtered[2] (Johnson, 1983; Xu, 1987; Chang, 1997; Zhu, 2002).

Indeed, the Nanjing death toll of 1937-38 may surpass the total casualties (estimated at 210,000) of the Hiroshima and Nagasaki atomic bombs that ultimately ended World War II (Chang, 1997). Chinese author Xu (1987), in the prologue his *"Words from the Earth,"* recounts an interview with a Xia Shu-qin, an elderly woman who had "cried blind" her eyes in grief over her family of seven slain (Zhu, 2002). In Xu's words, *"This bloody sea, this fiery sea is forever engraved on the sea of the human heart."*

In today's Nanking-Massacre Memorial Park (Plate 8), abstract sculptures symbolize the 300,000 dead and a line of bronze footsteps, woven about plaintive statues, calls out the voices, now silent, of the mangled and wounded victims. A bronze statute of author Iris Chang is dedicated in memory of her heroic effort recalling the Japanese savageries (Plate 8). A memorial to this bloody tragedy, a large tablet of blood-red 850 million-year-old limestone inscribed with the words *"In Memory of the 300,000 Nanjing Dead,"* can be found on a low hill at the back of the Academia Sinica's Nanjing Institute of Geology and Palaeontology, near one of the massacre sites at Jimingshi, in Nanjing's city center (see, *Frontispiece*).

Postwar Cover-ups. While Germany has made major efforts to atone for the atrocities of the Nazi era (Murphy, 1994; Watanabe and Walsh, 1995), Japan has apologized little for its crimes of WWII, most especially for the Nanjing Holocaust (Watanabe, 1994; Jameson, 1994; *Associated Press*, 1995). In 1970, West Germany Chancellor Willy Brandt knelt and presented a wreath at the memorial for Warsaw Jewish victims (Zhu, 2002). Yet for some seven decades after its occurrence, the Japanese-inflicted Nanjing massacre was simply ignored by the Japanese government as it continued its "don't ask, don't tell" policy.

In leading the official position of cover-up, Emperor Akihito refused to heed the denunciation of war horrors made by a member of his own royal family, the Emperor's 78-year-old uncle, Prince Mikasa, youngest brother of the war-Emperor Hirohito (Watanabe, 1994; *Los Angeles Times*, Op-Ed, 1994). Emperor Akihito, accompanied by his Empress during a visit to Los Angeles in 1994, sought to downplay this terrible episode by simply expressing, without acknowledging the Nanjing savagery, *"deep sorrow for the severe suffering"* (Moffet and Hamilton, 1994; Watanabe, 1994).

To perpetuate the cover-up, in 2004, the influential Governor of Tokyo, Shintaro Ishihara, continued to reject Japanese atonement even as the Japanese Prime Minister, Junichiro Koizumi, offered apology to the Asian nations (Wallace, 2004)—an apology Koizumi then undermined by his repeated visits to the Yasukuni War Shrine, his "Achilles' heel" (Wallace, 2006).

Remembrances. Despite omissions and cover-ups of the Japanese masasscre in Nanking, *given the chance, truth will prevail!* Today's Chinese have not forgotten the Japanese atrocities of WWII (Harney, 2004). Nearly seventy years later after their occurrence, on Memorial Day, 4 April, 2004, hundreds of Chinese schoolchildren placed wreaths of fresh flowers at the wall of the Memorial Museum in Nanjing (Plate 8; *Xin-Hua China Daily*, 2004). "People's views are shaped by their teachers," said Feng Zhaokui, a Chinese specialist on Japan (Harney, 2004), and "Chinese young people get a patriotic education."

The horror of the Sino-Japanese war has been remembered also in the United States. In Los Angeles, the *"Forgotten Holocaust"* exhibit assembled by Daniel Kwan (an American developer) at the Weingart Gallery and opened on the 50th Anniversary of the ending of WWII, focused on three especially horrific examples of Japanese cruelty during their occupation of China:

(1) Decimation of China's population, including the 1937 Nanking Massacre (an event still claimed in 1994 by Justice Minister Shigeto Nagano to be nothing more than a *"fabrication"*; Salonga, 2001).

(2) The infamous long-term experiments in germ warfare research—using anthrax, typhoid, cholera, and plague—conducted

by Japanese "Unit 731" in Harbin, in northeast China, on Chinese, Korean, Mongolian and Russian prisoners (Efron, 1994; Harris, 1994; *Associated Press*, 1995; Brazil, 1995; Kang, 1995; Trounson, 2001).

(3) The wartime use by the Japanese military of Chinese women as "sex slaves," so-called comfort women (Watanabe, 1994; Salonga, 2001; *Wire Reports*, 2002; Magnier, 2003; *Los Angeles Times*, 2005; Wallace, 2007), crimes for which formal apologies have been issued by several Japanese Prime Ministers (Jameson, 1992; *Wire Reports*, 1996), most recently, on the 50th anniversary of Japan's defeat, Japanese Prime Minister Tomichi Murayama (Jameson, 1994).

Yalta Betrayal. Beginning in July 1937, when fighting broke out at Beijing's Marco Polo Bridge (Tuchman, 1972), the Sino-Japanese War waged on for eight long years. Generalissimo Chiang Kai-shek's Nationalist troops, from 1941 to 1945 aligned with the Allied Forces, were at the forefront of the action. The Chinese people endured, barely, but China was savaged.

In February 1945, as WWII edged toward closure, the "Big Three" (Winston Churchill, representing the United Kingdom; Franklin Roosevelt, the United Sates; and Josef Stalin, the Soviet Union) reached an agreement at Yalta in the Crimea, "a hard-driven bargain [pressed chiefly by Roosevelt] to secure Soviet combat, in default of China against Japan" (Tuchman, 1972; Hsü, 1975).

In the Yalta Agreement, among the many concessions given to Stalin to secure the use of his troops against the Japanese, the Soviets were granted authority over China's Central Eastern Railway and the port city of Dalian in Manchuria, Liaoning Province. It was not until a year later, in the spring of 1946, that the terms of Yalta Agreement became known to Chiang Kai-shek and the Chinese people. Not surprisingly, it was greeted as a "great betrayal."

At the end of the war in 1945, and at that time without knowledge of what the Yalta Agreement had set in place, the Chinese government actively, if blindly, appointed governors and mayors to repatriate provinces and cities in Manchuria that had been lost to Japan (see, *Chapter 6*). In October of that year, my father, Dr. Shen Yi, the Author's husband, was appointed Mayor of the prime Manchurian port city of

Dalian (Plate 6). A month or so later, as he prepared to assume this post, he received word that his way was blocked by Soviet troops; he never reached Dalian.

Author Margaret Truman (1993), daughter of President Harry Truman, Roosevelt's successor, writes that when Fleet Admiral William D. "Bill" Leahy protested to President Roosevelt about the Yalta concessions to Stalin, "Mr. Roosevelt shook his head in resignation and said: Bill, I can't help it." According to Ms. Truman, FDR had been forced to negotiate "not from strength but from weakness" since he and his advisors had already concluded that Soviet troops would be absolutely "essential for the final defeat of Japan" (Truman, 1993). Ironically, on the 14th of August 1945, less than a week after the Soviets had entered the war, Japanese Emperor Hirohito ordered a cease-fire and the end to the hostilities (Hsü, 1975; Fu, 1984). The ensuing turmoil—as the Soviets sided with Mao's Communists, and the United States, with Chiang's Kuomintang Nationalists—was thus set in motion (Roberts, 1999).

In China, the resulting "Hot War" between the Communists and the Nationalists drew to a close four years later, when Chiang's army retreated to Taiwan in 1949. But the following Cold War lasted worldwide for more than four-and-a-half decades and in a less virulent form is with us still, as the successors of Mao and Chiang spar over the fate of Taiwan (Bullitt, 1946; Marshall and Magnier, 2004; Magnier 2005; *Times Wire Services*, 2005).

Civil War. The Yalta Agreement sounded the death knell of the Nationalist Kuomintang on the Chinese mainland. Chiang's government, riddled by corruption and confronted with rampant inflation (see, *Chapters 4, 8, 9*; Hsü, 1975; Roberts, 1999), was soon to meet defeat. The last half of the 1940s was unbelievably tumultuous— Mao Ze-dong's peasant movement rapidly gained popularity and power, first in the northeast and then throughout the land. By moving the seat of government in 1946 from the war capital of Chongqing to Nanjing, the Capital-of-Return ("*Hui-du*"), the Nationalists had hoped to staunch the flow of Mao's advance and achieve stability. By November of that year when the Author's husband, Shen Yi, arrived in Nanjing to assume the position of Mayor of the new capital, the fate of the country was already in doubt. The clouds of communism soon advanced on Nanjing as well.

Times were hard for her husband, her family and her country, but throughout it all, the Author retained her composure, her dignity, and even her sense of serenity. These reminiscences are her personal account, a chronicle of her triumphs and heartbreaks, her successes and failures, and of her heartfelt hopes and hopes unfulfilled. Nanjing's role as the seat of government, the Nationalists' *Hui-du*, lasted but three years, from 1946 to 1949, falling to the Communists on Sunday morning, April 23, 1949 (*Life Magazine*, 1949; Bodde, 1967; Hsü, 1975).

Footnotes:
[1]Adams' Pulitzer Prize-winning photograph, taken in Vietnam in 1968, was soon dubbed "*The shot seen round the world*" (*Parade Magazine*, 2004).

[2]Although the perpetrators of the Nanjing Massacre are known to be troops of the Japanese Army's Sixth Division, commanded by General Tani Hisao (Zhu, 2002), the precise number of citizens killed in the city during 1937-38 is somewhat uncertain, ranging into the hundreds of thousands.

Based on reports of the Nanking holocaust made by Europeans who were present at the time, Rabe put the number at 50,000 to 60,000 (Rabe, 1998). Basing her account on reports by local missionaries and members of the International Relief Committee, Pulitzer Prize-winning historian Barbara Tuchman (1972) estimated that some 42,000 civilians had been killed or raped and that an additional 50,000 Chinese soldiers were lost in the defense of the city. Historian Immanuel Hsü (1975) numbers the massacre victims at approximately 100,000.

Other estimates on the Nanking death toll are even higher. According to an *Associated Press* report (2004), historians generally agree that between mid-December 1937 and early February 1938 the Nanjing slaughter took the lives of at least 150,000 civilians. This estimate more or less tallies with that of British historian Paul Johnson (1983) who reports that during that two-month period some 20,000 male Chinese of military age were marched off to the countryside and killed—events documented by Rabe (1998) and also by Zhu (2002) who shows a photo of "*Japanese patrols rounding up Chinese* [civilians] *for execution*"—and that "the killing went on until 6 February 1938, and by then between 200,000 and 300,000 Chinese were dead."

The Japanese massacre records archived today in Nanjing suggest an even larger number—340,000 (Xu, 1994; Case no. 28, a summary of mass killings, together with Case no. 858, murders of individuals). After the cessation of hostilities, testimony given to the Far East Military Tribunal confirmed that more than 200,000 civilians and soldiers had been slain, a number that does not include an additional 150,000 bodies thrown into the Yangtze River or incinerated (Zhu, 2002).

Taken together, and assuming a 1937 Nanjing population of about 1.3 million (Rabe, 1998), such accountings assess the massacre to have annihilated as much as 25 percent of the city's population.

CHAPTER 1
SHANGHAI TO NANKING

It was a chilly but bright spring morning on the 27th of February, 1947. Though the wind was very strong, the sunshine spread warmth that soothed me to cheerfulness. When a clock at the station struck eight, the locomotive pulling a long line of cars started puffing and rolling its way from Shanghai to Nanking. My face pressed to the half-opened window; I could see Papa (my father), brothers, sister Duan [Plates 2, 4], and relatives and friends, all waving from the platform. Stretching out my arm as far as I could, I waved with my handkerchief passionately, again and again, until I lost sight of all of them. I was numb with joy, and sorrow, and aimlessness. But my senses soon returned when my two young children—newborn son, Shin-shin [Plate 3], crying in his rocking basket ("*yao-lan*"), and my little daughter Lan-lan, yelling with excitement—brought me back to reality.

It all seemed a dream, but it was real—I was seated in a private train compartment moving at fast speed northwestward to my husband, Yi, new mayor of the nation's Capital, Nanking. The trees, fields, brooks, and hairy huts ("*mao-wu*") flew away from my view, one after another. I stood in the cavernous compartment, neatly furnished but by no means luxurious, one end of which adjoined three smaller sleeping quarters with a WC and a pantry. Two strangers shared this compartment, a white-haired gentleman who sat serenely on a sofa reading a newspaper, and a young man standing by a window. When the latter noticed my glance, he approached me instantly:

"Shen '*Fu-ren*' (Mme. Shen), I am sent by the Director to attend you."

"Please do not hesitate to let me know your needs."

He bowed and handed me his card. I read it and noted that he was in charge of the section of railroad between Shanghai and Soochow. I thanked him for his kindness, but I was puzzled, and in fact rather disturbed, that Director Chen of the Nanking-Shanghai Railway ("*Jin-Hu Tia Lu*") was himself not on board this train. After all, it was

1

Director of the Jin-Hu Railway who just before I boarded the train had invited my children and me to join him in his private car for the eight-hour journey to Nanking. I accepted Mr. Chen's hospitality, but I had not realized until this moment that he had intentionally misled me into occupying this special compartment while Chen, himself, was not making the journey. I felt even more embarrassed when I was finally introduced to the white-haired gentleman, President of the prestigious Chiao-tung University in Shanghai and an acquaintance of Yi. He was effusive in gratitude for my allowing him to share the car.

In Soochow, a major station en route, we had a fifteen-minute stopover. The young man who had attended us had finished his assignment and left the train. Just before moving on again, I saw several brown-uniformed soldiers on the platform insistently attempting to get into our section of the car, only to be rudely turned away by the station guards. I heard their protests, "Why this spacious compartment with so few occupants, when we soldiers cannot get a single seat?"

As the soldiers were blustering I could feel their hostile glances directed again and again at my car. Their protests, like sharp blades, stabbed at my conscience. It was regretful that such inequity should exist. The steward rejected my plea of letting them share a section of the compartment, explaining that it was against railway regulations and, moreover, the soldiers were likely to cause trouble.

Our next major stop en route was Tzenjiang. We again waited for fifteen minutes. Through the window I could see a long line of trains, moving slowly by, with open-topped cars. All were crowded with shabbily dressed "*lao bai-shin*" (common people), men and women, young and old, pressed together like sardines. As their faces paraded slowly past my window, almost every pair of eyes was fixed on me— part in admiration, part in envy, and part in sheer resentment. The glances, decidedly different from those of the soldiers, were passive and humble, yet their honesty said a lot. A sense of guilt and regret welled up in me. My heart was heavy with remorse and I was burdened by the realization that I could do nothing to relieve the meager existence of these fellow countrymen.

After having fed my baby and lulled my daughter "*shao Lan*" (little

Lan) to sleep, I sat by the window enjoying the quietude and taking in the winding landscape. The vast plain, with bordered fields of rice, wheat, cotton, and new vegetables, sprawled beautifully in the sun. Rows of small huts made of bamboo and straw, humble and withered, lined the edges of the field. The picturesque scene, clumps after clumps of tall majestic willows, peaches, plums and apricot, bloomed before my eyes.

As I watch the vast span of land passing by my window, I saw straw-hatted farmers and their women folk immersed in their daily tasks—ploughing the fields, drawing water from the wells and brooks, stuffing rice sprouts into the flooded soil. Time and again I could hear farm songs from afar, echoing melodiously under the calm sky. Tall laughter issued from old folks enjoying themselves in the sun by their cottage doors, watching children at play in the meadows. "*Good earth, good people, the true treasures of China*," I thought to myself. A pity that these honest and diligent *lao bai-shin*, toiling days on end, have been so exploited by the upper tiers of the society that they could never make ends meet. My heart became heavy, once again.

At long last, the Purple Golden Mountain "*Tze Jin San*" [Zijin Mt., *Frontispiece*] came into view, the city's ancient stonewall stretching to the left; Hsuan-wu Lake [Xuanwu Lake] glistening in the distance; red earth and flocks of ducks here and there. All scenes heralded the approach of Nanking. The time was four o'clock in the afternoon when the sun let out its last glow of glory. As soon as the train pulled into the Nanking Sha-guan Station [Nanjing West Railway Station], passengers began to stream out, stumbling one over another in their haste.

Our train compartment was at the far end of the track. For the children's sake, I waited until the crowd had dispersed. I searched through the windows, in hope of catching a glimpse of my husband, Yi. But he was nowhere in sight. Then, a Mr. Shen Yu-fu boarded our compartment and introduced himself as a personal assistant to the mayor. He cautioned that several newspapers had gotten wind that the mayor's wife would be arriving on a special car, and that they might seek interviews. Not wishing to make news, Yi had not come to meet our train. I waited till everyone had disembarked. It was nearly five o'clock when my two children and I left the station and were driven to our new home on the west side of town.

Yi had been besieged by reporters from Nanking and Shanghai, ever since his inaugural speech in Nanking in 1946. The *Nanking New People's Daily* ("*Shin-ming Rer Pao*") had this to say: "The Mayor's maiden speech at the City Auditorium was like beautiful poetry, full of brilliance and hope, and promised a fine beginning." Within a two-week period, Yi had been inundated by newsmen who wanted to hear more about his plans. His comments to them were, "I shall put my eyes on broad views and my hands in little niches (*da-zu zoa-yen, shao-zu zoa-sou*)."

The City's main concern at that moment was an issue that to Yi was trivial—the prohibition of public dancing [Wakeman, 1955]. When this notion was repeatedly put to him, he replied that he had "no personal view on this very small matter." The very next day, the newspaper reported that "Mayor Shen insists that the prohibition of public dancing is a '*shao-shao*' (minute) issue." Little did Yi know that this prohibition of public dancing had come directly from Chairman Chiang Kai-shek, leader of the Nationalist Government!

As our car arrived at the Nanking home, the garden gate was already open and servants had been assembled to greet us. With arms opened wide and a warm broad smile, Yi greeted us on the front porch.

Our new Nanking home, standing in the middle of a block on 21 Tian-zu Lu (Rd), was a modest ivory colored house of Spanish motif, with a red-tiled roof. There was a small garden in the front, badly in need of trees and landscaping. A narrow path led directly from the gate to the front door. As soon as I entered the house, two of my daughters San-san and Chuan-chuan [Plate 4] rushed to me, hugging and kissing and hopping with joy. The girls had just returned from school. Interrupted by happy talk and laughter I learned that my older girls, Hwa-hwa and Pei-pei, were still at their Gingling[1] boarding school [Plate 8, *Frontispiece*]. All of us hugged again and again. Everyone spoke all at once.

The room was full of excitement with our reunion, but Yi was silent. I then realized that he was waiting anxiously to see our newborn son, Shin-shin, whom he had seen only twice since birth. The baby had already been carried upstairs. I immediately motioned to "Mama," our family nurse [Plate 9], to bring him down to meet his father. Yi cradled the boy in his arms, gazed at him for a long while, and spoke gently but for all of us to hear.

"Ah, little treasure (*shao bao-bei*), you are still a baby!" This brought laughter to everyone in the room.

"For Heaven's sake (*tian shao-de*), Papa, I am not quite two months old." I answered for my son.

On December 31st, 1946, when Yi received news in Nanking of the birth of our son in Shanghai, he was just on his way to a festivity at the residence of Chairman and Mme. Chiang Kai-shek. The party was given in celebration of the birthday of the American General, George Marshall[2]. The news of Yi's new son soon rippled through the party, adding extra spirit to the celebration. Guests congregated and congratulated Yi. General Marshall walked over and toasted him, and Chairman Chiang stopped by, adding his good wishes.

"This is your first son; you are indeed to be congratulated!"

Yi told me later that the congratutory words from Chaiman Chiang had touched an old wound, and brought tears to his eyes as he thought of Yee-zi [Plate 3], our first born, also a son, who had died in infancy.)

After the celebration for Gen. Marshall at the Chairman's residence, the next morning's newspaper described Yi as "having a son at an old age, the mayor's face was a broad sweep of spring breeze ('*man-mein tzuen-fung*')" and likened him to having "ascending to duty on a walking horse" (*zou-mah sun-ren*, full of satisfaction). I was not pleased with the words "having a son at an old age," since Yi was only forty-five years old! (He was not at all old in my eyes, but we Chinese have a habit of downplaying happiness—one reason why our national spirit had so often lacked enthusiasm and youthfulness.)

Because of the coincidence of birthdays, we gave our son, Shin-shin, the English name Marshall.

Footnotes:

[1]Ginling Girls School ("*Gin Nu-da Fu-zhong*") was the middle-school on the campus of Ginling Women College (later renamed Nanjing Teachers College but now known as Ginling College, Nanjing Normal University; Plate 8, *Frontispiece*), which was located in the "Safety Zone" during the rape and mass killings of Nanjing citizens by Japanese soldiers in 1937-38 (Xu, 1987; Chang, 1997; Rabe, 1998).

At Ginling College a memorial statue of Wilhelmina (Minnie) Vautrin (Plate 8), a native of Illinois and Dean of Arts and Sciences of Ginling during the period of 19937-38, stands on the campus today to memorialize her heroic efforts to shield women and children from the Nanking Massacre (Chang, 1997; Zhu, 2002). For her unrelenting courage, Vautrin is known locally as the "Living Goddess of Nanking."

[2]In 1945, U.S. President Harry S. Truman appointed his favorite military man, General George Catlett Marshall, to be Special Ambassador to China for the purpose of mediating an end to the civil war between Nationalists and Communists and unifying the country into a "strong and democratic China" (Hsü, 1975).

General Marshall convened the meeting between the Communists and the Nationalist leaders in Chongqing. "Extra! Extra!" yelled the evening newspaper vendors all over the city, punctuating the gravity of this face-to-face encounter between Chiang Kai-shek and Mao Ze-dong. Marshall did achieve impressive results, but he failed to convince the Nationalists to cease-fire. "After a year in China, Marshall unfortunately called it quits and returned to Washington" (Donovan, 1982) and the "American dream of mediation in China came to an end" (Hsü, 1975).

On January 6th, 1947, General Marshall was recalled by President Truman. He later became the U.S. Secretary of State who formulated Truman's renowned "*Marshall Plan*." To carry out this plan, designed to rehabilitate lands the U.S. and its allies had decimated during the war (mainly, in Germany and Japan), Truman requested 16 billion dollars from the U.S. Congress (Miller, 1984). An unparalleled success, English historian Arnold Toynbee regarded the *Marshall Plan* as the "signal achievement of our age" (Miller, 1984). In gratitude for the post-war reconstruction of Germany, in the fall of 1997 a special German postal stamp was issued to commemorate the 50th Anniversary of the *Marshall Plan*.

George Marshall's 1945-46 Nanjing headquarters, across the street from the administrative offices of the 1937-38 Nanking Massacre "Safety Zone" (see *Frontispiece*), is used currently by the Chinese military and has been beautifully preserved by the city government.

CHAPTER 2
A DAY ON HSUAN-WU LAKE

On the Lake[1]
A "*bai-hua*" poem by Hu Shih, August 24, 1920
Translation by J. Shen Schopf, Editor

A firefly on the water, one firefly in the water.
Side-by-side,
Softly, softly,
They pass our bow.
Closely, closely they travel in twain.
Slowly, slowly they merge in one.

My first excursion from our new home in Nanking was to Hsuan-wu[1] Lake. On its bank an umbrella of tall willows with entangled branches that had just begun to spread a tender green overarched an aligned array of moored rowboats. The morning air was soft and fresh, its breezes gentle and caressing. Spring flowers of varied colors were spotted here and there on the hills half-circling the water, and birds chirped merrily on their travels from branch to branch. All scenes welcomed the coming of spring. Sweet and fleeting thoughts sang in my heart, as Nature's loveliness unfolded before my eyes.

This was the second Sunday after my arrival in Nanking. Yi had brought our family to this lovely historical spot, where I had visited some twelve years earlier. A twelve-year interval is a mere blink of history, but to me it was a major span of my lifetime—a world war had been waged from start to finish; soldiers and civilians, both men and women, had been maimed or died; and children, my own included [Plate 3], had been born. My heart beat rapidly at the thought of my passage from being a young woman to now being a mother of six. Every person, every place, everything, in some respect, had changed in the intervening time—only the ancient wall standing sentinel by the lake [*Frontispiece*] still looked the same. Our baby son was yet too young to appreciate the surroundings, but his five sisters were enthusiastic [Plate 7], led by Hwa-hwa, "*lao-da,*" our eldest. They skipped, hopped, and clapped with joy, exuding an innocence of youth.

We strolled along the banks of Hsuan-wu and came upon a park. At the entrance between two sets of high gates placed closely together [see *Frontispiece,* Xuanwu Gate], stood a huge portrait of Generalissimo Chiang Kai-shek, our nation's leader. The portrait, badly done, fit not at all with the tranquility of the scene.

The grounds of the Hsuan-wu Park were not large, but the arrangement of trees, flowers, ponds, bridges, and pavilions had been tastefully carried out. Near the gate hidden in a nearby thicket facing the lake was the Lotus Hall (*"Heh-hua Ting"*), a small traditional-style building. This little building had been assigned to the Nanking Women Work Committee of the New-Life Movement, of which I had just been recently appointed Chairman. Because of this, since it would soon become our Headquarters [Plate 10], I had a special interest in seeing for myself how its remodeling was progressing.

A stone's throw from the Lotus Hall was the *"Hsuan-wu[1] Lo"* (North Tower), a large modern structure built by the Japanese during their all-too-recent occupation, now used for government functions. As our family wandered near the Tower we came upon a Mr. Mei, Chief of the Nanking Municipal Forest and Park Service. Out of politeness (and official protocol), he invited us in for tea. Seated at the tea table we could hear the laughter of approaching passersby, their expressions full of curiosity as they peered inside. As quickly we could, we took leave.

Yi hired a canopied rowboat and a boatman. Our boat glided soothingly among the thickets of drooping water willows. The lone sweep of the oars became the only sound. Sitting comfortably in our cushioned reclining chairs, we enjoyed the peaceful quietude.

(Thereafter, our family would have many pleasant outings on this lake. The children especially enjoyed summer evenings amidst fireflies and tall stands of looming lotus under a full moon while they relished treats of fruits, sweets, and cakes to fill their tummies. Another attraction of Hsuan-wu Lake was good fishing, and from almost every outing we would bring home catches. Fresh fish cooked to a savory tenderness provided Yi his most favoured meal, especially with a cold stein of beer.)

Gliding on the lake's gleaming surface, I could not have enough of

Nature's full beauty. For us all, it was wonderful! By noon, we opened our picnic baskets on board and hungrily enjoyed a sumptuous lunch. Partly from over-eating and partly from too much sun and excitement, one by one we fell asleep. As the sun was setting and we were preparing to go ashore, we heard a loudspeaker directed at our boat.

"Mayor Shen, Mayor Shen!"

We were stunned, but later learned that "Gimo" (short for Generalissimo, our private title for Chairman Chiang Kai-shek) had sent word for Yi to meet him immediately at his residence.

As we would later see, during Yi's term of office Chairman Chiang took a personal interest in the city government of Nanking. In fact, the activities in Nanking became for Chiang almost a "hobby," a weekend relief from his strenuous chairman duties, and Gimo would call on Yi frequently to accompany him to various regions of the city on inspection tours.

But at this time, as the loudspeaker boomed forth on the Lake, I was amused to imagine that Chairman Chiang's staff had had a difficult time in finding us. Our first outing on Lake Hsuan-wu thus ended with a summons of Yi, by the Chairman. Yi departed for his meeting, and the children and I returned home.

It was very late that night when Yi returned home in high spirits and excitement. He was especially pleased that something unexpected had happened regarding Gimo's portrait in the park.

When he had arrived at the meeting with Chairman Chiang, he was immediately asked to accompany Chiang to visit a camp of refugees from the province of Jiangsu, where, over the years, many battles had been fought between our Nationalist troops and the Communist forces of Mao Tse-tung. Jiangsu Province, the home of this large group of refugees, was also an area plagued by devastating floods, and was for that reason of special interest to Yi.

(To explain this connection, I must here briefly digress. Yi was schooled as a hydraulic engineer, and for quite some time was one of China's leading experts in the development of the Yangtze River Valley Authority project, YVA, China's counterpart to the TVA, the

Tennessee Valley Authority in America. Chief consultant of the TVA was a John L. Savage[2], the design-engineer of many of the "high dams" in the United States. In 1943 and 1944, Yi had accompanied Savage on survey trips along the Yangtze River, but not to its lower reaches, a region then under Japanese control and unsafe for travel. In 1946, after the Japanese had left, Savage returned to assist Yi and his colleagues. They then were able to traverse the entire course of both the Yangtze, including the possible dam sites at the Yangtze's Three Gorges [Plate 1; Xiling, Wu, and Qutang; Butler, 2004], and the Yellow River, known as the "River of Sorrow[3]." The Yellow River is so-known because over history of its devastating floods, even worser than that of the Yangtze [Shen-Y, 1974]).

By the time Yi had arrived for the meeting with Chairman Chiang, the day had become chilly with the setting sun. In the Chairman's limousine, his bodyguard ("*Fu-guan*") had put a blanket over Chiang's lap; Yi, seated to Chairman's immediate left, had the privilege of sharing the warmth. En route to the refugee camp, Chiang had asked Yi how he had spent the day. Yi related our outing to Hsuan-wu Lake with its beautifully landscaped park, trees, and buildings. Carefully, he prepared his words about the park's entrance, but he was not hopeful that Gimo would agree to remove his own portrait, standing so proudly between the sets of high gates. Yi's argument was simple but to the point.

"In such a setting, it is truly inappropriate to have such a huge portrait, especially a portrait of our Nation's Leader."

"Moreover, the portrait is poorly done."

These words caught the ears of Chairman Chiang. To Yi's surprise, Generalissimo replied:

"It shall be taken down, immediately!"

This eyesore by the Hsuan-wu Gate has never again been seen.

Footnotes:
  [1]Hu Shih's poem depicts the tranquility of Xuanwu Lake. Husan-wu (Xuanwu), the name of the lake, indicates a location to the north, a term that

dates from the Tang Dynasty, 618-907 (*Ci Hai*, 1976; note the northeastern location of the lake, *Frontispiece*).

[2]In 1928, John L. Savage (1879-1867), nicknamed "Jack Dam," began his career with the design of what was to become his favorite project, the Hoover Dam on the Colorado River, and ended with his initial design, in 1943, of his most exciting engineering project, China's Yangtze Gorge Dam (Rhodes, 1989), the world's largest dam designed and near completion.

Once built, this 750-foot tall dam structure of the Three Gorges will be appreciably more massive than the Hoover Dam; will produce five times the electrical power of Washington State's Grand Coulee Dam, the current record holder; and will create an enormous reservoir, some 250 miles long, while still permitting the passage of ocean-going ships (Kristof, 1993). The electricity to be produced from the Three-Gorges Dam is said to equal that of 18 nuclear-power plants (Hartz, 2005).

But while the Three Gorges Dam boasts the potential production of 85 billion kilowatt-hours per year, the price of such progress is high—the resettling of 1.3 million Chinese villagers and the inundation of 13 cities and towns along the way (Tempest, 1995). In 2004 (with construction scheduled to be completed in 2009), unexpected problems were encountered (Yang, 2004).

Among the potentially most serious problems of the dam construction are cracks (as much as 2 meters deep into the structure), structural distortion of the complex (at more than 1100 sites, due chiefly to some 40 earthquakes in this tectonically active region), pollution and rodent infestation in the yet-unfilled reservoir, and the large-scale loss of archeological relics submerged by the rising waters (Yang, 2004). At present, the project managers are in a state of last-moment appeal, "*linzhen bao fo-jiao.*".

Photographs by Linda Butler (2004) capture powerful images of the Yangtze River and the life of its people before and during the construction of the Dam. Hard-working farmers whose homes, land, and the river valley they had come to know and love will now be razed (See, 2003).

The roots of this project date at least to the 1940s, when the Nationalist government had imagined that such an ambitious project would spur China's arrival as a major world power. In 1946, Savage was in agreement with the U.S. Bureau of Reclamation's report to the Nationalist government that recommended the building of a conventional system of five locks around a major dam at the Yangtze gorges (Fleming, 1946; Rhodes, 1989).

Perhaps in an effort to save the three scenic gorges on the Yangtze, the Bureau's chief mechanical engineer, W. C. Beatty, proposed an alternate approach that modified Savage's design of providing a single lock basin by adding huge gantry cranes capable of lifting or lowering 10,000-ton ships. In the end, this design proved to be too costly and Savage's plan was selected (Rhodes, 1989). Despite its early formulation, the building of the Three Gorges Dam was not initiated until the regime of Chairman Deng Xiao-ping (Kristof, 1993).

In 1979, the author's husband, Dr. Shen Yi, an authority on China's waterworks (see, *About the Author,* this chapter), was asked by Deng Xiao-ping's government to comment on the plan for the Three Gorges Dam construction (Qian, 1998). Shen's younger sister, Xing-yuan (Plate 2), personally brought this request from Beijing to her brother, in 1979, during a visit to California where he was then living. Because of his concern about the potential buildup of silt (also see, Yang, 2004) that the proposed dam would cause and the problems that its construction would entail, Shen Yi was dismayed about the plan, but he reluctantly provided a few lines of suggestions (Qian, 1998).

In early 1992, Chairman Deng proposed, and the Peoples' Republic of China National People Congress voted for the construction of world's largest hydroelectric project on the mid-section of the Yangtze River at the Three Gorges (Holley, 1992; Kristof, 1993; Tempest, 1995). Deng may well have been looking to his place in history and his legacy for the future (Kristof, 1993; Tempest 1995), but the bases of this project were founded firmly in the past (Lin et al., 1998).

Savage, in 1944, had presented five alternative plans for the dam and power plant, all located within a 10-km section of the Yangtze Gorges, upstream from the city Yichang (Rhodes, 1989). Deng's Three Gorges Dam, now essentially completed, is located just upstream from Yichang, exactly as suggested by Savage 60 years ago.

The cost of this huge Dam project has been estimated to be at least 30 billion U.S. dollars (Kempster, 1995). Numerous environmental groups (as well as the Clinton administration) have opposed the project (Barton, 1994; Kempster, 1995; See, 2003). The Three Gorges region of the Yangtze is considered by the people of China to be a national treasure not unlike the Grand Canyon of the U.S. (Bengelsdorf, 1992). Nevertheless, a state environmental agency in Beijing was unable to halt construction on the project based on its lack of adherence to environmental protection laws (Ni, 2005) and this monumental undertaking will soon become a reality (Lin et al., 2000; *Reuters,* 2002; *China S&T Newsletter,* 2004).

[3]The Yellow River has historically been "China's sorrow" (Shen, 1974; Hillel, 1991). In July 1931, its flooding resulted in the death of one million people and the loss of crops over an area of 40,000 square miles (*Timeline China*, 1931).

Chinese engineers used to say that "a bowl of Yellow River water is half a bowl of sand." More recently, during the past decade, flood control has reduced the input of silt by some three million tons a year (*Beijing Daily*, 2000). But even as flood control has helped decrease the age-old sorrow associated with this great waterway, another sorrow is brewing—the overuse of the water it brings to the farms and the people it supports (Chu, 1999).

The once overly abundant water of the Yellow River is now being rapidly depleted, as more and more farms upstream divert water to their fields and staunch the flow to millions of acres of farmland downstream. As lamented by Wu Jiachun, a farmer in a small village in Shandong Province in the lower reaches of the Yellow River, "I haven't had water on my fields [this February] since sowing season last October" (Chu, 1999).

CHAPTER 3
"WHITE HOUSE" OF NANKING

It was amusing that a relatively small run-down house on a patch of vegetable fields would one day become known as the "White House" of Nanking. After World War II, this unprepossessing site was designated the official mayoral residence of the capital. It was here, during my husband's term of office that our family resided for nearly two years. And it was here that I first thought to write these reminiscences.

I never really knew where the nickname, White House, had come from, but its use was common among the circle of foreign diplomats. I heard it first from General Lucas, Advisor of the U.S. Military Command Group to the Republic of China [Melby, 1971]. Our newly restored house, he said, reminded him of the white stucco homes in California. In fact, because of its location, the General had wanted to rent the house for his own residence but had been told that the new mayor and his family would soon be its occupants.

The mayor's house was white and, to some, its circular shape as viewed from the east [Plate 3] bore a slight resemblance to the President's residence in the United States. Soon after its White House moniker had come to the attention of newsmen, they began to attack it with malicious and sarcastic pens, some hurtfully claiming that the house w as "the only high mark" of Yi's tenure in Nanking. In these reporters' views, all crows are black under the sky ("*tian-sha wu-ya yee-ban hay*"), that is—that all officials of the Nationalist government are corrupt.

My husband, however, has always been a person of honesty and perseverance, and he has always held that pure gold fears no fire ("*tzen-jin boo-pah whoa*"). So, never has he been discouraged by such nonsense. Still, the White House was, of course, our family residence in Nanking, the place where Yi and I and our children had all of our private moments together. Here, then, I want to put on record my account of the evolution of this residence, our family home.

After eight years of Japanese occupation, the nation's capital had been once again re-established in Nanking, the Capital of Return

"*Hui-du.*" Before World War II the house had held the office of a city sanatorium, which, during the Japanese occupation, was within the so-called "Safety Zone," the protected region near the site of the Nanking Massacre[1] where more than 100,000 Chinese citizens had been raped and murdered by the occupying troops [Johnson, 1983; Xu, 1987; Chang, 1997; Rabe, 1998]. After the war, only a skeleton of the building's former structure still remained.

The land behind the mayor's house-to-be was quite extensive, and over the years of war and continuous neglect had become transformed into a neighborhood communal garden. In the back, there was a circular pond, overgrown with weeds. An unsightly concrete structure, a wartime air-raid shelter stood awkwardly at the front of the pond. To the front of the property the land was bare except for three tall poplar trees lining a wall on the south, a guardhouse ("*mung-fang*") on the west, and a majestic evergreen that stood squarely facing the main gate. The whole area was a sad sight surrounded by four broken walls. Oddly enough, in the region surrounding this dilapidated ground there arose many grand mansions that housed families of foreign dignitaries. The property and the surrounding homes were situated on Peiping Lu[2] [now renamed Beijing Xi, *Frontispiece*], the most sought-after residential street of the international community [Rabe, 1998].

The prevailing tradition of the city government was that the mayor was to be given a residence, a house to be used for his lodging and various official city functions. So, this long-neglected site had been selected by the city of Nanking for an overhaul. According to the original plans of Yi's interim predecessor, Ma Chao-jun, who was Nanking's mayor before the city was taken by the Japanese in 1937 [Rabe, 1998], the envisioned restoration was to be a monumental project, requiring huge sums of money. This remodeling had a slow start.

By the time Yi arrived in Nanking in 1946, the work had progressed very little. To keep costs down, Yi altered the original plans, did away with much of the grandiose design, and for the planned expensive building materials he substituted those of lesser cost. After several months, the renovation was complete. I am sure that if it had not been for an outstanding City Architect, Tung Da-yo, the project would not have been nearly so successful.

Once moved in, our family soon faced the dilemma of not having enough furniture to fill the spacious rooms. The city government had provided only one pair of leather sofas, a bedroom set, and a wrought-iron oven—nothing more. I was given the job of furnishing the remaining space, a task that should have been that of the city but one I undertook with relish. Because of the sparseness of the furnishing provided us, I truly believed that someone in the city government had gotten wind of the rather large amount of personal furniture we had previously accumulated. And as I think back on the situation, it was really quite surprising that a family such as ours had amassed so much. But it was all merely a matter of chance.

My husband Yi, orphaned at a young age, was a self-made man who had long been without a home. Both of his parents died when he was fourteen and, as the only son, he had to make his way alone in the world. It was only after our marriage that he finally had a place to call his own, a small house built in *Jiang-wan* [Plate 9], the River Bay district of Shanghai's New Civic Center[3] ("*Shi Zhong-xin*"), a region at the northeastern reaches of the city that Yi was responsible for planning (when he was Chief of the Bureau of Public Works) and that he brought to completion in 1937.

Our family became the first occupants in this new residential area of Shanghai. With thirty percent down and a 10-year loan, we were able to purchase one of the smallest models, designated by the developers a Class "*Ting*" (Class 4), the least expensive grade in the complex. Located at 91 Minfu Lu (Road), this was our first very own home!

During the war years, our young family moved to the south of the country, then to the north. We lost nearly all our belongings. But we were blessed with five healthy bubbling daughters and, later, after the war, a baby son [Plate 3]. When Nanking, the capital, had fallen to the Japanese in 1937, and when the underground movement against the enemy ground to a halt, we quickly moved from Shanghai to Hong Kong. We left behind most of our belongings in our *Jiang-wan* home. A few favored pieces were put into storage in my sister-in-law's house, in the then-protected "*Fa Zu-jai*," the French concession[4] on Seymour Road.

During our three-year stay in Hong Kong we acquired a new set of furnishings. In 1940, when the war clouds drew ever closer to this peaceful peninsula, the Nationalist capital moved to Chunking. Yi followed as I and the children returned to Shanghai. When Shanghai came under Japanese attack in 1941 [Plate 8], we left in haste and took an airplane flight (a first for me and my children[5]), via Hong Kong, to Lanchow, the capital city of Gansu Province in northwestern China.

Unbeknownst to us, a well-meaning acquaintance from the Hong Kong-Shanghai Ocean Liner Company had transported all our furnishings from Hong Kong back to Shanghai where they had been stored along with our previous possessions, again with my sister-in-law. Our furniture had been saved, but the suitcases from Hong Kong that were to have been brought by truck to Lanchow were taken by the Japanese.

As it turned out, during the war with Japan, we lost almost all of that which we had truly wanted, but retained much of that which we would willingly have lost. In 1946, when our family returned to Shanghai after the war, we found that a year earlier, as WWII had drawn to a close our home in *Jiang-wan* had been destroyed by the bombs of the Allied Forces [Plate 9, *Chapter 10*]. Our house had been lost. And although losing the house could have meant losing everything, by miraculous good luck all our furnishings had been saved. Perhaps our collection of furnishings had been destined for its ultimate service to the municipal government of Nanking!

In May 1947, we moved into the completed Nanking residence at 38 Peiping Lu[6]. Within a short time, and to my joy and amazement, the house seemed filled splendidly with all our old furnishings salvaged from the war. Together with the staff, I gave every piece a good dusting and polishing. Each room was decorated rather elegantly with our "regained treasures"—lace curtains, carpets, scrolls, and artwork.

Soon, the unkempt land surrounding the White House was no longer so overgrown with weeds; trees were being planted, lawns had been spread, and a pleasing network of small stone paths was joined. I determined to devote my own labour to improve it even further. During the first three to four months, whether in rain or sunshine, I spent every morning working side-by-side with our two gardeners. (There is nothing better than a rainy day for the transplanting of trees, shrubs, and flowers!) Along the east side, adjacent to the house at the front, an open lawn was spread to form a badminton court for our girls.

The very large garden in the back of the mayor's residence was divided into two parts: a smaller one, near the west wall, for vegetables, and a larger part for further landscaping. A tall stand of junipers was planted to separate the two areas. The vegetable patch behind the kitchen quickly became lush. We had a profusion of greens, many of which were only rarely seen in the local markets. Near the vegetable garden, a small square area was fenced, and two sturdy wooden shelters were built for chickens and ducks. One can only imagine the number of fresh eggs I gathered every morning, a hobby I had acquired during the war years while we lived in Lanchow [*About the Author*].

I had high hopes of improving the landscape even more, but I was terribly vexed by one major obstacle, the awkward and ugly air-raid shelter that stood at the front of the pond in the back yard. This massive concrete structure was impossible to move. I lost sleep for many a night searching for a solution until one fine moment a perfect remedy came to mind—immediately a few labourers were quickly hired to expand and deepen the existing pool in the back, giving it a meandering shape around the concrete bunker. Mud from the excavation was then used to cover the unsightly shelter. With help from the Nanking Park Service (especially, Hsuan-wu Park Director Ho Ba-jen), within a short time we had built a small hill. The finishing touch was to dress this artificial hill ("*gia-san*") with dwarf trees and shrubs, interspersed with shapely boulders. More trees and flowers were added to the landscape. Flowerbeds edged and dotted the lawn, dispersed among the trees in studied disorder.

A traditional bamboo hut was erected behind the artificial hill and connected to a network of narrow winding walks. The hut itself was covered with leaves of trailing vines, and to its right stood a stand of banana palms, fanning and giving cool green shade over a stone table and stools [*Chapter 10*]. This soon became our summer haven—particularly for me, where I could read or write, or hide from the calls of the busy daily routine.

There was something mysterious about the pond. Its water was always clear and plentiful and it never dried, even during long spells of summer draught. I finally discovered that the pond was fed by a natural spring. This new knowledge gave me added incentive and enthusiasm to perfect the grounds further. As soon as work on the hill had been completed, I began to design and then have built a small red bridge across the pond to form a continuous path from the hill to the hut.

By moonlight, on summer evenings, I would go to the pool, preferably alone, and sit by its edge under the soft shadow of lazy willows. Buds of lotus and water lilies, running riot in the pond, gave off sweet light scents into the gentle breeze. Lapping fishes among dense lotus clumps murmured solitary notes of melody. Birds in sweet dreams, tranquil in the trees, softly interrupted the quietude. The whole garden, including my solitary self, would become completely entranced by the cool moon above. At such moments, and in this silken setting, I could not but indulge myself in romantic thoughts, of joy or sorrow depending on my mood at the time. A fine verse from the Sung period (~ 960 A.D.) would nudge me into consciousness:

> *Bewitching moon, sweet and fragrant blooms,*
> *With honors we have and groomed.*
> *Regret not but ponder, can duty and deeds be welded,*
> *When the first is certain, the other inerrant?*

At long last, this garden of phoenix had risen from the ashes! Although I was physically spent by the work, each improvement brought me immeasurable pleasure. Whether because of the house, or possibly the landscaping, our residence on Peiping Lu had by now gained notoriety. And our garden had become a marvelous setting for official functions (with me now known to the community as official "Top Gardener").

This was the same house that the newsmen, with their sarcastic pens, had attacked as the "high mark" of Yi's enterprise in Nanking.

Indeed, not all officials of the Nationalist Government are corrupt!

My garden was not only pleasing to the eye, but it was useful too.

We enjoyed the fresh produce—vegetables, fish, ducks, hens, and eggs. When an unexpected guest came to dinner, a sumptuous meal of appropriate variety could be prepared from my bountiful "little farm." Though I never actually tried, I often thought that a complete "home-grown" meal served to foreign guests might have proven more delectable than one of our formal banquets.

Life, however, is a dream, or a series of dreams, one after another. I now know that my two years in the White House were also nothing more than a beautiful illusion. Tears welled, upon arriving in Bangkok in 1949, when I opened the May 9th issue of *Life Magazine* [*References*]. I was numbed by the pictures taken in Nanking earlier that month, on the eve of the Communist takeover, showing mob scenes at our Nanking home [*"The looting of Nanking—At Mayor's House,"* photographs by the French photographer Henri Cartier-Bresson]. Local citizens (*lao bai-shin*) stormed and looted my living room of its radiator, wooden floorings, and, I had no doubt, stomping on and destroying my beautifully landscaped garden. The scenes were so vivid and familiar, the destruction so very painful.

My careful plans, my loving works were all too soon for naught.

Footnotes:

[1]This area, during the early part of Japanese invasion (1937-38), bordered the "Safety Zone," established by John Rabe (1998) and intended to protect civilians from the atrocities of war. According to his diary entries of December 1937, Rabe was in effect the acting Chief of Police and the Mayor of Nanking. He and members of an International Committee had organized in an attempt to curtail the looting, burning, killing and raping by Japanese soldiers.

According to Rabe, there were about 250,000 people in the city center. The Headquarters of the International Safety Zone Committee was situated at 6 Ninghai Lu, the former residence of Chinese Foreign Minister Chang Ch'un (Plate 1; *Frontispiece*; Rabe, 1998). The Ginling Girls School, attended by the Author's daughters, was located within this protected zone (Rabe, 1998; Zhu, 2002). To the north of this zone was the British Embassy, and to the south, the Japanese, German and American Embassies (Rabe, 1998). The mayor's residence, the "White-House" at 38 Peiping Lu (*Frontispiece*), was several houses to the southwest of the Ninghai Lu Headquarters.

²Peiping Lu (*"Northerly Peace Road"*) was originally named Peking Lu (*"North Capital Road"*), but when the Nationalists re-established Nanking as their capital after WWII, the name Peking was changed to Peiping.

³The new Civic Center of Shanghai (*"Shi Zhong-xin"*) was conceived in 1927, when Mayor of Shanghai General Huang Fu took office (Wakeman, 1995), and was completed under the supervision of Shen Yi, Chief of Shanghai's Bureau of Public Works and the author's husband. The development was dedicated in April 1934 as a symbolic center for the New Life Movement that had been formulated by Chairman Chiang Kai-shek (Wakeman, 1995).

⁴The French Zone (*"Fa Zu-jie"*), an area of Shanghai, was ceded to France after the Qing Dynasty succumbed in the 1890s to the demands of the eight nations (see *Historic Foreword*).

⁵The airplane to Lanchow had parallel rows of face-to-face seats along the windows, across a central aisle, resembling current military carriers. While the author and her daughters nursemaid were exhausted from their packing for the trip, the children were giddy with excitement and concern about their first plane ride, asking in wonderment: "Are we allowed to go to the bathroom?"

⁶Under the present regime, the name of the street, Peiping Lu, has once again been "elevated" to Beijing Road, and *"Xi"* (West) has been added to the section that includes the former site of the mayor's residence to distinguish it from the "Beijing *Dong*," Beijing Road East (see *Frontispiece*).

By 2005, the former White House was no longer standing, its grounds having been subdivided to accommodate two-storey townhouses. The landmark evergreen tree facing the front gate of the compound (Plate 3) was also gone, but the gray mansion across the broad Beijing Xi Road that once fronted the White House, the former Egyptian Embassy with its paired staircases rising from the sidewalk, remained essentially unchanged.

CHAPTER 4
MAYOR'S HOUSEHOLD

From time to time I saw passersby outside our wall peeping into the garden, fixing their glances on our home with more admiration than curiosity. They must have thought that whoever lived in this gorgeous mansion must be the luckiest persons in the world. Visitors calling on us would praise the house as the best residence in all of Nanking. But these people could never imagine that life in this palatial dwelling was, at least from time to time, unglamorous and even dismal.

Customarily, expenditures of an official residence were part of a city's budget. My husband and I rejected this practice, in spite of our underwhelming finances and meager income. The corruption of high officials in China was rampant and the norm, and well known to the world; but *there is still the purity of a lotus rising from a muddied earth* [cf. the author's painting, *White Sacred Lotus*, Plate 2]. For this reason, for his purity, I am so proud and deeply love my husband Yi!

It was a big job to run a household of about thirty people in the mayor's residence, the so-called White House. Of the staff, 13 were workers provided by the City Government. In addition to taking care of the daily needs of my children, my time was spent in training the staff in preparation for our frequent dinner parties and instructing the kitchen workers about how to prepare proper banquet meals. The sewing chores of my family had by now taken over by my godmother, "*Gan-niang*," who, being widowed from my father's third brother joined our household to help out on the family needs that I was not able to handle. Without her, I would have fallen to pieces.

In the White House household chores were divided into two sections, with official functions under the responsibility of Mr. Chu, the supervisor sent by the City. The family section was under my personal care. Mr. Chu was at a loss when it came to managing "facing out" diplomatic functions, so it soon became my job to oversee the entire household. Chu was a good and decent man who did help me a great deal wherever he could. Nominally, I was First Lady of Nanking, but in reality I became Chief Steward of the mayor's White House.

For me this was not really a hardship, but it did place our family in a financial predicament.

My husband's monthly salary was only barely enough to feed the whole household. Yet all the while we had to maintain a certain dignified lifestyle (both "facing out" and "facing in") in keeping with the rank of the Mayor of the Nation's Capital. As appreciative as my husband was of my efforts to keep up the expected attractive front, he lamented that our outwardly "presentable" lifestyle had attracted ridicule and even suspicion of corruption. Being born with an eye for the textures of beauty, the lines, the colours, the aesthetics, I could not help myself to not beautify my own surroundings, in spite of personal hardships and Yi's gentle "complaints." Though the following episodes are unpleasant for me to recall, I am proud to add that these hard times ultimately brought the joy and satisfaction of a respectable and honorable lifestyle to the household of Mayor Shen Yi of Nanking.

Family Life. We had two elder daughters in middle school, two younger ones in primary school, and two small toddlers, the youngest of the family. As frugal as I tried to be, we had no spare funds for our children's education, clothing, and occasional medical bills. Yi, of course, was laden with a tremendous official load, so I had not the heart to burden him with our own trivial problems.

Fortunately, our back garden was spacious enough for me to develop a small farm where we could produce food for our family to lighten our expenses. With the help of our two gardeners, we planted this small "dream ranch" with a good variety of vegetables and crops, and along the sides I raised a flock of ducks and hens [*Chapter 3*]. I seeded the lotus pond by the hillside with fish, and my elderly father, who lived with us, raised pigeons in the birdhouse he had designed. He was more than happy fishing in the pond to provide our family supper.

After a period of about three months, the production of our little farm at the back was enough to meet our daily needs. Rubbish accumulated from the farm and kitchen was made into a compost pile and recycled to the land as fertilizer (a trick I had learned from a Russian friend years before and saw to yield good results). I invested in my farm more labour than money. For most of the year, all we now needed was to occasionally buy fresh meat, fruits, and dry goods from the market. Our daily meal consisted of vegetables, fish, and eggs, and once in awhile we might splurge on a fowl—a chicken, a duck, or even pigeons. We were frugal, but we kept our nutrition up to standard. Our major food expenses seemed solved.

The success of our backyard farming was a great help. But we still needed to tackle the education expenses of our children. Fortunately, we had a small stash of gifts given to each of the children at birth. It was customary that in celebration of the first month of the birth of a child (we called it the making of the "month-let," "*tso yueh-tze*") the family would dye hard-boiled eggs a brilliant red and distribute them among friends and relatives who would be invited to a big feast. These friends and relatives would then each bring a gift for the new-born, invariably a present of gold—be it a ring, a bracelet, a necklace, or a dangle—all of considerable value. Because of these gifts, we had the wherewithal to secure the primary education of each of our four older daughters. Each season when their school sessions began, I would visit a gold shop in the central city for monetary exchange.

For us, the season of winter brought particular hardship. Our children rapidly out-grew or wore-out their clothing, so new clothes had to be provided. Being a packrat out of habit, I had kept all of my out-of-fashion wardrobe, even that from my girlhood, and I had most of my husband's old clothes as well. Quite a trunk of these potential cast-me-downs had accumulated. This ample pile now came to the use of my children.

My godmother was an expert seamstress, but she had no notion of the style of dresses that my girls were accustomed to [Plate 4]. I selected old materials from my stash, giving them each a proper cleaning, and using newspapers and a block of charcoal from the kitchen I took up pattern-designing which *Gan-niang* then followed-up with the cutting and sewing of "new" clothes. All the while when *Gan-niang* was with us, she occupied a small room on the first floor next to my study that was fitted with a foot-operated sewing machine made of heavy iron[1]. We listened to her labor—"*gedong, gedong, gedong ...*"—as she turned out refurbished dresses for my brood.

I, on the other hand, took care of knitting sweaters, socks, mittens, scarf and hats (and taught my daughters Hwa-hwa and Pei-pei how to knit some of the simpler items). Yarn from worn-out knitted woolen wear would be loosened stitch by stitch and the threads wrapped around and around the backs of chairs, bundle after bundle; the scavenged yarn was then soaked in warm water, straightened, and dried on clothes lines for another round of knitting.

My girls helped by offering their out-stretched hands and arms, holding the circular bundles of yarn like human looms and I would seek out the head of the thread and wind the yarn, all the while reconnecting broken ends, to make spool after spool of now reusable woolen threads. Our family dinning room, right next to *Gan-niang*'s sewing room, often looked like a garment factory! No one would have imagined that the lovely fashionable dresses and sweaters of my children came from vintage stashes of clothes worn tens of years before. This painstaking labor provided the clothing of my family, but it also brought piles of ridicule from people who had no understanding of how these nice clothes had come to be.

I give here one sorrowful incident that has forever remained fresh in my mind. During our first winter in Nanking, my eldest daughter Hwa-hwa was in high spirits as she put on her newly made slacks and coat before school one morning. After school, when she returned home, she had a long face and was obviously very sad. Before I could ask her what was the matter she broke down into a quivering voice and tears welled in her eyes.

"Mommy[2], I hope Daddy[2] will quit the government."

"This way no one will ever call us grafters."

What did she mean by this? I was at sea.

Hwa-hwa continued. "Maybe I shouldn't be so happy about my new clothes."

"I am proud of how they look and *Ah-dia*'s sewing." (*Ah-dia* is the name my children addressed my godmother.)

"I know how they were made, but when I got to school the other kids shouted. '*Everybody, come and see how smart the mayor's daughter looks today! … What a rich girl she must be!*'"

"Mommy, what do they mean by rich corrupt big bosses?"

Hwa-hwa broke down crying aloud. I cuddled her in my arms and felt defeated and terribly sad. There was a deep-seated feeling throughout the country (even among children) that not a single government official was above corruption [see, "newsmen's black crows," *Chapter 3*]. I could not blame them for thinking this way. Corruption was a commonplace in our society as a great many in high places used their position and power to exploit the wealth of the nation [*Chapter 5*]. But, still, to me this insult to Hwa-hwa was so unfair—so unfair to her, so unfair to my family. I felt terrible!

Both Yi and I embraced morals, not money. We did our best to find peace with our own conscience, not burdening our minds with unimportant matters, each night hoping to have a good sleep. No one on the outside really understood our situation. Friends from out of town heard of our "mansion" and would ask to stay with us. Our hearts were full of hospitality, but we were much burdened by this friendship. Though we had several guest rooms at the back, when visitors came we needed to be presentable and provide our guests with an appropriately fine meal [this being so-called face-saving[3], "*yao mian-zi*," a deep-seated central part of Chinese culture], the cost of which had to be scrounged from our shallow purse. Our guests would never have fathomed that we lived in a constant fear of embarrassing humiliation.

Another sorry moment I recall happened one day when my children returned home for lunch. I was in the pantry instructing the chefs about the various dishes to be served that evening to our houseguests. The children got a whiff of the good smells and jumped with joy.

"How tasty, are these for us?"

My heart sank. I did not know how to answer. I could not say "*no,*" and disappoint them, so I said nothing (and swallowed my tears). Hwa-hwa sensed my problem—that the dishes were meant for our guests, not for the children—and jokingly said to her younger sisters,

"You gluttonous little things '*Shao tung-shi*' (a phrase of endearment), these are for tonight's guests!"

"Mommy will give us the same next time."

The children fell to a stone silence. I saw the disappointment in their little faces, and one after another they filed out of the pantry. Something inside me suddenly sprung forth, and as I pointed to the wall behind them I asked in a happy tone.

"Can you guess what is in this cupboard?" Their cheerfulness instantly returned.

"Mommy has prepared *your* tasty dinner for tonight."

They could not wait to open the locked cupboard.

"Oh no," I said, "hurry up with your lunches and wait for your surprise!"

Mixed with laughter and jostling, they scampered into the family dinning room and forgot all about the good smells from the pantry. (All this, of course, was a trick. There was no such "tasty dinner" in the cupboard. I busied myself that whole afternoon putting together the nice dinner they now expected. How could children understand the agony of a mother's heart?)

Remembrances like these—of my children and their heartfelt desires—cause me to recall a childhood moment when I had an overwhelming penchant to act in school plays. As it turned out, this experience (despite its cost in labor and pocket-money) helped me greatly as it could now be applied to my real-life living.

Gift Giving. In China, following the lunar calendar, three big holidays are celebrated: May 5th "*Duan-wu Jie*" [the Midsummer Festival for remembrance of patriot Qu Yuan[4]], the Mid-August Moon Festival, "*Chung-cho Jie*," and the Chinese New Year, "*Shin Nian*." During such times, one was expected to pile his/her bosses with presents. When Yi and I became married, I was unaccustomed to this practice.

So, during one big festival, when I was a first-year bride and gifts began to pour into our home, I did not know how to react. In fact, I was so uncertain that I told the delivery men to wait until my husband Yi returned from his office. When Yi came home I told him about the deliveries. He turned angry and muttered to himself, "This is absolutely absurd, *'wan-chang'* [a nasty phrase, literally, 'muddled accounting']! What kind of person do they think I am?" I secretly congratulated myself—I loved his purity, he was a very good man—and I felt comforted that I had not accepted any of the presents.

Yi told the delivery men that he wished *not* to accept any of the nice gifts sent by their clients. One person had sent a truckload of banquet food to our door. Yi asked the driver to return it to the sender. Upon its return, the gift-giver ordered the driver to deliver it once again. Yi, again, ordered it to be returned. After three such back-and-forth deliveries, the truck driver dumped every crate of the food by our door and angrily announced:

"I give up. I am through delivering today to you people."

"You can settle your own accounts!"

During Yi's tenure at the Shanghai Bureau of Public Works, from 1927 to 1937, many of his colleagues at the Bureau, for the most part able young men of about his age who looked up to him as their leader, were just as incorruptible as he. Developers and contractors would drop "red envelopes" containing bribes at the office door. Yi was proud that his colleagues, whom he much respected, reported the bribes. During his term in Shanghai the Bureau donated these monies to Shanghai charities, in the names of the bribers, and then sent to each of them a donation receipt that showed how their money had been "spent." News of the attempted bribes, and the refusal by Yi's department to accept them, spread throughout the city. After such episodes, and as Yi's reputation of gift refusal became well known, the presentations gradually decreased[5] and my anxiety slowly went away.

The custom of gift-giving was of course also followed in Nanking, and was unavoidable among close friends and relatives. Though we had no budget to handle the matter, I devised what seemed to me a clever scheme by which to exchange one gift for another so at the end we spent nothing and received nothing in return.

During Christmas, it was our place, in the diplomatic circle, to make friends with notable foreign visitors, and it was customary to exchange presents. I first managed this task by looking into our collection of local arts and crafts, "*tu-chan,*" to find gifts that might be to the foreigners' liking. After only a single Christmas season, however, I found that our stash was exhausted. I luckily then came up with another scheme. I took the potted plants I had raised in my hothouse in the backyard and, decorated with festive bows and ribbons[6], I sent them as presents to our distinguished friends.

Official Entertainment. At the beginning of our years in Nanking we catered all our formal banquets from restaurants. The results were always disappointing, both the food and its presentation. (Yi and I had both developed a particular eye and taste for flavoury dishes of brilliant colors and varying textures that could be properly presented, and most restaurant food did not measure up.) I therefore took it upon myself to organize the preparation of such banquets from our own kitchen, and to train our household staff to serve according the proper rules on such occasions (with *Gan-niang*, my godmother, having the added assignment of outfitting the staff in the smart white uniforms I had designed).

We had two cooks, one we had hired for family meals who had been with us before and after the recent war [WWII]. This cook, Ben-yao, not only knew Chinese cuisine but had been trained for Western food in Russian and French kitchens. The other cook came from the City Government. When this cook came to work at the house he was young, inexperienced, but eager. Under our tutelage he soon became facile in preparing many dishes. The third expert in our family staff was the children's nurse, "Mama" [Plate 9]. Coming from the town of Yangchow, well known for its cuisine, Mama brought a tremendous knowledge of good dishes to our kitchen. With this three-part collaboration, plus my own knowledge of what we ought to be preparing, we could present a very fine feast at the mayor's table.

At the beginning of entertainment, we tested our performance by giving small dinner parties to a close circle of foreign guests. A great success came with our very first attempt. Later—helped, I think, by my zealous collecting of Chinese dinner settings and European porcelains that started from the time when I first ventured to Europe with Yi in 1934[7] [*About the Author*]—we gained versatility in entertaining Chinese dignitaries with European meals, and foreign guests with Chinese banquets. Rather soon, the "*Shen Kitchen*" won high praise from local and international company. We had weaned ourselves from the caterers, saving the municipal government considerable expense.

Despite this progress in banqueting, we had problems. We needed receipts for reimbursement of our entertainment purchases of food ingredients from the mass markets. The accounting of such things, and the red tape and hassle from the City Auditing Department, became a maddening headache. One day Mr. Chu came to me to beg Yi to give up this practice of buying on the open market and to resume the catering of our dinner parties. I raised the matter with Yi, but he firmly refused, saying that our way of banqueting was not only refined, with "wholesome" smartness[3] ("*ti-mian*"), but could save the City Treasury a great deal of money that could be applied elsewhere for public needs.

We had problems also for dinners Yi hosted at Nanking municipal buildings. I actually was quite astonished to hear of the red tape involved for one particular such dinner party given by Yi at the City Hall at *Futze Miao*[8], a dinner he had arranged for bankers to thank them for facilitating a loan to the City of Nanking. This was an official and rather formal affair, and to soften the rigid atmosphere he jokingly ended his speech by saying,

"Although this is a formal occasion, and a speech by the host is unavoidable."

"In this case, many of you are my friends and old acquaintances, so this customary formality might have been dispensed with."

"However, as you have seen, I have kept it I say this with good reason."

"After all, if there were no speech given on this occasion, the bill for this dinner would have been red stamped by the municipal Audit Department."

His guests burst into laughter. Yi then explained.

"I heard a story from my good friend, O.K. Yu, the former Acting Mayor of Shanghai [Plates 6, 9]."

"On one occasion when Yu gave an official dinner, the Audit Department of the municipal government of Shanghai rejected the bill, arguing that since Mayor Yu did not give a speech, the dinner could not be considered an official function."

Municipal governments, more a hindrance than a help in such matters, were notorious for their useless bureaucratic waste! I was not in a position to complain, notwithstanding the fact that I gave my services free and whole-heartedly, but in return got a "*dan*" of grief! All in all, Yi and I and our family faced a major financial burden.

Given this dilemma, I began to check how we could further cut-back our family expenses so that we could offset the deficit from our public functions. My heart grew heavy as I could not find even a single not-needed cost in our daily expenses. Surprisingly to me, I found that fresh milk and butter occupied a full one-sixth of our monthly food bills. Perhaps we could dispense with these luxuries. I gathered our four older girls in one room and in a relaxed fashion tried to get them to answer some serious questions. I gathered a bowl of candies and peanuts and told them that I would award tasty prizes to those who could come up with the best answers.

"Do you consider us a rich or a poor family?"

They looked at each other with blank faces—but swept desiring glances at the bowl of sweets—and knew not how to gauge their reply. After a while, in unison they chimed.

"Mommy, we are not rich, but we are not as poor as many."

"You answered perfectly, but do you wish you were richer?"

"Of course you do."

"And you'd like to have plenty of good treats after school and have pocket money like your friends[10]."

They paused, shook their heads.

"No, Mommy, we do not want Daddy to become corrupt in order to provide us with such things."

I was impressed to tears. I kissed Hwa, Pei, San, and Chuan, one by one.

"You are right, all of you are right, my precious little ones!"

I then divided the sweets and peanuts into four equal portions and gave each a pile. While they enjoyed their treats, I softly told them that from now on we all would have soybean milk and peanut butter for breakfast, and I then explained the reason. At first they were a little disappointed, but that quickly passed and they then happily responded:

"Oh, soy milk and peanut butter are tasty too! We love them." Hwa-hwa then piped up, "May we save some beans and peanuts to be roasted and smoked for snacking?"

"Sure, of course you may." Everyone smiled. To cheer them on further I added,

"Let's each of us spend a Sunday picking beans and digging up extra peanuts for our snacks."

Our cozy little room was instantly filled with a clamoring, "Mommy this and Mommy that," and of pure happiness among mother and daughters. Often I have thought of this. The happy scene stands out in sharp relief in my memory.

Crisis. Inflation came to a climax in the summer of 1948. The most serious items of increased cost and low supply were the staples, the so-called "rice mob" [see, *Chapter 10*]. Every civil servant got a monthly rice ration from the government (and for oil, salt, soy sauce and vinegar as well), everyone, including our service staff. But when the city granaries stopped supplying rice, the rice ration came to a halt. I was informed one day by one of the kitchen staff that our whole household had only one or two days of rice left.

This staple crisis was an emergency. For Chinese, rice is the main dish required for each meal. Many of the younger folks consume up to four bowls of rice at a single sitting. To make things worse, we also were nearly out of cabbage oil and pork lard. Some of the young staff came to me and demanded that I provide oil for their meals, threatening that if I couldn't come up with it they would quit and find a household that could provide them adequate foodstuffs.

"Calon-tong" ["Oh my," the sound of a rock hitting ground], a stone lodged in my throat! Much of the crew was under the jurisdiction of the City Government, and the possible abandonment of their service would create a crisis for our household. Not only that, but diplomatic invitations had been mailed two weeks in advance for an upcoming function at our home, and it would be embarrassing, to say the least, if we were forced to cancel a function at the mayor's residence.

I sympathized with the needs of rice and lard of these workers and offered my best efforts to find oil for their meals. I even told them that I would get oil to them before our family got ours. About this, they didn't care. To them, our supply was of no concern. After this fiasco finally passed, after the crisis of the rice and oil shortage had ebbed away, Mr. Chu came to let me know that I had done wonders to "snuff out this smoldering ash."

To meet my promise of food stuff for my staff, I sent our own cook, Ben-yao, to do his best to search for oil at whatever it cost, and I went door-to-door to my friends to borrow oil and rice. After an afternoon of hunting we were able to gather 200 catties[9] of rice and 15 catties of oil, enough to last our household for one more week.

The newspaper said that many people in Nanking were failing to find supplies and that there was a close watch whether the mayor would still, under these harsh conditions, get rice for his own household.

By nightfall, in the dark, I sent Mr. Chu in my car with my driver to collect the borrowed foods. This was done so secretly that even my own staff, except the gatekeepers, did not know how the food came to the house. I was exhausted, and worried, for at the same time I was preparing a dinner party that we were to host. No one at that party would have imagined that this "most blessed person" (that's me)—living in this palatial surroundings, lording over a troop of servicing crew, and resplendent in my evening clothes as I bumped elbows with our fine guests—was in actuality a beggar of the night!

Only Mr. Chu sympathized with my predicament. One day, when I asked him to purchase 100 catties of yams for the children's afternoon tea, he broke down and cried (knowing full well that yam[11] was considered a food for the poor).

"No one would have imagined that the living conditions at the mayor's house could be so minimal, so low as to be well beneath those of lesser-rank officials."

"Even the lower ranking families enjoy better meals than the Mayor."

Chu was so touched that he offered to go out to neighboring villages and purchase food there, where the cost could be much lower. This was a good idea, which I readily accepted. But I would still have to come up with the money needed.

Inflation. Nanking was known throughout the country as one of the three "boiler" cities in China. Summer of 1948 was particularly hot, an unending series of the "dog days" of summer. Watermelons were an item all families coveted to quench the thirst. Because of high prices in the city, my chauffeur suggested that we drive to the melon patches outside of town to stock our needs.

The next morning for the purchase of watermelons, I gave Mr. Chu 500 Jin-yuan Juan [gold notes], enough for 100 catties. Our children eagerly awaited his return. But at the end of the day, Mr. Chu returned empty handed. The money I had given him was enough to buy only half the watermelons I had ordered. And he did not want to lose face by bargaining with the farmers, as he was representing the First Lady of Nanking. The children were downtrodden, I deeply dismayed. I found my chauffeur, hopped in the car, dashed off to a nearby market, and brought home six big watermelons instead of the 100 catties I had hoped for. The children munched happily and forgot their earlier disappointment.

On this same day, Yi had an audience with Gimo [President Chiang Kai-shek] and had a very interesting talk with the old man. When Yi came home, he and I sat down and I cut him a piece of watermelon without telling him about our problems in getting it. While eating, he began to tell me the gist of his conversation with Gimo, most of which concerned municipal finances.

At the end of Yi's meeting with the Chairman, Gimo inquired about Yi's personal financial condition, whether he had encountered difficulties. It was far beyond Yi's expectation for Gimo to ask about such a personal matter. Yi's response was that his situation was hardly worth mentioning when almost all employees of Gimo's government were suffering deeply [see, *Chapter 10*]. Gimo was silent and did not ask further. But Yi noted an expression of embarrassment on his face. Yi soon took leave and returned home to me and our family.

I have written this chapter with great trepidation. I have tried here to present a realistic picture of how the mayor's household managed to have a presentable lifestyle of honorable living at a terribly difficult time in the history of our country. But despite the problems we had to overcome, I have no regrets, and I am not ashamed of our poverty and frugality. Rather, as I now look back on those days, I am proud and happy to have gained from this novel experience of living!

Footnotes:

[1]This foot-peddled sewing machine was left with the author's godmother after the Shen family departed Nanjing. *Gan-niang* was grateful for this gift which she used in her later years to provide her livelihood in Shanghai under the new regime.

[2]All of Author's children addressed their parents as Daddy and Mommy, familial terms not customary in China. Evidently, the Western education the author received at an early age (see *About the Author*) led her to adopt some Western ways of life, especially with regard to food and the style of clothing for her children (see Plate 4).

[3]In traditional Chinese culture, a person must at all costs "save face" ("*yao main-zi*"), maintain the respect of others even to death ("*si yao main-zi*"). One who loses respect, who "loses face" ("*diu lian*"), loses all. It is a deep insult to tell a person that he has lost face to the death of him ("*si bu-yao lian*"); the opposite is a wholesome face ("*ti mian*"), meaning that the person or his action is presentable, smart, and appropriate.

[4]In despair over the country's turmoil during the period of the Warring States of Chu (476-221 BC), poet patriot Qu Yuan committed suicide

by plunging into the Mi-lou Jiang (River) in Hunan Province. According to tradition, the suicide occurred on the 5th of May and the citizens who witnessed his courageous death threw packets of glutinous rice wrapped in bamboo leaves ("*zong-zi*") into the river to protect him from being devoured by water animals. Today, this event is celebrated on May 5th of the lunar calendar as the Midsummer Festival, "*Duan-wu Jie*". On this festive day, wrapped sweets or meats in sticky rice, "*zong-zi*," are eaten, and dragon-boat races take place on rivers throughout China (*Xinhua Zidian*, 1982). A large bronze statue of Qu that overlooks the Yangtze River stands astride the Qu Yuan Temple.

[5]In Taipei, when Shen Yi was Minister of Communications of the Republic of China (1960-1968), his reputation for the refusal of festival-time gifts became more and more well known, and fewer and fewer gifts found their way to his house. One New Year's Eve, his family cook came to the author and told her that a particular family had received gifts of at least a dozen *Jin-hua* hams (a well known variety of outstanding quality, having a flavor like that of a Virginia ham or Italian prosciutto). The cook suggested that if Minister Shen wished to obtain an excellent ham at a minimal price, the cook would go to the house of that family and offer to buy one.

To the author it was dismaying to learn that the habit of gifting and gift-acceptance was followed even on Taiwan, the island to which the Republic had retreated.

[6]The author had mastered the talent of wrapping presents with exquisitely constructed bows of beautiful and ingenious designs. This special ability was an artistic and inexpensive way of being presentable, "*ti mian*."

[7]See, In (1935) "*Diary from Europe*" (*References*).

[8]"*Fuzi Miao*" (Confucius Temple), site of the Nanking City Hall (1946-49), is situated by the Qin-huai River. Established some 4000 years ago, this old-town area along the river of historic temples, tea houses and restaurants is flourishing still, and decorated with display of splendid lanterns.

[9]One *dan* equals 100 *catties*, with one catty ("*jin*") being equivalent to 0.5 kilogram; a "*dan* of grief," is a heavy ("50 kg") dose of headache.

[10]The author's children, unlike many of their schoolmates, were given no pocket money of their own. They watched with admiration (and some envy) as their schoolmates, walking together across the street after school, bought small snacks, or on weekends ventured into movie houses to see the latest films.

Author's children felt left out, despite their many family group activities—gardening, raising chickens and ducks, weekend family outings, badminton and softball games on the family lawn, swimming in the city pool, and riding borrowed bicycles (round-and-round the evergreen tree in front of their house).

Frequently, if the author permitted, the children had the great fun of putting on the phonograph full-blast and dancing in the spacious formal dinning room to the house-rattling beat of "*boon-za-za, boon-za-za*." At other times they were treated to watching home movies (taken and laboriously edited by their dad) to which they yelled and howled. And on rare occasions the whole family would venture to the cinema to see cartoons and their favorite Chinese and Hollywood actors.

Poor or not, in the author's eyes her children were wonderfully blessed.

[11]In fact, baked yams were one of the author's favorite foods (in addition to other sweet dishes). In her old age, when she lived at the Bentley House in Los Angeles (see About the Author), she occasionally became feisty and refused to eat her meals; whenever this happened, the Bentley House cooks were instructed to feed her yams—which, of course, she devoured with great gusto.

CHAPTER 5
AUDIENCE WITH THE FIRST LADY

Background ----------

The First Lady of China, Mme. Chiang Kai-shek (Soong Mayling, 1897-2003), came from a wealthy and privileged family. She was reared and schooled in the United States, spending her ten most formative years there [Hahn, 1941]—*first, at the Piedmont School in Demarest, Georgia (which she entered at age 10, in 1907); then, at Southern Methodist Wesleyan Female College in Macon, Georgia (1912); and finally, at Wellesley College, Massachusetts, from which she received her B.A. degree in 1917* [Lin, 2000]. *Soong Mayling's attachment to her American southern upbringing was deep; years later she still fondly remembered her happy times at Piedmont.*

Her English was impeccable and spoken with a slight Georgian lilt. Biographer Emily Hahn [1941] *writes: "Few Americans can say that they know their country as well as Mayling does." Soong Mayling Chiang once told the U.S. Congress, "I will always look upon America as my second home"* [Meisler, 1995]. *Counting her ten years of schooling and the subsequent time she spent in the United States until her death at the age of 105 in New York City in 2003* [Woo, 2003], *Mme. Chiang lived a third of her life in her U.S. "second home."*

Journalist B. W. Lin [2000] *lauds her as having "no predecessor before or successor behind," and describes her as being intelligent, stubborn, sharp, and steel-hearted. Others describe her as being precocious but not especially hard working, a person who relied on wits and flair and had a quick tongue that helped her to charm her way out of trouble* [Seagrave, 1985]. *British Field Marshal, Lord Alan Brooke, described Mme. Chiang as using "sex and politics" to achieve her goals* [Bryant, 1959; Lin, 2000]. *Indeed, throughout China and much of the Western world as well, Soong Mayling's wedding to Chiang Kai-shek (Chairman of the Kuomintang), on December, 1, 1927, was hailed as a major political event* [Seagrave, 1985; Lin, 2000].

Toward the end of WWII, from November 1942 to May 1943, Mme. Chiang made a triumphant visit to the United States, staying for a while in the White House as a guest of President and Mrs Franklin Roosevelt. "[She] captivated the U.S. Congress with a speech which brought the members to their feet, for a four-minute standing ovation. The press was overwhelming in praise of this charming First Lady of China" [Service, 1974]. Newspapers headlined her address—"The First Lady of China Smiled, Spoke, and Conquered" [Meisler, 1995] and publisher Henry Luce put her picture on the 1943 March cover of Time Magazine *[Lin, 2000].*

More than 50 years later, in 1995, Mme. Chiang's triumph was still recalled; as reported in the Los Angeles Times: *"In Washington, a World War II icon dazzles dignitaries once more. Lawmakers flock to honor Mme. Chiang Kai-shek, 98, at a reception co-hosted by Bob Dole* [Senator, R-KS]*" [Meisler, 1995]. The occasion was to commemorate the 50th anniversary of the end of WWII. Co-host Senator Paul Simon (D-IL) introduced her as "the only remaining major figure of that time." Among the many attendees who paid their respects to the "tiny elegant guest with jade earrings" were Senators Strom Thurmond (R-SC), Phil Gramm (R-TX), and Tricia Nixon Cox (daughter of former President Richard Nixon).*

(During his service as Vice President, Richard Nixon had embraced the Chiangs and had been houseguest at their Taipei residence on several occasions [Lin, 2000]. Mme. Chiang had felt bitterly betrayed when, in 1979, President Nixon formally recognized the People's Republic of China, the Communist regime that had driven the Kuomintang from the Chinese mainland [Lin, 2000]. Nixon's change of heart well illustrated that the drama of international relations is a gauge of "enlightened self-interest" and political expediency [see Chapter 7] rather than of personal friendship, and that such changes can come abruptly, cold and steely. Still, to Mme. Chiang, Nixon's betrayal was a hurtful wound [Lin, 2000].)

In 1943, Mme. Chiang lived in the White House as a guest of the Roosevelts for several weeks. Her extravagance and demeanor during this visit were roundly ridiculed in a book by the White House head butler, Alonzo Fields, "My Twenty One Years in the White House" *[Miller, 1984]. In one entry, Field wrote: "Mme. Chiang brought her own silk sheets and they had to be changed from top to bottom as many as four to five times a day. They had to be changed even if she took a ten-minute nap. She was very mean to the help in the White House."* In another entry, Fields opines that *"any opinion of the Great Lady of China depends on what status of life an observer might happen to belong to"* [Miller, 1984].

In fairness to Mme. Chiang, it should be noted that during this period she suffered from urticaria, a chronic skin ailment that *"produced angry red patches all over her body whenever she was nervous"* [Seagrave, 1985].

Because of her proficiency in English, Mme. Chiang was almost always present at her husband's meeting with foreigners. U.S. General George Marshall considered her a nuisance, always *"butting into things, always hanging around"*—but he nevertheless allowed that she was of great help in negotiations [Melby, 1971]. In fact, at such times Chairman Chiang was virtually at a loss without her. Her U.S. publisher friend, Henry Luce, idealized the Chiangs and nominated them as *"Man and Wife of the Year"* for the year-ending 1937 cover of Time Magazine [Tuchman, 1972]. And, *"In* Life Magazine, *Henry Luce intentionally caricatured the Generalissimo and his lady, turning them into romantic stereotypes that became hot commodities at the newsstands"* [Seagrave, 1985]. The couple appeared on the cover of Time on no less than ten occasions, beginning in 1931 [Lin, 2000].

Publisher Luce promoted the Chiangs, but according to writer Laura Hobson, perhaps not without second thoughts: *"The trouble with Henry is that he is torn between wanting to be a Chinese missionary like his parents and a Chinese warlord like Chiang Kai-shek"* [Seagrave, 1985].

In some quarters, Madame's husband, Chiang Kai-shek, was regarded a dictator, even by his own people. He evidently was often uninformed about what was happening in the war and he refused to listen to anything but favorable reports. Chiang Monlin, a respected educator and close associate of Chairman Chiang, put it this way: *"He does not know what is going on. He writes orders by the thousand like snow flakes, and everybody says yes, yes and he never knows what has been done"* [Tuchman, 1972].

To avoid Chairman Chiang's wrath, people close to him gave him bogus reports. His power was supreme; in 1948, during the first constitutional session of the National Assembly in Nanjing when he was elected President

[Plate 6], *"the Generalissimo had made it clear that he, and he alone, would make all decisions" about new appointments* [Melby, 1971].

According to historian Barbara Tuchman [1972], *in 1943 a large number (some 200 to 600) of disgruntled younger officers within the regime had conspired to cause the removal of corrupt and inefficient officials (particularly, Ho Ying-Chin, Dai Li, H.H. Kung, and the Chen brothers, Li-fu and Kuo-fu). Yet Chiang paid no heed. Instead, he ordered his confidants to execute 16 generals, the most high-ranking of the revolting officers. And though the corruption of Chiang's regime was even at that time widely known among the press corps, it was not widely reported only later coming fully to light.*

In 1975, for example, 30 years after he had witnessed the event, Journalist E.J. Kahn, Jr. [1976] *reported that "In late 1948, while Chiang Kai-shek was offering his last frail resistance to the Communists, [U.S. diplomat] Melby had stood at the Peiping airport and watched planes coming in and unloading two kinds of cargo that some of the Generalissimo's subordinate generals evidently considered high priority: their gold bars and their concubines." Such incidents were the norm. Journalist Seymour Topping* [1999] *of the* Associated Press *reported that on the eve on which Nanking fell to the Communists: "I watched in disbelief as a Nationalist General shouted orders to soldiers to load his piano and other furniture abroad a military plane."*

H.H. Kung and T.V. Soong, President Chiang's brothers-in-law, served, respectively, as Minister of Finance and Prime Minister in Chiang's Nationalist government, positions that they later exchanged—Kung becoming Prime Minister, Soong, Minister of Finance. Kung's control over foreign aid (both that provided by the United Nations Rehabilitation and Relief Administration and that by the American Lend-Lease Program) seemed absolute [Service, 1975].

The U.S. Lend-Lease Act of 1941 was formulated by President Roosevelt who asked the U.S. Congress to lend or lease arms and material to "the government of any country whose defense the President deems vital to the United States" [Tuchman, 1972]. *China received a loan of U.S. $100 million* [Seagrave, 1985]. *"The Kungs and Soongs, and their various brothers, nephews, and nieces made up a palace clique under the* *matriarchal control of Mme. Kung [Soong Eiling; Plate 6] who dominated her younger sister, Mme. Chiang Kai-shek."*

"Mme. Kung was a frequent theme of foreign service-reports to Washington" [Tuchman, 1972]. *Relatives of Kung and Soong assisted Mmes. Kung and Chiang in pocketing some 50 million U.S. dollars from foreign exchange, currency reform and stock market transactions* [Lin, 2000]. *While H.H. Kung was Minister of Finance, Mme. Kung was credited, according to historian Tuchman* [1972], *"with receiving a moderate but invariable commission on all purchases of military planes. She and her sister, Mme. Chiang Kai-shek [Plate 6], were whispered to have manipulated government bonds and raked in huge profits from speculation in silver in the course of currency measures put through by Dr. H.H. Kung."*

According to an FBI report at the time, "The real brain of the group is reputed to be Mme. Kung [Soong Eiling] ... She is characterized as a clever and evil woman. She sits in the background and directs the family" [Seagrave, 1985]. *U.S. Ambassador Johnson suggested that Dr. Kung and his brother-in-law T.V. Soong were in no position to give "unbiased consideration" to China's problems because of their various personal financial interests* [Tuchman, 1972].

In April 1943, the leftist Chinese newspaper Changsa Da-gon Pao *reported on the marriage in the United States of H.H. Kung's number one daughter, noting her dowry of eight large trunks that had been shipped from China* [Lin, 2000]. *The expenses for airfreight and the dowry itself were claimed sufficient "to feed and bring smiles to 10,000 Chinese refugees," and the amount of time spent on preparing the dowry by women from the military unit of the Ministry of Finance was said to be "enough to produce uniforms for two army units" or to have provided "new garments for workers at 50 army hospitals." Indeed, the total spent on Kung daughter's dowry was reported to have been "enough to endow a fully equipped university"* [Lin, 2000], *a huge expenditure that prompted M.R. Nicholson of the U.S. Shanghai Finance Bureau to lament,*

"It's Mme. Kung, not Japan, who is killing the Chinese dollar" [Seagrave, 1985].

Given power by Chairman Chiang, the Kung family held sway. In 1946 *alone, Kung Eiling's oldest son, Ling-kan, together with the Chairman's in-laws, amassed some U.S. $350 million from business transactions* [Lin, 2000]. *When the Kung Villa (95 Feeks Lane, Locust Valley) on New York's Long Island was sold in 1998, it netted over U.S. $3 million; sales of their real estate in Florida yielded another U.S. $20 million; and when they sold some 400 acres near Disney World in Florida, additional tens of millions of U.S. dollars found their way into the Kung coffers* [Lin, 2000].

According to journalist Sterling Seagrave [1985], *Chiang Kai-shek's brother-in-law, H.H. Kung, and his wife, Eiling, "together were worth somewhere close to U.S. $1 billion (by modest estimates)." Chiang's other prime brother-in law, T.V. Soong (Mme. Chiang's brother), was said to be "the richest man on earth," having an unparalleled umbrella of wealth that cast a long shadow over London, Paris, Moscow, Tokyo, Rio de Janeiro, Hong Kong, Singapore, Johannesburg, Manila, Taipei, and even Peking* [Seagrave, 1985].

President Truman was disgusted, in his unique style stating plainly that "Chiang Kai-shek and the Madame and their families, the Soong family and the Kungs, were all thieves, every last one of them, the Madame and him included … They stole it [aid given by the U.S. government], *and it's invested in real estate down in São Paulo and some right here in New York"* [Miller, 1984]. *President Truman might have done something to correct the matter, but he did not—for political reasons—and so, "nobody spoke for the victims"* [Seagrave, 1985]. *In the Epilogue to his book "The Soong Dynasty," Seagrave* [1985] *asks: "What would Charlie Soong* [the family patriarch] *say about how his children turned out? … with but one exception* [Soong Chingling], *they passed through life like a team of pickpockets."*

Journalist Seagrave's heroine, Soong Chingling, the wife of Sun Yat-sen [Plate 6], *was independent and upstanding, a woman who staunchly carried the torch of her husband, founder of the Chinese Republic in 1911, who actively promoted his ideal of the Three People's Principles ("San Min Zhu Yi"): People's rights, people's governance, and people's livelihood* [Kahn, 1975; Tuchman, 1972]. *In doing so, she found herself in strident opposition with her brother-in-law, Chiang Kai-shek* [Seagrave, 1985]. *Soong Chinling, co-founder of the "Third Force Movement[1]"* [Seagrave,

1985; Chapter 8], *ultimately sided with the Communists and in 1950 became Vice President of the People's Republic of China.*

The immensely powerful Soong sisters were known well by the Chinese public. A popular saying at the time had it: "One loved money [Eiling Kung], *one loved power* [Mayling Chiang], *and one loved China* [Chingling Sun] *"* [Seagrave, 1985].

Ironically, a small fraction of the loot appropriated by the Kungs and Soongs—money from the U.S. given to China after WWII—miraculously returned home. On March 27, 1997 (Mme. Chiang's 100th birthday), Wesleyan College in Macon, Georgia received an anonymous donation of U.S. $2 million (sent by the Hong Kong attorney's office of Tsang, Chan, and Woo) in honor of Soong Mayling [Lin, 2000]. *Later in that same year, two more donations of U.S. $2 million each arrived at Wesleyan, in honor of the other two Soong sisters, Eiling and Chingling* [Lin, 2000]. *In May of 1997 an anonymous donation of U.S. $6 million from the same Hong Kong attorney's office was received by Oberlin College, the distinguished liberal arts college in northeastern Ohio from which Eiling's husband, H.H. Kung (by then 30 years deceased) had graduated in 1906* [Lin, 2000].

By this time, the only survivors of the Soong Dynasty were Mme. Chiang and her eldest niece, the "dowry endowed" Kung Ling-ye; all of the others had passed from the scene, interred at the Ferncliff Cemetery in a New York city suburb [Lin, 2000].

China was a nation of bureaucrats who secretly revered high places to which they hoped to ascend sooner or later. Becoming a high-level government official was an obsession at every level. Dictated by long-held tradition, men enjoyed the privilege of monopolizing the positions of most importance. But in recent years, women had gotten a share, too. To me, it was still a novelty to be in the same room with Nanking's lady officials ("*neu-guan*").

One afternoon I was summoned to meet the First Lady, Madame Chiang Kai-shek, who was then Vice President of the Women Supreme Advisory Committee of which I had been designated Chief of the Nanking Branch. Upon my arrival at the official residence, I was ushered into an office by Mme. Chiang's General Secretary, Mrs. Wang, a middle-aged woman with pretentious modesty.

(I was told later that Mrs. Wang attended the same school as Mme. Chiang, the McTyeire Girls School in Shanghai, where all the Soong sisters were alumnae, and that Wang later went to college in America. I was told also that she had become a Christian, yet she maintained an old-school officious authoritative attitude and exuded a strong flavor of red-tape dominance. I felt no kinship with her, even though for a while I also attended McTyeire.) Mrs. Wang made me uncomfortable. I soon began to regret coming to this place.

The official residence of the Chairman and Mme. Chiang (on Huang-pu Road, to the back of the Ministry of Defense) was tightly guarded by brown-uniformed soldiers. I gave up counting the number of gates where my car was detained before we finally arrived at the First Residence. Fortunately, however, I had earlier received a visitor's pass, so my visit might not have been as difficult as it was for others.

The Chairman's house was simpler and smaller than I had anticipated. It was a red brick building, set at one corner of a garden that gave the impression of a park filled with lovely trees. The home itself looked neat and comfortable, though it was by no means luxurious. It could not match homes in the wealthy neighbourhoods of Shanghai, nor the mansion of Prime Minister T.V. Soong, brother of Mme. Chiang.

The Chinese people were much impressed by the simplicity of the lifestyle of the Chairman[2]. (Nevertheless, Chiang was still regarded widely as a dictator, despised by many, a leader who permitted widespread corruption—the appropriation of public funds and of American aid by his wife's family and his subordinates. All these funds, of course, belonged to the Chinese people, not the Soongs or the Kungs or the other members of the Chaings' extended families.)

As I waited in the entry hall of the Chiang residence, I glanced through a door leading to a room on the left. It was a small drawing room, decorated in the old style Chinese setting—elegantly carved beech wood furniture, its walls harmonized with scrolls of ancient paintings. Adjoining this room was a study. Although it was out of my complete view, I could see a desk near a north window with bookshelves along one side. Soon, a butler ushered me into a huge parlour next to a dining room. Many visitors, men and women, were already there. This room was said to be the grandest in the house, but its furniture was monotonous and clumsily arranged: brown leather sofas with low tables sat on a dark-brown floor, forming small groupings around a large fireplace. The warm glow of the fire was the only happy note in the entire hall.

I was, however, much attracted by the vases of fresh flowers that had been placed on each table. Fresh flowers in early spring were a luxury especially the carnations, daffodils, and sweet peas—wonderful varieties—that were totally beyond the reach of common people. And, they were my favorites. But the vases were so overstuffed with these rare blooms that they swept away all sense of beauty. I glanced quietly at one arrangement on the nearest table, trying to remedy its imperfection in my mind's eye.

As I sat, lost in flower arranging, a man in "*Tzong-sen tzuan*" (the trademark uniform of the late Dr. Sun Yat-sen) loudly announced the arrival of her Ladyship. I rose with the others for our now long-delayed audience. The blue brocade curtains in front of an archway were parted. A tall slender woman of fine appearance (deflated by what I took to be a supercilious air) immediately emerged. With a quick gait, ignoring her visitors, she inquired insistently, again and again, about the whereabouts of Shen *Fu-ren*, Mme. Shen. She was asking for me!

Suddenly overwhelmed, I stepped forward with a sense of correctness—rather than pleasure—and timidly greeted her. She gave me her hand, and in an earthy Shanghai tongue she rambled off a litany of words of greetings.

"How are you, Mrs. Shen?"

"Oh, you are getting plump!"

"I have to congratulate you on the birth of a son that I read about in the paper."

She left me with no time to respond. Fortunately, before I could muster the few words that I might have thought suitable, she moved on to receive other visitors. This, I greeted with a great relief!

Her words to me had been perplexing. Madame's husband had at one time been a close friend of my husband's sister and his brother-in-law, Huang Fu [*About the Author*]. Moreover, during the revolution-days led by Dr. Sun Yat-sen, Chiang, Huang and Chen Ying-shi had become bonded as "blood brothers[3]." As Chiang was the youngest of the three bonded brothers (Chen being the oldest), he and the Mme. had always treated my widowed sister-in-law, Mrs. Huang[4] [Plate 2], with a certain amount of deference.

(In fact because of the special bond of brotherhood, during one of our family stays at the Huang's home in Shanghai [*Chapter 10*], the First Couple, just after their return from the war capital Chunking had come to call on my sister-in-law Mrs. Huang. They were received in a drawing room directly across the hall from where I was sitting. Urged by curiosity, I peered through the doorway to see what was going on. Now, sitting amongst the throng in Mme. Chiang's residence, I recalled this moment from years ago and wondered whether I had been caught in the sight of the First Lady. I felt very embarrassed.)

When Mme. Chiang left me to greet the other guests, I was pleased to be left alone, a pause that gave me a chance to sketch my impressions of the First Lady. She was in her late forties and had a pale but seemingly healthy complexion [Plate 6]. Her fine eyes, though perhaps a little cunning, were bright and bewitching, eclipsing weaker points of her face[5]. The First Lady's hair was black and thick, combed in a style similar to that of women of the Tang Dynasty. She wore a gown of gray silk dotted with small black prints, and a black velvet jacket. The gown was long, long and tight; the jacket was distinctly Western. But at the base of her long gown I was taken aback by what I saw—a pair of black leather high-heeled shoes speckled with gold. Such apparel did not seem to fit a woman of her age and status. Her whole appearance, especially her face, bore striking resemblance to a skillfully and carefully crafted painting.

Mme. Chiang possessed a noble and self-controlled air, yet she seemed from time to time to feel the necessity to remind herself to keep her dignity. She was civil to all, but she was always conscious of her rank, displacing a self-importance that to me seemed unattractive. She stood very erect, her left hand on her hip clutching an embroidered white handkerchief, while she greeted her visitors, and she shook hands with her right hand. This was the first time that I had ever observed such a male civility, a Western custom, among Chinese women!

After having greeted everyone the First Lady abruptly walked to the fireplace, hands locked behind her back, as she continued to intently whisper a word or two to a few of the visitors (members, I later learned, of her Advisory Committee). Relaxing her statuesque pose, she then invited everyone to be seated. She herself took a seat by the fireplace facing the assembled flock. With a deliberately imperious manner, her Ladyship then rapidly turned her head and glanced around the room as though she was searching for something. Her General Secretary, Mrs. Wang, understanding the gesture, promptly stepped forward fetched a cigarette case from a nearby table and offered it to her. She accepted the cigarettes with an expressive smile, placed the case on the table by her side, and began to smoke. After a long pause she began the audience.

I listened to her words with a mixture of bemused interest and boredom. All the while I occupied myself by counting the number of cigarettes[6] consumed by our leader; the tally was nine in two-and-a-half hours.

Without much tact, Mme. Chiang began the audience by putting us in our place.

"Well, what do you have to tell me ladies and gentlemen?"

"No doubt, the problem you are having and the motive for all of you being here is money—you want to ask for money."

"But you must know I am not a magician."

This preface of Mme. Chiang delivered in a half-comical, half-sarcastic tone did not quell the pleas of the assembled group. In choppy waves, proposition after proposition, plea after plea were put forth. Each of her visitors had an agenda, and each one deemed his or her issue to be the most important and most deserving. As for myself, since I had just came on board as Chairman of the Nanking Branch Women

Work Committee, I think that I was the only one in the room who had neither an official report to give nor anything in particular to ask for. I felt uninvolved and relieved.

(Had I been on the job of my Women Committee a while longer [*Chapter 9*], I, too, might have merged with the group of "beggars" for more and more money for my Committee from the Madame. But from what I learned that afternoon, such begging would probably not have helped.)

In dealing with the numerous requests from the visitors, Mme. Chiang, her Ladyship showed an endowment of rare eloquence and a quick wit. After analyzing one or another matter within the scope of her understanding, she quickly formed her own conclusions (albeit more theoretical than substantive). Finally, she clearly became anxious to terminate the discussion. But her visitors remained tenacious. At long last, given an opening she concluded the audience by stating forcefully,

"You know how to ask and ask more and more of me. But to whom do I appeal?"

"In such matters even your Chairman Chiang has no special solution."

"He has no support for me to offer."

Tea was served in the residence, but when it was over the discussion was rejoined with much buzzing and boisterousness. After a time Mme. Chiang became impatient and bored. And when the discussion became especially tumultuous, a butler came to her side and in an intentionally loud whisper said, "*Fu-ren* [Madame], *the car is ready—the Chairman is waiting.*" The guests, almost all with their missions unaccomplished, rose politely from their seats and nodded that they, too, had to take leave.

I was the last one to depart. When it came my turn to say good-bye, Mme. Chiang turned to me good-naturedly, in a seemingly changed manner. Graciously and with intimacy she held my hand firmly and asked me to "do your best with the Nanking Branch [of the Women Work Committee]." As we parted she said,

"Please give my best regards to the Mayor."

I was surprised by her warm and friendly words, given to such an unimportant person as myself. I thanked her repeatedly.

On my way home, I thought to myself that without doubt the First Lady was an intelligent and highly perceptive woman of knowledge and ability; she could, and should have done a great deal more to the well-being of her country. With her fine education and high position she could have contributed much of value. Still, deep within me, I continued to wonder whether a person of lesser education and status, but one who understood and wanted to help the people of our country, might well have been a greater asset to our society than Mme. Chiang— who, with her privileged upbringing and high position, was nothing more than a robber-baron! In my heart of hearts, I thought that Mme. Soong Mayling Chiang and the other members of the Soong clan who called themselves Christians[7] were sinful.

Footnotes:

[1]The third Force, organized in 1927 in Berlin by Soong Chingling and Teng Yen-ta after Dr. Sun Yat-sen's death, was "a movement that would provide an alternative both to Chiang's reactionary Kuomintang and the Communists" (Seagrave, 1985).

[2]"Chiang [Kai-shek] had power, but no purse. T.V. [Soong] knew how to fill a purse" (Seagrave, 1985).

[3]During Dr. Sun Yat-sen's revolution in the early 1920s, "Chiang Kai-shek, Ch'en Ch'i-mei (Chen Ying-shi), and Chief of Staff Huang Fu (Huang Ying-bai, brother-in-law of the author's husband, Shen Yi) took a ritual oath of becoming blood brothers" (Boorman and Howard, 1967; Seagrave, 1985). The oath of blood brothers is a solemn vow "swearing to look after each other's kin as if they were of the same clan" (Seagrave, 1985).

[4]Mrs. Huang, visiting the author's parents in Shanghai and speaking on behalf of her brother, Shen Yi, formally requested the parents' permission for her brother and the author to wed (see *About the Author*).

[5]Soong Mayling, Mme. Chiang Kai-shek, the youngest of the three Soong sisters, was not considered a beauty, as was the middle sister, Chingling,

Mme. Sun Yat-sen. Her eldest sister, Eiling, Mme. H.H. Kung, was reputed to be unattractive, having a "pie pan" face (Plate 6; Seagrave, 1985).

[6]From her heavy smoking, Mme. Chiang ultimately developed a sinus problem. During the war years with Japan, when signs prohibiting of the extravagance of smoking were posted throughout China, a foreign newsman, during a lunch meeting with the Madame, observed her smoking expensive Camel cigarettes one after another. When the reporter reminded her about the prohibition on smoking, Mme. Chiang casually replied that such rules were only for the common people (Seagrave, 1985).

[7]President Truman noted that "when people [of the stature of the Soongs and the Kungs] get into politics, all hell breaks loose. It kicks the hell out of the country" (Miller, 1984).

Plate 1. *UPPER Row*, L-R: President Chiang Kai-shek (left) and Advisor Dr. Shen Yi (Author's husband), 1968, Taipei; Dr. Hu Shih, 1958, Taipei. *MIDDLE Row*, L-R: Silver Anniversary, members of the Author's original wedding party, left to right: Mrs. Chang, the Author, Shen Yi, Hu Shih, Presidential Advisor Chang Ch'un, 1953, Taipei; Reception, left to right: Shen Yi, the Author, Anna Chennault (wife of General Claire Chennault of the "Flying Tigers"), 1965, Taipei. *LOWER Row*, L-R: Shen Yi's friend and colleague, U.S dam designer Dr. John L. Savage (hat) and other experts, 1944, Three Gorges Survey Yangtze River; birthday party for biographical novelist Irving Stone, left to right: Editor J. Shen Schopf, Irving Stone, J. William Schopf, Mrs. Jean Stone, 1987, Los Angeles.

Plate 2. *UPPER Row*, L-R: Chinese calligraphy of the Author's name, "Inyeening"; as a student at the University of Oregon, 1958, Eugene; with her proud husband Shen Yi, upon receiving her Honorary Doctorate in 1976 from the Chinese Institute of Culture. *MIDDLE Row*, L-R: With Grandmaster Artist Chang Ta-ch'ien following the traditional "Disciple Ceremony," ~1951, Hong Kong; the Author's painting, White Sacred Lotus, which was praised by the Grandmaster (who at the upper right penned the phrase "The essence of scholarship is purity"), ~1959, Bangkok; the Author's painting exhibit by the Brazil Art Council, Chinese Embassy, 1969, Rio de Janeiro. *LOWER Row*, L-R: Portrait of the family of the Author's husband, Yi, Left to right: sister Xing-yuan, Yi's mother, second sister Xing-ren, elder sister Yi-yun, Yi's scholarly father, and 10-yr-old Yi (his queue having been cut off for this portrait), 1911, Shanghai; 16-yr-old Yi (3rd from left) at a Tong-ji University engineering class, attended also by Guo Tiemei (4th from left), a colleague in developing the wartime NW "hinterland" at Lanzhou (1940-45), and by Zhao Dun-fu (far right), another Lanzhou colleague, 1917, Shanghai.

Plate 3.*UPPER Row*,L-R: Pensive 15-yr-old Author, 1921, at Shanghai school-grounds; the Author's siblings and their spouses, left to right: Author (seated), husband Shen Yi (standing), sister Duan (seated), elder brother Ying Yi-san (standing) and wife (seated), second brother Huai-san (leaning), and wife (seated), talented younger brother Jin-san (standing), 1928, Shanghai. *MIDDLE Row*, Baby photos of the Author's seven children, L-R: The first-born, son Yee-zi, daughters Hwa-hwa, Pei-pei, San-san, Chuan-chuan, and Lan-lan, and the youngest, son Shin-shin. *LOWER Row*, L-R: Wedding of King of Siam Bhumibol Adulyadej (on throne) and Queen Rajawongse Sirikit (kneeling), 1950, Sri Pathum Palace, Bangkok; "White House," newly finished mayor's residence (38 Peiping Rd; see Map of Nanjing), with its rounded end (right) and its roof covered by a bamboo mat for the "Dog days of summer," 1947, Nanking.

Plate 4. The Author's family. **UPPER Row**, L-R: Author's multi-talented father, ~1908, Shanghai; Wedding portrait of the Author and Shen Yi, 1928, Shanghai Carlton Hotel; the Author's educated mother, with "fashionable" small-feet ("three-inch golden lotus"), ~1904, Hangzhou. **MIDDLE Row**, L-R: Author in costume for the Peking opera "Susan Qijie" performed at the 1943 Annual Meeting of the Chinese Society of Engineers, Lanzhou; Author giving a piano lesson to daughter Hwa-hwa, 1947, Nanking; Author showing brush painting to husband Yi in the studio he built for her at their home in Bangkok, 1952; Author's daughters in the pretty frocks she and her godmother sewed for them, 1940, Shanghai. **LOWER Row**, L-R:Three generations of the Author's family (grandson Tenni not present), 1975, Indiana Chinese Summer Camp; Golden Anniversary family photo with the Author (center) in a 50-yr-old wedding reception gown, 1978, California.

Plate 5. The Author's husband Shen Yi. *UPPER Row*, L-R: Outfitted for field work, ~1955, Israel; with Shah of Iran Mohammed Reza Pahlavi (right) in Teheran where Minister Shen Yi headed China's Delegation to the 1964 UN-ECAFE Conference; Israeli Prime Minister David Ben-Gurion (standing) and Shen Yi (far right), at the 1955 ECAFE Conference, Tel Aviv; U.N. Secretary General Dag Hammarskjöld (left) greeting the Author (right, shielded from view), 1956, UN-ECAFE Reception, Bangkok. *MIDDLE Row*, L-R: Shen Yi as a Ph.D. student at Dresden Technischen Hochschule, 1922; in a formal portrait as Chief of Shang-hai Bureau of Public Works, 1937; as Chief of the ECAFE Bureau of Flood Control Water Resources Development and "Father of the Mekong River Project,"1956, Bangkok. *LOWER Row*, L-R: Minister Shen as China's Chief Delegate at the 1967 ECAFE Conference of the International Civic Aviation Organization,Buenos Aires;as Ambassador of China, presenting his credentials to President of Brazil Artur da Costa e Silva,1968, Rio de Janeiro; with head bowed, greeting King of Thailand Bhumibol Adulyadej at the 1963 UN-ECAFE conference in Bangkok.

UNITED NATIONS ⬡ NATIONS UNIES

NEW YORK

CABLE ADDRESS · UNATIONS NEWYORK · ADRESSE TELEGRAPHIQUE

FRU 60   22 June 1960

Dear Mr. Shen-Yi,

I wish to acknowledge your memorandum of 1 June 1960, in which you convey to me your decision to resign your permanent appointment with the United Nations. It is with sincere regret that I accept your resignation.

By your devoted and excellent service to ECAFE as Chief of its Bureau of Flood Control and Water Resources Development from the time of your appointment to the United Nations in April 1949, you have indeed made a very valuable contribution to the work of the United Nations. I am pleased to know of the high esteem in which you are held by your Government and wish you happiness and every success in your new assignment as Minister of Transport in the Government of the Republic of China.

I greatly appreciate your expression of continued interest in and support of the work of the United Nations.

Yours sincerely,

Dag Hanmarskjold
Secretary-General

Mr. Shen-Yi
Economic Commission for Asia
 and the Far East
Bangkok, Thailand

Plate 6. *UPPER Left*: U.N. Secretary-General Dag Hammarskjöld's letter commending Shen Yi at the time of his resignation from UN-ECAFE, 1960; *LOWER Left*: May 20th 1948 Inauguration of President Chiang Kai-shek (front, 2nd from right) and Vice President Li Teng-jen (front, far right), together with Mme. Chiang (Soong Mayling, front, 3rd from right), Nanking Mayor Shen Yi (the Author's husband, third row, 2nd from left), and Finance Minister O.K. Yu (third row, far left), at the Nanking President Building. *UPPER Right*: Mme.Chiang (front right) hosting the Author (left) at the Nanking residence of the Nationalist President,1947. *MIDDLE Right*: The Soong sisters, left to right: Eiling (Mme. H.H. Kung), the eldest; Mayling (Mme. Chiang Kai-shek), the youngest; and the comely Chinling (Mme. Sun Yat-sen), ~1943, Chongqing. *LOWER Right*: Present-day City Hall of Dalian in Liaoning Province; in 1945, Russian troops prevented the Author's husband, Shen Yi, from assuming the position of Mayor of Dalian.

Plate 7. *LEFT Column*, top to bottom: The Author and husband Shen Yi in Bangkok, 1950. Author with her friend Morris at Bentley House, 1993, Los Angeles; the Author's daughter Chuan-chuan (2nd from right) at the 60th Anniversary 2003 of the completion of the Yuan-yang Reservoir, constructed under Yi's directives by engineers S.X. Yuan and T.Y. Lin, Mt. Chi-lian, Gansu Province; Author with her daughters in Lanzhou,1944. *MIDDLE Column*, top to bottom:The Author at the "Chico" Villa construction site (Villa of "Belated Doves") with son Shin-shin, 1962, Taipei; "Chico Double Internment," Chinese calligraphy on the headstone of the grave-site of the Author and her husband, Oakland, California, 2000; Yuan-yang Reservoir (retained by a 36-m-high mud dam), 60 years after its construction, 2003; the Author's family, during husband Yi's U.N. home-leave, with grandson Tenni (front, right), at the Wanda Dam site, Taiwan,1959. *RIGHT Column*, top to bottom: New Chico Villa home at Grass Mountain, 1964, Taipei; Author's birthday celebration with son-in-law Bill Schopf (center, standing) and friends at Bentley House, Los Angeles, 1993; lush vegetation supported by waters of the Yuan-yang Reservoir at Mt. Chi-lian, 2003; the Author's family, left to right: Pei-pei, San-san, Hwa-hwa, husband Yi, the Author, Chuan-chuan, Shin-shin and Lan-lan, Indiana Summer Camp, 1975.

Plate 8. Sino-Japanese War. ***UPPER Row***, L-R: Local schoolchildren commemorating the Nanking massacre at the Memorial Wall of the Nanking-Massacre Memorial Park on Memorial Day, April 4, 2004; "Burn-Shanghai-Burn," prelude to the invasion of Nanking, photo taken by the Author's husband Shen Yi at Shanghai Nanshi November 11, 1937. ***MIDDLE Row***, L-R:Memorial to 300,000 fallen citizens at the Massacre Memorial Park, Nanjing, 2005; Memorial to Iris Chang, author of "The Rape of Nanking," at the Nanking-Massacre Memorial Park, 2005; ***BOTTOM Row***, L-R:Gingling Women College (attended in middle-school by the Author's daughters), site of the "Safety Zone" during the1937 Nanking massacre (see Map of Nanjing); statue of former Dean of the College Minnie Vautrin, who during the Japanese occupation of the late-1930s used her office and personal influence to protect thousands of women and children.

Plate 9. *UPPER Row*, L-R: The Author's children and nurse Mama (center, seated), with the two eldest daughters (center back) in lovely cast-me-downs from Tania, daughter of the family's good friend Tann Bai-yu (son of the Republic of China's 1st Prime Minister, Tann Yen-kai), 1950, Bangkok; traditional small shoes like those worn by the mother of the Author, Shanghai, 2005. *MIDDLE Row*, L-R: Hangzhou's beautiful West Lake, with a profusion of lotus and the historic Song Dynasty Sudi dyke in the background, 2002; the Author's family and friends during husband Shen Yi's 1952 U.N. home leave to Taipei, with Yi (front, 6th from left), Presidential Advisor Chang Ch'un (behind, 9th from left), Minister O.K. Yu (front, 10th from left), daughter Lan-lan and son Shin-shin (front, right), the Author's close friend Mrs.Yu (Yu-sen; 2nd from right), and the Author (4th from right, behind her children). *LOWER Row*, L-R: The Author and family at their Shanghai Jiangwan home, bombed by Allied Forces during WW-II, 1946; the Author's Wutai San house in Nanjing, at 4 Baibu Po (see Nanjing Map), the metal window frames for which were retrieved from the family's bombed Shanghai home shown at the left, 2005.

Plate 10. Nanking Women Work Committee. *UPPER Row*, L-R: Original office of the "City of Nanking Women Work Committee," proclaimed on the wooden plaque at the right of the entrance to the dilapidated building, 1947; capable and faithful Executive Secretary Wu Wan-Tzen (right, front) and her hard-working colleagues in 1947 at the new headquarters of the Committee. *MIDDLE Row*,L-R:Thirsty children at the UNRRA "milk station" (with the Chinese characters at the upper right proclaiming: "Get Milk"), 1948; Children's Health Station at the Committee's original site, 1948. *LOWER Row*, L-R: Blankets and warm clothing provided by the Committee brought relief from the winter cold (note the snow-laden branches, at left), December, 1948; group photo of recipients of aid from the Committee, under the banner "1948 Winter Relief, New Life Movement Nanking Women Work Committee" at the Committee's new Headquarters near Xuanwu Lake (see, Map of Nanjing).

CHAPTER 6
EVENTS LEADING TO MY BAPTISM

Early Years. Though I was raised in a family of devout Buddhists, for much of my early adult life I was a confirmed atheist. Spurred by motives known only to my mother, I was sent by my parents, from the very beginning of my formal education, to missionary schools. Despite how conservative Chinese traditions then were, religious choice was, as in my family, a matter of personal preference, not one dictated by family tradition.

During childhood, I had an immense fascination both for Buddhism and Christianity. The truth was that, on the one hand, I could share with my family the pleasures of colourful Buddhist festivities, and on the other, I could be part of the annual Christmas pageantries at school. But on no occasion had I knelt before a statue of Buddha in order to please my mother and grandmother, nor had I ever attended a Sunday service in school (notwithstanding the numerous demerits I received for this behaviour from my teachers). In light of my early attitude, I would never have thought that a person of my stubborn and preemptory nature would one day choose to become a Christian.

I vividly remember my student days at MacNair [Plate 3], a private English Christian school in Shanghai. One afternoon during a scripture class, the Head Mistress, Miss Ramston, imposed on me the severe chastisement of locking me in a darkened room for three hours. The cause for this disciplinary action was my inability to recite a sentence from the Bible, "*Jesus turneth the water into wine.*" I was indignant and outraged by this punishment. It was so harsh, over such a trivial matter. But though my resentment was deep, I held back my tears. Never in my life had I been subjected to such shame. I had never been so humiliated. Even at that early age, I had a strong sense of self-pride. The humiliation was unbearable.

As I now see it, it was unfortunate that my faith in Christianity did not take this opportunity to bloom. Instead, an abhorrence of this religion and all things Christian began to ferment. I withdrew from MacNair soon afterward, mostly to show Miss Ramston my displeasure;

and I vowed not to see her face again. No doubt, Miss Ramston understood the cause of my departure, for on several occasions she visited my home and urged my parents to have me returned to school. Supported by my father, I firmly rejected all these overtures.

A year later after this incident, a feeling of self-reproach began to gnaw on me, and made me ill at ease. When I thought of my stubbornness, I realized the hurt I had caused Miss Ramston. But it was too late to mend my rash behavior, for by this time she had returned to her home in England. This remorse has followed me for all these years. To be truthful, Miss Ramston was actually a kind-hearted woman who loved all her charges as though they were children of her own. And I know that she had a special fondness for me. Unfortunately, her discipline in religious doctrine was too severe for young girls of my age to appreciate. She was not able to comprehend the delicate nature and the depth of our feelings.

Out of respect and remembrance for Miss Ramston, I have to this day kept the English name "Jenny" she gave to me on my very first day of school at MacNair.

In the spring of 1921, after our family had returned to Hangchow, the city of my birth, I began high school at the Hong-dao Girls School, a Chinese missionary school. I was very unhappy at being placed in this cloister-like environment, and I especially disliked being a boarder. For quite some time I was unable to adapt.

Most of the teachers and students at the school were Christians. Their conversation frequently included a heavy dose of religious doctrine, notions that I found superficial and boring. I felt alone and isolated. Few of the other girls would make friends with a non-Christian such as me. However, as I grew more accustomed to the school my impression of Christianity gradually and subtly changed. I came to recognize the supreme personality of Jesus, but I still did not believe that there was a God or that Jesus was a God. Instead, I was of the opinion that if one possessed a steadfast spirit and devoted oneself to justice—beneficence to the poor, willingness to sacrifice for others—then that person, herself, could be a follower of the supreme.

My schoolmates at Hong-dao, of course, did not agree with

my views, which generated endless debate. Not a single person was on my side, and the drawn-out debates yielded no resolution at all. Nevertheless, I eventually came to acknowledge, to at least some extent, the importance of religion, of any religion, in my life. I saw it as filling a spiritual void indispensable to human beings, important particularly to those who lacked self-confidence. In other words, it seemed to me that religion sustained people when there seemed to be little other reason for hope. Religion helped where education seemed to fail. My schoolmates laughed at my self-concocted notion, but I fiercely maintained my unpopular point of view.

Peer Pressure. One evening when I was attending a mandatory service at the school chapel, Juliet Woo, a classmate sitting next to me, whispered in my ear that she now fully understood the root of my views about God and religion. I was astonished by what I took to be this fellow student's change of attitude, for in our endless debates Juliet had been one of my staunchest adversaries. Because the evening service was still in progress, I did not ask for an explanation, but I was inwardly very pleased. Soon after the service, we walked together to the schoolyard, stretched out on the soft lawn, and looked to the dark sky sprinkled with stars. Juliet was stern and serious. She stared me in the eyes.

"Now listen, Inyeening, I have something important to say to you."

"You have studied the Bible, and you now regularly attend services.

"Why aren't you baptized?"

Her words came like a torrential flood, accented with vigor. I was breathless and lost for words. After a silence she continued once more.

"I hope you will not mind my frankness, but I have seen how unhappy you have been lately."

"Obviously, you are troubled. I can see it in your face." Juliet continued.

"You are intelligent with rare gifts, but you seem not to be able to face reality and overcome your difficulties."

"This is the reason why I want you to know God, from whom you can obtain relief."

"God is an invisible power that will give you strength when you feel alone and weak."

Juliet's words had touched a secret pain deep within me and my heart throbbed rapidly. Yes, I was troubled. The fact was that I had come from a traditional Chinese family and my mother, having a strong and conventional view, had recently become keen in having me betrothed to a certain young man from a wealthy and distinguished family, the so-called "*mung-dang hu-dui*," gate-for-gate accordance. I had firmly rejected her plans for this arranged marriage. After all, I was only fourteen years old! But, of course, my mother was angry at my disobedience, and a great gap had opened between the two of us. I was very sad and fearful of losing my mother's love, and by the time of my conversation with Juliet, my mother and I had not spoken to each other for more than three months.

As I listened to Juliet, I became increasingly troubled. I did not know how to respond; my head was crowded with worries.

"Tell me, why are you not baptized?" Juliet insisted again. I could not be silent any longer. In a soft but defiant tone, I uttered,

"Ok, I will."

"Then when?" Her eyes fixed on mine again.

"At any time as I wish." I was hoping that she would drop the subject, but she continued to coerce me.

"What about this Sunday when most of our classmates will receive baptism?"

"Join them. Give them a surprise!"

Most youngsters are prone to hasty decisions, made on the spur of the moment and based on sentiment rather than reason. I was no exception. After a slight hesitation, I blindly consented, agreeing to be baptized on that Sunday along with the others. I thought this was a show of courage, and at the same time I much wanted Juliet's friendship.

Soon that Sunday came. It was a crisp rainy morning in the spring of 1922. I got up earlier than usual, for no particular reason, and did not give much thought to the pending events. When breakfast was over, everyone was ready to go to church, about a mile away. With a raincoat clutched under my arm, I did not join the group but instead climbed the stairs to the school's chapel where I stared out the window, watching my many classmates marching by below. I dared not think of anything but Juliet, who probably was anxiously searching for me among the gathered throng. After everyone was out of sight, I headed for the church myself, carefully keeping a distance from the rest.

With slow and heavy steps, I trekked the muddy path toward the church. I restrained myself from all thought, except the sheer joy of the beautiful surroundings—the crisp morning, the remote hills, the tranquil Hsi-hu [Hangzhou's West Lake, Xi-hu] with boats floating near and far, teeming apricot blooms, and huge boughs of budding willow trees lining the banks of "*Sue-tee*[1]." The lovely scenes [Plate 9] passed from me one by one, and brought sweet memories and forgetfulness of my present plight. Walking on, I suddenly found myself staring up at the foreboding church standing solemnly before me. A nervous agitation swept over me, as I asked myself:

"Inyeening, is it right to take baptism without the knowledge of your parents?"

"Do you really want to do this—do you truly believe in Christianity?"

"Or, has what you are about to do stemmed merely from a deep longing for friendship?" In my mind the questions and their answers poured forth, and my decision about the baptism came clear, a definite "No." With a quick turn, I fled the scene. To home I marched.

War Years. In the fifteen years that followed that school episode in Hangchow, I moved from girlhood to wifehood to motherhood, the springtime of my life. I had become thirty, but I still craved for the love of my parents and the love of my husband, loves that so often had helped me overcome the sorrows of life. But the sudden death of my mother in the spring of 1937 shocked me into deep pain. Life was no longer as good as I had thought it to be. Close on the heels of this deep sadness, on July 7, 1937 the long-festering Sino-Japanese war burst wide open in Peiping at *Loo-go Chiao,* the Marco Polo Bridge [*Historic Foreword*]. Ironically, this coincided with a grand celebration near our home in *Jiang-wan,* some 20 miles northeast of the Shanghai city center, the opening of a new Civic Center that was Yi's masterpiece, the result of ten years of his efforts as Chief of the Bureau of Shanghai's Municipal Public Works [1927-37].

I recall vividly that evening's celebration of the grand opening of Shanghai's new Civic Center [see, Wakeman, 1995]. Commencing at six o'clock there was a colossal lantern parade featuring a multitude of delightfully diverse designs, shapes, and colors. Beginning from downtown Shanghai, the long happy procession worked its way to the new Center at *Jiang-wan.* From high up in the banquet hall of the new Municipal Building, where Yi and I were attending an enormous dinner party, we could hear a thunderous roar from below. From the windows I could see the on-coming lights, and lights that silhouetted the grand new buildings, each of distinctive Chinese style.

But I could not bring myself to properly enjoy this glorious scene of celebration, an occasion that had been awaited expectantly by my dear mother when she was alive and who was now resting forever at a grassy knoll in the Municipal Cemetery but a stone's throw from the site of our festive gathering. Though I was lost in sadness, at the same time I was aroused by the roaring crowd of the parade procession. Tears welled as I saw my husband and O.K. Yu[2], acting Mayor of Shanghai, standing side by side on the grand balcony receiving cheers from the huge throng as they repeatedly roared: "Long Live China! Long live the Nationalist government! Long live the City of Shanghai!" The cheers were full of passion and enthusiasm—but to me the sounds were but the pitiful cries of a lost flock seeking protection from the invading Japanese army as our government now prepared to move its capital from Nanking to Chunking. Silently I uttered,

"God bless our people. God save our country." The more boisterous the crowd became, the more sorrowful I remained.

According to an old Chinese saying, "trouble does not travel s ingly" ("*huo-boo dan-shing*"). I had been devastated by the death of my mother, by the encroachment of the Japanese forces, and by the seemingly unending war. And I was soon saddened again, by separation from my husband Yi, who in 1938, after moving our family from Shanghai to Hong Kong, had gone off to the war capital, Chunking. I was alone, now with my four children, feeling bleak and helpless. It was unbearable. My husband and I had never before been parted for longer than three days.

In China, family relationships were intricate and often unreasonable. In spite of the changing times and the progress brought by education, rigid traditions remained. In the eyes of in-laws, a young wife was regarded as the least worthy of the family, and the deeper the husband loved his wife the greater was the dislike for her by his family. I was no exception. Yi's family regarded me as no more than a delicate "hothouse flower."

For me, the first four years of the Sino-Japanese war were incredibly difficult, the first three spent in Hong Kong (1937-40) and the last in Shanghai (1940-41). Over that time, Yi was almost always away from the family. If I had not had the warmth and sympathetic friendship of Yu-sun [Mrs. O.K. Yu, wife of the former acting mayor of Shanghai; Plate 9], life would have been unlivable.

Yu-sun "*Jie*" (sister Yu-sun), as I fondly addressed my friend, was a devout Christian, a virtuous wife and a warm and wise mother. We were neighbors in Kowloon, across the bay from Hong Kong, where both of our families had lived on Prince Edward Road ("*Tai-zi Tao*"). Many times Yu-sun told me bitter tales of her life as a young wife, of how she was able to overcome her troubles with in-laws and of how she had sometimes managed to convert her detractors into friends. She embraced the Christian commandments "love your enemies, do good to those who despise you, and pray for those who persecute you or make false statements against you." She urged me to use this approach in my own family relations. In my own way, I did try to follow her lead. But as much as I was impressed by her success, I was not able to fully embrace her Christian faith.

San-san's Illness. "Worry about nothing, but be patient with any difficulties. Be calm when you are in trouble, for it is God who is arranging your way." These were the words Yu-sun had said to me as we parted in Hong Kong in the autumn of 1940, when my children and I sailed for Shanghai, once again. Because we could not manage to obtain a private berth, we were placed in a large dining hall ("*tung-tzang*") filled with the masses.

Less than an hour after our ship had left the harbour of Hong Kong Japanese soldiers approached my children and questioned them as to the whereabouts of their father (who by then had been on their "blacklist"). Immediately, memories of the water torture inflicted in Shanghai on my brother Huai-san [Plate 3] at the hands of the Japanese welled in me. To show their might, with a loud thump the soldiers splashed a can of my children's candies on the table. Jolted, my two older girls became frightened and tongue-tied. I ached with agony. Luckily, at that very moment two fine young fellow passengers came to the rescue. Taking a liking to my children and pity on me, they led us to their private cabin, and they themselves, then gallantly moved into the public hall. I was so deeply grateful.

Suddenly, soon after we had settled into our new cabin on the ship, my number three daughter San-san [Plate 3] developed a high fever. When I noted the color of her stool, I immediately realized that she had contracted dysentery. It was this very disease that had taken the life of my first-born son, Yee-zi [Plate 3]. I felt helpless—alone on a large ocean liner with four small children in tow and a single nursemaid to help. Worst of all, there was no doctor on-board. The only medicine I had brought along was a small bottle of Milk of Magnesia, a cure for indigestion. I gave this to San-san every three hours, and stayed by her side all night. By midnight, her temperature had skyrocketed. Memories of son Yee-zi's illness returned in waves. The agitating tide of worry, one swell after another, was overwhelming.

Strangely, the parting words of Yu-sun came to mind. I slowly calmed myself and became less worried. I prayed aloud for San-san. As dawn began to break, I dozed off. In this semi-repose, as if in a dream, I heard a voice whispering in my mind.

"Garlic, garlic can cure dysentery!"

With my eyes half-opened, I sprang out of my chair and hurried to the ship's kitchen where a morning steward was already cleaning the floor. I asked urgently if he had raw garlic. When I got that precious bundle in my hand, I returned to my cabin and minced and squeezed it with all my might to extract the precious little liquid I could get for my daughter. I fed it to San-san. The juice was hot and spicy, burning in her little mouth.

Miraculously, after a second dose of garlic juice, San-san's fever broke, her stools returned to normal, and she was hungry. After another night, the fever had gone. Imagine, a little clove of garlic[3], prickly hot, can heal so well! (Ever since this episode, I have fed my children pickled garlic, particularly at the onset of each winter. And later, when I raised chicks and ducklings in Lanchow and Nanking, I used the same garlic cure on my sick birds.)

On the fourth day our boat reached Shanghai. I was never so happy as when I saw land that morning. These four days of troubling time had strengthened my faith in God, and my whole heart melted in gratitude to Him for healing my daughter and making her well once again.

A year later, in 1941, my husband moved from Chunking to Lanchow, the so-called "*Da hou-fang,*" the great hinterland, far removed from the Japanese, where he had been sent to help develop the Great Northwest. By this time, Shanghai was no longer safe [Plate 8]. My children and I quickly flew to join Yi in Lanchow. Embarrassingly, a life of tranquility for the next four years in this peaceful setting diluted my faith. Meanwhile, our fifth daughter was born, Lan-lan [Plate 3], named after Lanchow. I thought less frequently of God. Life was busy but quiet and unthreatened. To me, in the hinterland, God was not so important. My faith was not yet firm.

Manchurian Experience. After the unconditional surrender of the Japanese in the autumn of 1945, and unbeknownst of the contents of the Yalta Agreement, the Central Government appointed my husband, Yi, Mayor of Darien[4], a major port city in Manchuria on the Liaotung Peninsula that had been long coveted as a year-round warm-water port by both Japan and Russia. By this time, our family had moved from Lanchow to Chunking.

After eight years of war, the exaltation that accompanied this peace was beyond words. Soon thereafter, while the children and I remained in Chunking, Yi was ordered to travel to Peiping to await the handing-over of Darien by the Japanese. To my dismay, we now heard nothing but bad news: Soviet troops, who had taken over Darien from the Japanese, had no intention of giving it back to China. This bitter fruit of betrayal stemmed from the secret agreement made at Yalta in February 1945, without China's knowledge or agreement, by the so-called "Big Three" (Churchill, Roosevelt, and Stalin).

Upon the Japanese's defeat in August 1945, their forces were to surrender Manchuria to the Nationalist Government. But the troops of the Soviet dictator, Josef Stalin, immediately encroached upon the territory and blocked the entry of the Nationalist army into Manchuria by air, land, and sea [Shen-Y, 1985]. The Russians kept close surveillance over the group of the eleven Chinese officials, Yi included, who had been appointed by the Chinese Central Government ("*Zong-yang Tzen-fu*") to repatriate the cities and provinces in northeastern China [Shen-Y, 1985; *Chapter 10*].

The safety of Chinese officials in Manchuria was in serious jeopardy; assassinations and military confrontations occurred, one after another. A most shocking incident was the cold-blooded murder by the Soviets in 1945, on the Central Eastern Railway, of Chang Shin-fu, a highly respected mining engineer. During this time I received no news from Yi. Reports in the papers were all discouraging. And later, when the Russian forces finally began to withdraw from Manchuria, the papers reported that they had looted all the cities, taking for their own use China's industrial machinery [Hsü, 1975; Roberts, 1999].

One evening in late 1945 I read in a newspaper that Soviet troops had completely destroyed the airport at Chang Chung, where the Chinese officials were located. All flights had been cancelled. This was the city from where my husband was waiting to be dispatched to Darien.

In Chang Chung, my husband had been assigned a troop of 500

policemen to accompany him, but the Soviets had already set up a blockade to prohibit all ships carrying Nationalist troops into the Darien port [Plate 6; Hsü, 1975]. I went to the home of Yi's friend, Yin Chun-yun, where we talked deep into the night trying to devise a scheme to rescue my husband. I returned home in pitch-black darkness with a heavy heart. The sound of raindrops on the leaves was the only reality. I could not sleep. I sat up and lit a candle by my bed. I was once again led to the solace of the Bible and I began to pray. In a semi-daze, I prayed, as an inner voice came to me, "Be calm Inyeening, your husband is safe, he will be back to you soon." It was a clear voice. I relaxed, physically and mentally. I fell asleep.

After a late breakfast the next morning, I again went to look for official word, but none was to be found. I began to entrust my destiny to fate. It was drawing toward twilight. I sat knitting by a window in our Chunking living room, trying to quiet my nerves. Suddenly, I heard familiar heavy footsteps climbing the hill, approaching the door. They came closer and closer. Then, abruptly, happy voices burst through the window. When I looked out, it was my dear Jun-yi, smiling and walking toward me, followed by a cheering crowd. I could not believe my eyes. I stood like a statue as my husband hurried to me and took me in his arms.

In spite of my prayers and their help in overcoming difficulties, I still hesitated to join the Christian faith, for by now I had seen far too many people who called themselves Christians but behaved like heathens, doing unconscionable deeds to China. Among these, I counted people such as the Kungs, the Soongs [*Chapter 5*], and a number of other top officials of the Nationalist government, who had filled their own pockets and indulged in luxury while they cast the country into misery. I would cite these examples, this despicable behaviour, whenever my friends began to urge me to become a Christian.

Shin-shin's Fever. In 1946, when the war was finally over, we returned to Shanghai where our son Shin-shin was born. Shortly thereafter, in 1947, our whole family moved from Shanghai to the capital city, Nanking, where Yi had been appointed Mayor. It was in Nanking, on the 28th of August, 1947, when my son, just eight-months old [Plate 3], became ill with an unusual sickness.

At the beginning Shin-shin had a slight fever and a running nose, the symptoms of a cold. A doctor came to the house and gave him a prescription of sulfa. But his fever rose that very evening; his face was burning like fire while his hands, arms, legs, and feet were icy cold. His fingers and toes were scarlet, and deep red spots covered his little body all over. The doctor was puzzled.

After a night of consultation of our son's illness with all available experts at Nanking's Municipal Hospital, the suggestion was to give him an injection of the newly marketed antibiotic, penicillin[5]—but no one was able to guarantee that it would be effective. The diagnosis was that baby Shin-shin was suffering from severe blood poisoning. An injection was given, but my little baby's condition worsened. I was terrified and heart-broken to see his swollen lips, as big as the snout of a little pig. He was not even able to suckle my milk. At this moment, I could think of nothing but to turn to the Holy Bible.

A knock came on the door to my study. A servant ushered in Mr. Wang, Commissioner of the Bureau of Public Health, who had with him Dr. Chi So-nan, an eminent physician. By the time I hurried upstairs to the baby's room, the doctor was already at his side. Dr. Chi was Dean of Medicine of the Ginling Men's University for men [now Nanjing University; *Frontispiece*]; he rarely made house calls.

Dr. Chi's decision was to keep administering penicillin, but to step-up the dosage from 5,000 to 16,000 units, once every three hours. Miraculously, within two days the baby's fever had dropped and the red spots had begun to fade. The doctor visited again on September 12. Shin-shin's temperature had returned to almost normal. Finally, the heavy load was lifted from my shoulders as my baby's fever left him completely the next morning.

My faith in God had solidified, and my gratefulness for His blessings had profoundly deepened. I had at last realized that we human beings are weak and fragile, and that there is, indeed, a Higher Power that can lift us when we are down.

Baptism. Some weeks later after Shin-shin had fully recovered from his illness I sought out Sister Yu-sun[2], who, by this time, had also moved to Nanking. I asked her to advise me how to arrange baptism for my baby son and for myself. On my behalf she promised to talk to a Bishop Koo Chuan, who would then counsel me.

On the 7th of December, 1947, at 2 o'clock in the afternoon, I had an interview, a sort of oral examination for the qualification of bapticism, at the Union Mission of Ginling University for men. I was not questioned in great depth on the knowledge of scripture obtained in my youth, but I was examined at some length about my reasons for wishing to become a Christian. In reply, I related my personal experiences—but I also revealed my shameful habit of smoking as well as my utter disdain for the activities of certain people who called themselves Christians [*Chapter 5*]. The examiners did not interrupt me as I poured out my thoughts and related the various events that had led me to this moment. After a few minutes of discussion among themselves, I was told that I had been accepted for baptism.

Three days before Christmas, on the bright Sunday morning of December 22, 1947, I brought son Shin-shin and my number four daughter Chuan-chuan [Plate 7], who had asked to be baptized with her brother and me, to the service at Ginling Men's University. Yi, my father, my godmother (*Gan-niang*), my niece Ah-ping and my four other children accompanied us. Yu-sun Jie, who had led me to embrace the Christian faith, was present among my many friends. I was beckoned first to the altar to receive the Holy water, which was sprinkled over my head and trickled down my body. One by one, my two children took their turns. Words were inadequate to describe my calm and peacefulness. My whole heart melted as we recited the Psalm,

"The Lord is my shepherd,
I shall not want.
He maketh me to lie down in green pastures.
He leadth me beside the still waters
He restoreth my soul."

At long last, I had become a Christian—but out of my own conviction, not by the coercion of others. I realized that a Christian life cannot be attained by the mere act of baptism alone, that one has to sincerely emulate the goodness that Jesus Christ had showed us all. On our way home from this joyous event, I cheerfully joined my children in the singing of,

"Onward Christian soldiers, marching off to war,
With the cross of Jesus going on before ...."

Footnotes:

[1]Sue-Tee (*"Sudi,"* new pinyin), a beautiful dyke across West Lake in Hangzhou, with flowering apricots, peaches and drooping willows lining its banks (Plate 9), bears the name given it during the Song Dynasty by the famous poet Su Dong-po. Popular still for hundreds of years, this site is a favorite spot year-round.

[2]O.K. Yu (Yu Hong-jun; Plates 6, 9), acting Mayor of Shanghai in 1937 (and later, in 1947, Minister of Finance in Nanking) was considered by the U.S. government to be an especially able administrator (Melby, 1971; Seagrave, 1985). Years later in Hong Kong, the author's good friend Yu-sun (Mrs. O.K. Yu, Plate 9), helped her to prepare wardrobes for her daughters as they set sail for college in the United States.

[3]Garlic (*Allium sativum*) is claimed to be a remarkably effective medicinal herb (Duke, 2002). Besides its use for herbal treatment of dysentery, it is reported to be an effective treatment for arthritis, diabetes, and various fungal, bacterial, and viral infections (Duke, 2002). Evidently, the author's prescience in using garlic to treat daughter San-san's dysentery was right on the mark.

[4]By the late 19th Century, during China's weak Qing administration, governance of the strategic year-round port of Dalian had repeatedly passed between Russia and Japan. At the end of the Russo-Japanese war of 1905, Japan was in control of Dalian (Chang, 1997; Roberts, 1999). Though the status of China's northeastern lands changed in subsequent years, during the Japanese invasion of 1931 they once again fell under Japanese rule. Manchuria was prodded by the Japanese for its agricultural and mineral wealth.

The ensuing Japanese "military immigration" brought millions into northeastern China well before 1937 and the beginning of the full scale Sino-Japanese War (Hsü, 1975; Roberts, 1999; CCTV Station 9, 2005). During the 1945 "Big Three" Yalta conference, among the various concessions made to Russia's Stalin by Roosevelt and Churchill was the ceding of Dalian to the Soviets (Melby, 1971). Russia had long "cast covetous glances at the ice-free port of Darien … at the southern tip of [the] Liaotung [Peninsula]" (Hsü. 1975).

⁵The antibiotic effects of the fungus *Penicillium notatum* were discovered by Alexander Fleming in 1928. The active principle of the bactericide, penicillin, was isolated and formulated for medicinal use in the 1940s.

CHAPTER 7
FRIENDS OF "WINE AND MEAT"

Never in my life had I met so many dignitaries from so many countries of the world. Never before had I been in such a swirl of entertaining, or being entertained, by diplomats of foreign lands. China had rarely if ever before encountered such an onslaught of envoys. Some might view the opportunity to be involved in such activities an honor, but I regarded it a misery for I was neither used to, nor interested in this "whirlwind" of social interaction.

My first glimpse of the diplomatic circle occurred at a dinner gathering hosted by British Ambassador and Lady Stevenson. There was a huge crowd, very few of whom I knew. I was left alone, quiet and tongue-tied; my meager capacity in conversational English was inadequate for small talk, not to mention meaningful dialogue. My hostess, Lady Stevenson, was a genial and eloquent woman who tried many times to relieve my obvious embarrassment.

Minister from Brazil. In my boredom, I spotted a person standing alone who seemed particularly unusual. A man of medium height and large build, with a face brushed with a humorous smile, he kept his hands absolutely still whenever he spoke. In spite of his exuberant cordiality he did not seem able to attract many conversations. Without an introduction, he walked up to me and began an erratic dialogue that left me speechless and at sea. He had not introduced himself, nor had he inquired my name. With more curiosity than interest, I listened and observed his nonchalant yet excited manner.

During dinner, I learned that this gentleman was the "Doyen du Corps Diplomatique" Minister from Brazil. At the end of dinner he approached me again, by now having learned who I was. Holding the posture of a confident "old-timer," he began another conversation.

"How long have you been in Nanking ... how many places have you seen?"

He blurted questions in such a rapid succession that I was left breathless.

When I mentioned a series of places—the "*T'song-san Ling*" (Sun Yat-sen's Tomb), the "*Ming-shao Ling*" (Ming's Tomb) and the "*Tann Mo*" (tomb of the Republic's first Prime Minister, Tann Yen-kai[1]), he burst into laughter.

"Yes, yes, I know you Chinese—you are excellent in paying great respect to the dead."

Had he not been a diplomat, I perhaps would not have been surprised at such rudeness. But, intuitively, I sensed an intentional insult. Suppressing my reaction, I replied:

"Mr. Minister, I am so very sorry, indeed, that you should hold this view of the Chinese." "However, we *do* know how to revere people who prove deserving, regardless of whether they are dead or alive."

I was afraid that my reply to the Brazilian diplomat might have created an awkward situation, but the man took my reply as though it w ere merely a breeze passing by the ear ("*er-bian fung*"); he was oblivious of my displeasure and continued his effusive questioning. I learned later that rather than being intentionally obnoxious, he was a person who was simply prone to ramble. And his thoughtlessness was nothing compared to the sarcastic remark of a British diplomat who arrogantly asserted:

"The most outstanding accomplishment of your government is the massive tomb of Dr. Sun Yat-sen."

To me, these words were a deep insult.

Ambassador of India. In the early morning of January 30, 1948, I was awakened by the sound of someone reciting scripture. I thought at first that it might have come from a nearby temple, and put it out of my hearing. The next morning, the recitation repeated again. This time it caught my attention, for it was ponderous and melancholy, filled with sadness. I learned later that it had come from the house next door—the residence of the Indian Ambassador, His Excellency K.P.S. Menon[2].

The mournful sound from our neighbors told of the death of Gandhiji[3], India's beloved leader, who had been shot and killed by an unknown assassin. The following day I accompanied my husband to pay our condolences. We left our cards at the entrance. From the gateway I could see the main hall, overflowing with Indians in mournful prayer. My heart went out to Ambassador and Mrs. Menon, who at other times had been most jovial.

Living in close vicinity with the Menons for over a year, our families became well acquainted. Both the Ambassador and his wife were intelligent and well educated, and they were very approachable. He had the air of a scholar, rather than a high diplomat, and had a fine reputation among the people of Nanking.

Irrespective of the fine regards from the Chinese, one distraction, which seemed to me rather typical of many Indian nationals, was the Menons' air of self-importance (no less a British affectation). They gave the impression of regarding themselves as the most brilliant, and certainly most interesting persons to grace any group, as being the "great power" among all powers that might be present in any gathering. Interestingly, however, and notwithstanding their evident self-esteem, they were unable to pull themselves free from the shackles of humbleness and deference they paid to the British. The following is an example.

One summer evening, the Menons had invited us to dinner. The evening was sultry, but the dress code was formal. There were twenty guests. The British Ambassador, not accompanied by his wife, was the last one to arrive. Before the Englishman could enter the parlour, where the other guests had already assembled, his thunderous laughter preceded him into the room, disrupting the polite atmosphere.

Emerging from behind a curtain in the splendid living room of the Menons, with a slow rolling gait (one might call it a waddle), the British Ambassador's appearance immediately attracted attention. The exquisitely dressed ladies were taken aback by this intrusion, and in unison they quietly uttered a long, soft, "Aaah." The British Ambassador was wearing an ordinary shirt and trousers, but his attire for this formal occasion was anything but ordinary. His shirt was short-sleeved and his wrinkled pants had not seen an iron for days. He tried to cover the embarrassing situation with a continuous stream of laughter, seemingly uttering whatever nonsense entered his head.

As the tension built I began to have the notion that this ill-mannered Englishman truly believed himself to be the supreme personality in the room, and I could feel how insulting this must have been to the Menons. But true to their upbringing as subservient to the British, our Indian hosts maintained their cordiality and in fact showered the Ambassador with deference, despite his boorish behaviour.

This occasion recalls to me a story about my favorite grandfather, Ying Bao-shi, who held the official title of "*Toe'tai*," Top Desk of the Shanghai government from 1865 to 1869 during the Ching Dynasty [*About the Author*]. A *Toe'tai*, whose rank was higher than that of a present-day mayor, was in charge of all foreign affairs, including all matters concerning military operations of the Western deputations.

One summer day, *Toe'tai* Ying paid a courtesy call on a British general. Following the rules of etiquette for the official attire of the Chinese Imperial Government, Ying had come in full attire. The British general received him in a short-sleeved shirt, without a tie. My grandfather hid his dismay at this lack of proper respect, feigned a polite exchange with this supposedly civilized Westerner, and quickly made his exit.

A few days after grandpa's visit, the distinguished British general made a return call to my grandfather, who was still quite affected by their earlier encounter. When the arrival of the guest was announced, *Toe'tai* Ying swiftly changed clothes into a pair of Chinese linen trousers and a house vest, and came forth to receive his guest. The general took one look at his host and, immediately recognising his earlier error, quietly apologised for his breach of etiquette during the previous visit. (I suppose this story must be true; I found it in the archives of a library in Shanghai.)

Consul from Egypt. Almost without fail, when I worked or played with my children in our back garden a man in a nearby little yellow house would lean out of his upper floor balcony. Upon being noticed, he would immediately retreat. My children and I had felt awkward about this intrusive behavior.

Later, during a large cocktail party, a dark European gentleman came forward to greet me as if we were long lost friends. His knowledge of my daily routine, my gardening, and my raising of fowls and vegetables, greatly surprised me. He could tell me how many pigeons we had, their colors, and on which days I had been in the garden. He was even able to recount the color of the gowns I had worn on various days. Such personal minutia was extraordinary from a total stranger. Had he not introduced himself as the man in the little yellow house, the Consul of Egypt, I would have taken him for a spy!

From that day on after the party we became better acquainted with our Egyptian neighbor. He was shy and timid, and would talk only to those who came into his path. His peculiar behavior attracted my attention, so out of curiosity I began to observe *his* daily activities. During the day he would be a spinster, quiet and alone in the house. But in the evening, almost every night, the little yellow house would be fully illuminated with elegant cars aligning its gate. After some time, Yi and I were invited to join his parties. At first we had been only occasional guests, but by-and-by we became frequent invitees. I had been puzzled by his endless rounds of entertaining, parties that had become more and more boisterous over the months, and I wondered whether this was his sole function in Nanking.

Finally, the Consul of Egypt trusted me enough to confess that his life in Nanking was lonely, insipid and colorless. He longed for Cairo and was constantly homesick for the bazaars, teahouses, and a span of quiet sand stretching far into the distance. He thus plunged himself into this evening ruckus, just to amuse and divert himself.

Governor of Hong Kong. It was like a comic performance when we entertained the Governor of Hong Kong, Sir Alexander Grantham, and his wife, on their official visit to Nanking. On October 1st, 1947, we were informed that the Granthams were to arrive in Nanking at four o'clock that very afternoon. Punctually, Yi went to the airport and greeted their party.

In keeping with the protocol of the Western world, Mrs. T.C. Pao, wife of the Chief Protocol of the Nanking Foreign Affairs Division, represented me in welcoming Mrs. Grantham, presenting to her a bouquet of flowers. I stayed home to organize a welcoming dinner in their honor, scheduled for eight o'clock that same evening. The entire household was mobilized for this hastily organized event.

Having thespian training as a youngster I was not at all ignorant of the theatric experience on a stage (having had considerable success in my school days in several plays), but on that day I was absolutely at sea, and found myself a puppet in a most strange drama. Before the evening festivities began, a protocol officer prompted me about the proper formalities. A formal toast to the host and hostess was to be given by our honored guests; but I was cautioned not to stand or drink when Yi and I were being toasted, as Western protocol would consider this part of the traditional Chinese etiquette to be rude and impolite.

The banquet for the Governor and Mrs. Grantham was a big one. Four round tables were set in our formal dining room and elegant Chinese banquet dishes were prepared from our own kitchen by my favorite chef, Ben-yao, and his eager helper. High officials of the Chinese government and distinguished guests of various nationalities were gathered for the festivities. At first the atmosphere was stiff, but after the unavoidable formalities had been completed the guests became relaxed.

Sir Alexander was a tall, slender, middle-aged man of a very civil and thoughtful demeanor. But, by nature, he like all such British officials obviously held himself in high esteem. To me, due to her white hair and well-lined face, Lady Grantham looked older than her age. She was an American, petite and almost dwarfish, nimble in movement. After a time the guests became quiet and Sir Alexander broke the awkward silence by telling of his experience in physiognomy[4], a subject that had preoccupied his attention for the previous 17 years.

After regaling us for a time about the Governor's ideas on the study of human features, he then hesitated and, with a penetrating glance, began to examine, closely, my husband's face. He then turned to me and in a whisper said that Yi's features, especially his face and hands, identified him as a hard-working man devoted to his duty.

"A great benefit to others, often at his own expense"—in Chinese parlance, a "*lao'lo ming*," a person having a destiny of selfless hard work.

I replied that Yi had experienced many difficult appointments, but that this one, in Nanking, was by far the most onerous.

"That's nothing; he shall have harder ones yet to come," predicted Sir Alexander.

His expression was so serious, and so definite, that it depressed me. He noted my distress, smiled, and added,

"Don't worry Mme. Shen, following hardship there is the glory of success."

"Your husband is a wonderful man for China, and China needs such a man."

Whether it was logic or diplomacy, I listened with a faint smile.

Early in the morning, October 4th, three days after our entertaining the Governor of Hong Kong, a small group gathered at Ming Gu'gon Airport, to the south of the city, for the departure of Governor Grantham and his wife. The Granthams arrived late, just minutes before take-off. I was the only woman among the "seeing-off" party. Surprisingly to me, the attitude of our departing guests seemed indifferent and dispassionate.

"A short stay of three-and-a-half days might have been more than enough for the Granthams," I thought to myself,

"After all, on the happy peninsula of Hong Kong, they are treated as King and Queen."

"But they would be wrong to think that Hong Kong[5] could remain Britain's forever!"

The departure of the Granthams, I thought, would be the last scene of the final act of this little drama. But I was mistaken. A week later, via the British Embassy, I received a parcel from Lady Grantham. It was a handsomely hand-painted vase, in silver and gold, sent in reciprocation of my gift to her, a set of Nanking fine brocade cushions and embroidered tablecloths.

To my surprise, when I un-wrapped the parcel from the First Lady of Hong Kong I found a card that read: "To Lady Chen Chak, with Compliments from Lady Grantham." Thinking that the package had been misdirected, I quickly rewrapped the vase and immediately returned it to the British Embassy. But the Embassy delivered it to me once again, apologising with the explanation that the card had simply been miswritten. (In my mind, it could not have meant for me, especially when I saw the price tag on the bottom of the vase, "400 H.K.," four hundred Hong Kong dollars; our brief association did not call for such an expensive a gift!)

I remembered that Lady Grantham had said to me several times that they would be more than honored to have my husband and me as their guests in Hong Kong, so as to give them the opportunity to reciprocate our hospitality. In the years that followed, Yi and I traveled to Hong Kong on many occasions. Each time I thought of Lady Grantham's words, and wondered whether she would have remembered her offer and would still have wished us to visit[6].

Charge d'Affaires of the Soviet Union. In the Nanking diplomatic arena, I was intolerant of people who outwardly appeared humble and human but inwardly hid the "eye of a black heart" ("*hay shing'yen,*" bad motives)—people who had what was to me the annoying habit of using odd metaphours and sharp and piercing words, or who treated others as antagonists or enemies. But no matter how much I disliked such people, I did my best to maintain a civil presence. Among the worst were the diplomats from Russia.

One afternoon at a reception, on the hottest day of summer, we had the misfortune of meeting a Charge d'Affaires of the Soviet Embassy, a good-looking young man whose appearance was flawed only by his steely eyes, in which I discerned certain ruthlessness. He spoke fluent Mandarin, his accent being more authentic than some Chinese not native to Peiping. But he also used "crocked words," slang and even worse, that were not suited for polite company. On this occasion we stood face-to-face, very close, saying nothing. I felt the uneasy silence. My husband began the conversation, noting what terrible hot weather we were having and asking him if summers in Moscow were like this one in Nanking[7].

"Oh everything is different between the two capitals, not only the weather."

I was taken aback by this rudeness; his attitude and expression made my hair stand on end. Yi was a man of pacific disposition; he pretended not to be affected. I, more easily agitated, tartly replied,

"Yes, of course, our capitals are different!"

"We Chinese are different from the Russians, fundamentally because we are a peace-loving people."

Whether he heard my remarks or not he seemed to have felt the disagreeable atmosphere. He quickly moved on.

At just that dramatic moment after our unpleasant meeting with the Soviet diplomat, out came Mr. Wen Yuan-ning, China's newly appointed Ambassador to Greece, who was our houseguest at the time. His face had the colour of burning amber and his voice was quivering, out of breath. It happened that, he, too, had had a encounter with this same Russian fellow, who had flippantly told the Ambassador that his appointment to Greece was a ridiculous assignment[8]—there being only a single Chinese national living in the entire country—and that he seriously doubted whether there would be any business at all for a Chinese Ambassador in Greece. Though furious, Ambassador Wen, a British-educated experienced diplomat, quietly rejoined:

"The main purpose and mission of my country in sending an envoy to Greece is to develop friendship and understanding between the two nations."

"It is totally irrelevant whether there are many or only a few Chinese living in that country."

Soon after this unpleasantness, it became our turn, according to protocol, to entertain the Russian diplomats. On the appointed date, Ambassador A.A. Petrov and his wife were not in Nanking, having returned home to Moscow on holiday. Regrettably, the newly hatched *"shing'zu mao'lu"* (wet-behind-the-ears) Charge d'Affaires, with whom we had the unpleasant encounter, was our guest of honour[9].

Very strangely, the unpleasant Russian fellow now showed a complete change of attitude. He and his wife were exceedingly natural, polite, and even sincere. I almost mistook him for a different person! His wife was an unaffected woman, young and handsome. When she saw the diamond ring on my finger, she asked, in a childlike manner, whether I had many more. I told her that the ring was an engagement gift from my husband and that I did not accumulate diamond jewelry.

In spite of the repeated nasty lessons we had learned at the hands of the Russians—whom I regarded as hypocritical, tricky, and insidious—I reminded myself that, at the end of the day, human beings are all basically the same, the Russians being no exception.

"For Heaven's sake," I thought,

"I should have at least some compassion for these poor people who are being ruled by that heartless dictator, Josef Stalin."

For it was Stalin, I believed, who had made the Russians virtual slaves to the doctrine and devices of his tyranny—forcing them into barbaric acts that were totally in defiance of their own wishes and the laws of nature. To my mind, Stalin was a tragedy brought from Hell to millions and millions of innocent people[10].

Wife of Ambassador of Italy. Certainly, Mrs. Fenoletti, wife of the Italian Ambassador, could not be regarded in the same light as Lady Stevenson, wife of the British Ambassador; nor Mme. Merrier, wife of the French Ambassador[11] nor Mrs. Davis, wife of the Canadian Ambassador—a group of superficial and conceited women who hovered in a mist of self-centered importance, with Lady Stevenson leading the pack.

Mrs. Fenoletti, wife of the Italian Ambasador, on the other hand, was sincere and accessible. Indeed, she was truly admirable, perhaps though more as an exemplary housewife than as the wife of a diplomat. However, recognising what she viewed to be her "inadequacy," she became keen to emulate the three "accomplished ladies." The result was awkward and humourous. Among other things, she wanted to move into a house that would be far grander than the one she currently occupied. Clearly, she had an inferiority complex, in part stemming from realising that the embassies of the other three ladies were larger and decidedly more elegant.

One fall afternoon, I strolled into my front garden enjoying the beautiful chrysanthemums in full bloom. I heard footsteps behind the wall of wintergreens and saw a figure of a woman. It was Mrs. Fenoletti. I invited her into the house for tea, which she more than gladly accepted. She was anxious to tell me about a house she had found which was just being built; she liked the design and had given it a thorough study. Upon inquiring, she had been told that this house was being built for a relative of ours and wanted my help to persuade these relatives to rent it to the Italian Embassy when it was finished. When I saw the blueprint, I was taken aback; it was the exact house design on which Yi and I had just started construction at *"Wutai San"* [*Chapter 10*; Holy May Hills]. I was embarrassed when she insisted on having me to introduce her to the owners.

To avoid unnecessary attention on the house construction on *Wutai San*, Yi and I had had the deed of the buiding listed under the name of our oldest daughter, Hwa-hwa, Shen Yu-hwa[12]. As I listened to Mrs. Fenoletti's plea, I tried to conjure a suitable reply. In order to satisfy her (and to give me more time to think), I told her a white lie—that the owners were presently away in Shanghai. I promised to inquire on her behalf to find out if the house would be for let. This, as it turned out, was not to be.

The story as to how we acquired the property at *Wutai San*, then under construction, is circuitous [see *Chapter 10*]. When we were in Lanchow, during World War II, my husband brought back from Chunking, a gift set of Sheaffer fountain pens. He knew I loved Sheaffer. I was thrilled. I kept the pens in my treasure chest. This prize possession, however, had become known to some acquaintances. One day, a person came to call and asked about the pens, wondering whether I would be willing to part with them. Having no such intention whatever, I jokingly replied, "Sure, for ten gold bars". To my surprise—and utter dismay—the person immediately accepted my offer. I regretted it terribly, but I was too embarrassed to go back on my word.

After the regretful telephone negotiation I parted with my treasured pens—for nine *"jin-tiao"* (gold bars, strand of gold[13])! With these plus added savings I purchased nearly three *"moo"*[14] of land, on *Wutai San* to the southwest of the city [*Frontispiece*]; and with six more strands (from a long lease of our apartment in Shanghai to my sister), and loans and savings we were able to begin construction of the new house. To cut building costs, all the usable steel window- and door-frames from our bombed-out house at *Jiang-wan* in Shanghai [Plate 9; *Chapter 10*] were shipped to Nanking for the new construction[15].

In spite of cutting costs everywhere we could on the *Wutai San* construction, we still ran into debt and had to borrow from brother-in-law, Tao Moon-ho[16]. So I actually did have the notion of letting the house when it was finally finished. Sadly, this dream came to naught when the Communists captured Nanking in 1949. Despite our plans, we never lived in this house.

Minister of Australia. Each time when I had tea or dinner with Mr. and Mrs. Douglas Copeland, our good friends from Australia, I had the feeling of returning to my old school days once again, for it was like being in the home of a former teacher where the atmosphere was pleasant and congenial. Sweet memories returned one after another whenever we entered the home of Minister and Mrs. Copeland.

On several of our visits the Copelands included our two elder girls, Hwa-hwa and Pei-pei, who were a few years younger than their only daughter, Rose Maria. Situated on the top of a low hill [see *Chapter 10*], their house, neither gaudy nor pretentious, was comfortable and pleasant. Both the Minister and his wife were affable and sincere, without the hypocritical politeness that I had so often seen as the only social amenity of many of the other diplomats. We were never at a loss for words. Our conversations were interesting and free, and we would chat on any subject where our thoughts led us. My one regret was that my and Yi's limited capacity in English prevented us from fully expressing our views. Frequently we became "good listeners."

The Australian Minister was very pleased that we addressed him as Professor Copeland, rather than his official title. Indeed, he was better known for being a scholar than a diplomat. He was an educator and an outstanding economist in his own country. World economics seemed to be his prime concern. He frequently presented lectures in Nanking, at universities and other educational institutions. He also took pleasure in going to other cities in China by invitation from local universities. We met more often in academic gatherings than at diplomatic functions. On one occasion, a meeting of the Chinese Institute of Economic

Reconstruction was held at our home and presided by my husband Yi. Professor Copeland was the guest of honour, speaking on issues concerning reconstruction of the world's post-war economy. This lecture was greatly lauded by the Nanking newspapers.

The friendship between the two families of Copeland and Shen was strong among the parents, but not quite as harmonious among the children. One afternoon, a children's party was given on board a British naval ship. Our four girls were guests of the Naval Mission of the United Kingdom. But when the girls returned from the outing, they appeared downtrodden. At length, Hwa-hwa, our eldest, told us that they had met the Copeland daughter on board the ship, and that not only had she acted as if she did not know them but that she had joined the group of Western children who then teased the local Chinese youngsters.

My four children were burning with embarassment, but they harboured their fury within. Without rudeness or revenge, their young minds had become aware of the all-too-prevalent Western attitude. Unanimously, and sadly, all four girls proclaimed that they wished to be friends with Rose Maria Copeland no more.

This incident reminds me of my own experience during my stay in a British school in Shanghai. There it was obvious that the antagonism among the children stemmed from the attitudes of their parents—and, sadly, that it had been fostered intentionally by the Western parents, especially by those who had long exploited the local Chinese and who had filled their children's innocent minds with tales of ridicule.

Yet, as long as this feeling of arrogance and "superiority" existed among the Western people, how could there be real cooperation in forming a stable and peaceful world? No matter how famously "inscrutable" the Chinese might appear to outsiders to be, the long pent-up fury would one day burst forth when their pride became so deeply hurt that their endurance finally came to an end.

(Now, as I write this, I think the consequences can be seen on the mainland, under the Red regime. From my experience, I am convinced that the majority of Chinese inwardly dislike the Reds—Russian and

Mao, both—but because of their even greater disdain for the Western world, they stoically stand by the Chinese Communists.)

Friends of Wine and Meat—"Jo'rou Peng'you." Toward the end of our two-year stay in Nanking, the capital seemed to be entering a moribund state like the quiet before a storm. The pale-coloured sky of winter looked somber, as if snow would soon fall, and the usually crowded and noisy streets were still and empty. Sycamore trees stood stately, but now naked, on both sides of the roadways. Occasionally, one or two passing cars and tricycles and rickshaws jarred the silence. Dusk crept in, and the hazy twilight plunged the city into an immense darkness. There was not a light on the streets and hardly a light in the homes. What a profound bleakness Nanking had become! My heavy heart could not help my deep despair. I had come face-to-face with the hopelessness of my surroundings.

Oddly, however, the mood of the foreign diplomatic circle remained cheerful, as though all was well. As if on some other planet, the diplomats kept themselves at arm's length from the misery around them. They felt no dismay, no sympathy for those whom they had once regarded as friends. They were not concerned at all about the desperate state of the Nationalist Government. Secretly, they had begun to cherish the hope of bonding new friendships with a new power, one they had previously considered their enemy. Like a flock of aimless sheep, childishly and ignorantly they began to strike agreements with a wolf.

Social diplomatic functions continued, one after another. On the eve of the great disaster of the fall of Nanking, a grand dinner party was underway in the mansion of the British Ambassador and Lady Stevenson. This was the last time Yi and I would attend a formal social in Nanking. The dinner was given in honour of the Minister of Siam and his wife and the newly arrived Minister of Belgian.

"When could we start our mutual language education?"

I was startled at the end of the dinner by this query from Mrs. Lamb, wife of the British Minister. At one point, she and I had made a reciprocal agreement to teach each other English and Chinese [*Chapter 11*]. Minister Lionel Lamb was fluent in Chinese and his wife wanted to learn more. I did not know what to say, as my heart was heavy with hopelessness. I answered her with an awkward smile. She seemed to understand my mood and dropped the subject.

On that very evening of the social at the British Embassy, at eleven o'clock, a census was to be taken, organized by the Municipal Government [*Chapter 11*]. The dinner party dispersed early so that everyone would have time to get home. As I was walking toward the host and hostess to thank them for the evening, my husband stopped me and told me that he and Mr. Yeh Gon-tsao, Deputy Minister of Foreign Affairs, wished to speak with the host.

Given that opportunity, Mr. Yeh asked the Ambassador of Britain, Ralph Stevenson, his opinion on the perilous situation in China. Stevenson shrugged his shoulders, smiled knowingly.

"By now, it is too late," he replied.

"All is too late, my friends."

"There is no way, and no one, who can save this government, a result of her own foolish reliance on the United States."

"You still believe that they are your only friends."

"But, look at them now. They are throwing you away mercilessly."

The Ambassador might well have been right[17], but his words were unfit to have issued from the mouth of a diplomat! I never believed that there could be real justice, righteousness, or friendship, either in politics or among the diplomatic circle. In such arenas, empty words are used to achieve self-interests. We have a term for people such as that: "*Jo'rou Peng'you,*" friends of wine and meat. Shakespeare, in "*As You Like It*", phrased it well:

> *Blow, blow, thy winter wind,*
> *Thou art not so unkind*
> *As man's ingratitude ...*
> *As friendship remember'd not.*
> *Heigh ho! Sing heigh ho! Unto the green holly:*
> *Most friendship is feigning, most loving mere folly ....*

Footnotes:

[1]Tann Yen-kai, first premier of the Nationalist Government, was one of the three official guests invited by Huang Fu (Shen Yi's brother-in-law) to participate in the marriage of Shen Yi and the author on February 12, 1928 (Shen-Y, 1985). Tann's son, Tann Bai-yu, was Shen Yi's good friend (*Chapter 10*), a fellow student in Germany. In Nanjing, Tann's only daughter, Tania, had given Mayor Shen's family quite a number of her nice out-grown clothes, hand-me-downs that were much appreciated by his daughters (Plate 9).

[2]Ambassador K.P.S. Menon was later designated Minister of India's Foreign Affairs. At about the same time, the author's husband, Shen Yi, was appointed Chief of the U.N. ECAFE Bureau of Flood Control and Water Resources Development in Bangkok (Shen-Y, 1985). In 1949, Menon, together with hydraulic engineer Dr. A.N. Khosla (Indian Central Water, Irrigation and Navigation Commission), was instrumental in assisting Shen's U.N. Bureau in the selection of an Indian engineer to form a "Three-expert Committee" (Shen-Y, 1985). Later, during a visit by Shen to India, Khosla arranged a much publicized courtesy audience with Prime Minister Jawaharla Nehru that was broadcast on radio throughout Asia.

Shen Yi's ECAFE Committee—had included Albert Normandine (France) and B.K. Kapur (India)—made numerous visits to countries in Asia and formulated the Bureau's overwhelmingly successful Mekong River Project (see *About the Author*).

[3]Mahatma Gandhi, the leader of India's passive-resistance movement for independence from the British, was assassinated in January 1948 by one of his own countrymen (Johnson, 1983).

[4]Physiogamy is the art of assessing the character of a person on the basis of physical, particularly facial features.

[5]Following the Opium Wars (1839-46), Hong Kong was ceded by the Qing Dynasty to the United Kingdom. In 1997 it was returned to the People's Republic of China.

[6]Sir Alexander was Governor of Hong Kong until 1957. Lady Alexander, Maurine Samson, was his first wife (*Google*).

[7]Nanjing is one of the three so-called fire pots ("*huo-lu,*" boilers) of China. The other two are Wuhan and Chongqing. Each summer, all three cities, situated on the banks of the Yangtze River, are overwhelmed by hot, sticky weather (the so-called "dog days" of summer; see *Chapter 4*).

[8]Wen Yuan-ning not only served as Ambassador to Greece, in which post he remained for more than 20 years, but became the acknowledged leader of the Diplomatic Corps in Athens. He fostered a close friendship with the King of Greece. Indeed, in the presence of Wen, the King once admonished his son, the royal prince who later succeeded his father to the throne. The son, King Constantine II, was often ill at ease thereafter in the presence of the Ambassador (In, 1971).

[9]Ironically, this neophyte Russian Charge d' Affaires was entrusted to transmit a strong protest, from the Nationalist Government to Moscow, against the Soviet Union's refusal to relinquish authority over Dalian and Port Arthur (Durdin, 1946; see *Chapter 6*).

[10]According to journalist Paul Johnson (1983), during Stalin's reign of terror, beginning in 1929, tens of millions of peasants (kulaks) and others who opposed him were killed.

[11]His Excellency, the French Ambassador Merrier, forwarded an invitation signed by Charles de Gaulle, President of the Paris Municipal Congress to Mayor Shen Yi, inviting the mayor to attend the World-Capitals Mayoral Congress to be convened October 2-8, 1948 (Fang, 2004). In view of the precarious position of Nanjing in the on-going war with Mao, Mayor Shen declined, requesting Prime Minister Wong Wen-hao to appoint a New York-based representative delegation in his stead (a delegation that was led by the mayor's old friend Jiang Jiping, a member of the Chinese delegation to the United Nations; Fang 2004).

[12]Shen Yu-hwa (Hwa-hwa; Plate 7), the author's eldest daughter, was chosen by Mayor Shen Yi and his wife to be listed on the deed as holder of the *Wutai-San* property (*Frontispiece; Chapter 10*). The deed was registered with the Nanking City government in 1948; the house is still extant (see *footnote*[15], below).

[13]Under the rampant inflation of that time (see *Chapter 9, footnote*[2]), strands of gold ("*Jin-tiao,*" gold bar) were the only "currency" worth keeping (*Chapter 10*). These bars were small nuggets, "coin-size" but thicker, about the width of a pencil.

[14]One *moo* ("*mu*"), a unit of area, is equivalent to about one-third of an acre.

[15]The house on the hills of *Wutai San* (Plate 9; *Frontispiece; Chapter 10*), owned and paid for in full by Mayor Shen and the author, is situated at 4 *Bai-bu Po* (Slope of Hundred Steps) where it neighbors the former homes

of the then-Nationalist Prime Minister, Wong Wen-hao and mayor's good friend Tann Bai-yu.

Today, the Shen's house at *Wutai San* (Holy May Hills)) sits opposite a newly completed sports arena and is on top a busy street, up a long flight of steps from the "*Gudu*" Hotel (Old Capital Hotel). From 1949 to the time of the editor's most recent visit (2005), the house was occupied by high-ranking military families. At the generosity of one of the present occupants, Hong Zi-Ming, the son of a deceased high-ranking military officer from Shanghai, the editor was ushered into the house and grounds.

Surrounded by huge evergreen trees and painted a pleasant pastel yellow (Plate 9), the *Wutai San* house is still equipped with the steel-frame windows salvaged from Author's Shanghai bombed-out house at *Jiang-wan* (see Plate 9; *Chapters 3, 10*).

[16]Tao Moon-ho (Tao Meng-he, new pinyin) was the husband of Mayor Shen's sister, Shen Xing-ren (Plate 2). In the 1970s, Tao, a distinguished scholar, served as Vice President of the Chinese Academy of Sciences, Academia Sinica. Grateful for his brother-in-law's loan for the house construction at *Wutai San*, in 1949 Shen Yi repaid the borrowed sum from the first paycheck he received from the United Nations ECAFE (see *Chapter 10*).

[17]In January 1950, Britain granted *de jure* recognition of Mao's regime. British Prime Minister Ernest Bevin justified this action by asserting that there are "some factors which affect us specially, not only our interest in China, but the position in Hong Kong" (Donovan, 1982).

CHAPTER 8
ENVOYS FROM THE UNITED STATES

Background -----------

When Harry S. Truman became president, in 1945, he held the same view as his predecessor, Franklin D. Roosevelt, that the U.S. should continue her support of China so that the Chinese Nationalist Government could be helped to fill the impending post-World War II power vacuum in Asia [Hsü, 1975; Donovan, 1982]. This chapter highlights visits to Nanjing after WWII, during the final days of the Nationalist regime on the mainland, of U.S. government officials and their meetings with Nanjing Mayor Shen Yi (the author's husband). Primary among such visitors and resident dignitaries were William C. Bullitt, U.S. Ambassador to the Soviet Union during the Roosevelt era; General Albert C. Wedemeyer, Trumans's Special Envoy to China; and John L. Stuart, the U.S. Ambassador to China.

William C. Bullitt (1891-1967), Ambassador to Russia during FDR's administration [Tuchman, 1972] and an experienced "China hand" [Kahn, 1976], came to Nanking in 1947 as a private citizen and journalist. He later made several more visits; the last one, in late 1948, was shortly before the capital fell to the Communists.

General Albert Wedemeyer paid a visit in July 1947, a fact-finding mission made at the suggestion of Republican Congressman Walter Judd [Hsü, 1975]. When he departed China a month later, he issued the following statement: "To gain and maintain the confidence of the [Chinese] people, the Central [Nationalist] Government will have to affect immediate drastic, far-reaching political and economic reforms. Promises will no longer suffice. Performance is absolutely necessary. It should be accepted that military force itself will not eliminate Communism" [Tuchman, 1972]. A full report, prepared by Wedemeyer upon his return to the U.S. and recommending "sufficient and prompt military assistance" and economic aid to the Nationalists, but was later "politely received and quietly shelved by [General] Marshall" [Hsü, 1975].

In 1948, following General Wedemeyer's visit, Chiang Ching-kuo, son of President Chiang Kai-shek (and in 1975, successor of his father to the presidency in Taiwan), was given the task to carry out drastic economic reform[1]. "Having found out the vested interest was stronger than he" [Melby, 1971], young Chiang resigned in November of that year.

The China-born U.S. Ambassador John Leighton Stuart—appointed in 1946 and the last U.S. Ambassador to the Nationalist Government on the mainland—was previously a missionary to China and later President of the prestigious Yenjing University in Peiping (now Beijing University) [Melby, 1971]. Ambassador Stuart was much admired and respected, both by the Chinese and by the Americans. According to Professor John Melby [1971], Stuart "passionately loved the Chinese people and was heartsick over what was happening to them." The Ambassador himself wrote in his memoir: "We Americans mainly saw the good things about the Chinese Communists, while not noticing the intolerance, bigotry, deception, disregard for human life, and other evils which seem to be inherent in any totalitarian system" [Kahn, 1975].

In the spring of 1949, toward the end of his tenure, Stuart's steadfast loyalty to the Chinese people was apparent in his meeting with Huang Hua, Chief of the Alien Affairs Office (later, Head of the Chinese delegation to the United Nations), who extended overtures to the U.S. government to formally recognize Mao's Communists regime. Stuart's reply, judicious and to the point, was that because the civil war was still in progress, no Chinese communist government existed to be so recognized [Donovan, 1982]. On August 2, 1949, nearly four months after the fall of Nanking and as a further rebuff to the communist proposal, Ambassador John Leighton Stuart departed China [Topping, 1999].

Though less than fully trustful of people in the Nationalist Government, many knowledgeable Americans had high regard for some members of the government a number of them are noted in this Chapter:

Dr. Wong Wen-hao, said to have "an international reputation as a geologist" [Time Magazine, 1948], was regarded to be "a man of unquestionable integrity" [Melby, 1971; see Chapter 7, footnote[15]] and "one of the finest and most respected of China's public officials" [Tuchman, 1972].

Chiang Monlin [see Chapter 5], a former Chancellor of Peking

University and a leading academic figure in China [Tuchman, 1972], was highly regarded and actively cultivated by General Joseph W. "Vinegar Joe" Stilwell, U.S. Commander of the China-Burma-India theatre—despite the fact of being Military Attaché to China from 1935 to 1939 [Tuchman, 1972], had become intolerant of President Chiang to the extent of gaining the reputation of being Chiang's severest American critic [Donovan, 1982].

And, Yü Ta-wei—a mathematician, graduate both of Harvard and Heidelberg Universities, and the Minister of Ordnance of the Nationalist government—was an admired man, cultured and thoughtful [Tuchman, 1972].

During the immediate post-WWII period, a "Third Force" merged to play a pivotal role in the unfolding saga in China. Initially organized in 1927 in Berlin by Soong Chinling (wife of the founder of the Republic, Sun Yat-sen, and the sister of Chairman Chiang's wife, Mme. Chiang Soong Mayling) together with Chinese General Teng Yen-ta [Seagrave, 1985], this Third Force stood squarely between the Nationalist Kuomintang and the Communists. The members of this group, who seemed to have the ear of U.S. General Albert Wedemeyer (see text) were almost all educated abroad and considered themselves intellectuals of liberal views. On the one hand, their interest was to maintain close support and cooperation with the Communists [Service, 1985], and on the other, was to give the Nationalists at least lukewarm support by "writing ambiguous editorials for Kuomintang papers" [Melby, 1971].

American Journalist. The first trip of William C. Bullitt to China, in July 1947, received very little attention from the Chinese community, which regarded him as merely a U.S. journalist comeing on behalf of *Life Magazine.* My husband Yi, however, was of another opinion; he thought that though Bullitt may well have been on a personal mission, there could be more to his visit than met the eye. Mr. Bullitt had not only been a distinguished diplomat, but at one time had also been an important figure [U.S. Ambassador to Russian and to France] in Franklin D. Roosevelt's White House. Chairman Chiang, of course, knew all this, and had therefore personally requested that the Ministry of Foreign Affairs provide special treatment to Bullitt. Even more notably, Chiang had assigned his personal secretary, Mr. Shen Chan-huen, to serve as Bullitt's escort.

Soon after Bullitt's arrival in Nanking, Yi received a call from the Ministry of Foreign Affairs informing him that Mr. Bullitt was to call on him shortly. Another call came soon thereafter from Chairman Chiang's secretary, Mr. Shen, inquiring whether Yi had been notified of Bullitt's intended visit. Yi instinctively felt the magnitude of this call and indicated that, of course, he would be very pleased to meet with Mr. Bullitt. Instead of an official dinner at the City Hall at *Futze Miao*, a more informal dinner was to be held in our home.

For that next evening's gathering, following the phone call from Chairman Chiang's office, we invited a few people whom Bullitt had wished to meet, including Dr. Wong Wen-hao[2], Chairman of the National Resources Commission; Mr. Yü Ta-wei, Minister of Communications; and Dr. Chiang Monlin, educator and Secretary General of the Executive Yuan. These were admirable and much respected men, all of whom were close friends of Yi, especially, Wong and Yü.

During the evening's gathering at our home, the group of Chinese officials and Mr. Bullitt huddled for a long discussion to which I was not privy. And Bullitt and Yi had two or three more conversations in the weeks thereafter, each one lasting more than two hours. Fortunately, both men were fluent in German, so language was not a barrier. Furthermore, their views were in perfect accord.

"China is in the midst of a bad time, but not as bad as I thought." Bullit said.

"On the contrary, it appears that things are brighter."

"An especially encouraging sign is the appearance of people on the street, going about their normal way, cheerful and high-spirited."

"They look clean and tidy, with no sign of bitterness."

These were Bullitt's parting words to Yi on the day he left Nanking, where he had stayed for nearly a month, from July to August of 1947.

The Chinese people acquired their own impression of Mr. Bullitt's views after an article he had written ("*A report to the American people on China*") appeared in *Life Magazine* in October, 1946. A second article (December, 1947), longer and more explosive, caught the attention of the American public as well. In it he argued that because it was the United States that had allowed the Soviets to gain influence in Manchuria, through the Yalta agreement, it was now the job of the U.S. to step-up its aid to the Nationalist Government so that Stalin could be prevented from dominating China. If this did not happen, he warned, the U.S. might be drawn into an all-out war that would inevitably involve the 450-million-strong Chinese nation [Bullitt, 1947].

In the *Life Magazine* article of 1947 Bullitt further emphasized that "Neither China's internal reforms, without American aid, nor American aid without China's internal reforms, can solve the problem of protecting the vital interest of the U.S. and the well-being of China." He steadfastly maintained that close cooperation between the two nations was essential. Though for the Nationalist Chinese this report generated a sliver of hope that positive U.S. action might be forthcoming, such progress was not apparent when Bullitt returned to China again on May 5th, 1948.

The festivities accompanying the second of Bullitt's visits to Nanking were unprecedented. Never had I witnessed an occasion so grand as that given in Bullitt's honour on the third day after his arrival by Brigadier General Kaiser at the American Officers Club on Tzong-san North Road [now, Zhongshen Bei Road; *Frontispiece*]. The Club, itself, said to be the former residence of the Japanese-backed puppet-president Wong Jin-wei[3], was gloriously decked-out. My husband was absorbed in conversation with Bullitt during the entire gathering. Yi told me later that Bullitt was appalled by the precipitous decline of the situation in China that had occurred in the ten months since his earlier visit[4].

Meetings of Mr. Bullitt with members of our government and a great many social engagements had overwhelmed his schedule. It was not until May 29th that we had a chance to again invite him home for dinner. He made it clear that he wished us to also invite Yü Ta-wei, whom he had met at the previous dinner in our home. In one of Bullitt's *Life Magazine* reports he had written that Yü was regarded as the most honest of all cabinet ministers in the Nationalist government, and was both a true patriot and a person of good judgment and first-rate ability, qualities Bullitt found lacking in most other Nationalist officials [cf. *Time Magazine*, 1946].

There were only the four of us (including Bullitt) dinning at our house. Before, during and after dinner, the three men huddled together, their discussions continuing deep into the night (again, mostly in German, since Yü, like Yi, had been educated in Germany and was also fluent in that language). Though just a bystander, I was keenly interested in their views. But as I quietly listened, my mood changed from elation to depression. Indeed, this was one of the most disturbing discussions I had ever heard. Bullitt ended the conversation by poking fun at me.

"Well, Mrs. Shen, I think you would make a good Minister of Defense; then everything would be fine in China."

This was shortly after President Chiang had fired General Pai Ch'ung-hsi[5] from that position, and the selection of his successor for Defense was well underway. This vacancy had been a major concern and a great obstacle to the newly formed cabinet, headed by Dr. Wong Wen-hao, the new Prime Minister [*Chapter 10*].

Later that year, on October 6th, Mr. Bullitt arrived for a third visit. In order to have the opportunity to meet with him again, Yi declined an invitation from France's President Charles de Gaulle to attend the World-Capital Mayoral Congress in Paris [see *Chapter 7, footnote*[11]]. By this time, the situation in Nanking was so grave that there seemed no hope at all. War clouds had moved closer and closer to the capital gates. The general mood of the people had become numb; they showed no fear, no sorrow no hope. The majority harboured no kinship with the Communists, but they were tired of their own government and its inaction. Yi had a very gloomy conversation with Bullitt; both sighed and lamented the opportunities lost by President Chiang Kai-shek.

It was on a chilly evening on the 6th of December, 1948, when my husband went to the Nanking station to see Mr. Bullitt off after yet another visit, his fourth trip to China. In retrospect, the three days of that short visit might well be considered historical, for no one then could have predicted how very soon the capital would fall to the Communists. As Bullitt boarded the train, his parting words were:

"To save the Nationalist government, you will need immediately to have a war cabinet well organized, immediately to have new blood in the organization, and immediately to have American aid increased."

"Things are bad, but certainly they are not incurable." Yi's rejoinder was equally serious.

"Even without making reforms in politics and improving the standard of living, the government must be saved with urgency."

They parted with heavy hearts and never met again. Sadly, the title of Bullitt's 1947 *Life Magazine* article, "How We Won the War and lost the Peace," turned out to be right on the mark. The end was all too near [with Nanking falling to the Communists in April, 1949].

General Albert C. Wedemeyer. During Mr. Bullitt's first visit, in 1947, Lt. General Albert C. Wedemeyer had come to China as a Special Ambassador sent by President Truman to gather a firsthand report on China's plight. Regretfully, my husband was so snubbed by the General during that visit that Yi had serious doubt whether America was still China's friend.

On July 22nd, 1947, Yi entered the following in his diary [Shen-Y, 1985]:

"I had come to meet General Wedemeyer punctually at eleven fifteen this morning, in the residence of the American Ambassador John Leighton Stuart. After an extended wait of 35 minutes, we terminated our interview in just two minutes.

"I came to this meeting with great enthusiasm and hope because Wedemeyer was the first person who suggested and offered the Generalissimo a proposal of establishing public works in China. He had directed Colonel J. S. Golinsky to be the liaison between the two countries. I fully understood

and appreciated his suggestions, for I have had 10 years of public-works experience in the Municipal Government of Shanghai [Shen, 1970; Wakeman, 1995]. And, for Wedemeyer's proposed project, I had devoted more than one year's time studying and developing a program for China to adopt.

"In accordance with his brief, I, together with experts, outlined a prodigiously detailed plan[6]. We were of the opinion that if this project could come to fruition it would not only be the solution to the unemployment of enlisted men and officers, but would also be a fulfillment of China's economic goal, one that could have paved the way for our country's post-war reconstruction and industrialization.

"On the morning of my appointment with Wedemeyer, I was pleased by the fact that I had very little business to attend to at the City Hall so that I could concentrate my full attention on discussion of the important topics with the General. I had admired Wedemeyer's proposal and held him in high regard as a good and helpful friend to China. For this visit, I had spent a great deal of time preparing my thoughts. To my astonishment, when I finally shook his hand he instantly said:

'I have a busy schedule; we shall have only five minutes to talk.'

"How could this be possible, that his attitude had changed so much and in so short a year since the submission of his far-sighted proposal, in 1946 in Chunking, to the Generalissimo? Faced with this restriction I was at a loss. In deep disappointment and frustration, I finally decided to say nothing and concluded the interview in just two minutes.

"During my wait for the appointed meeting I had noted that Wedemeyer was having an enthusiastic exchange with some of the so-called middle-of-the-road group, the fence-sitters ('chi-chian pye'). I was bewildered by the sudden and unreserved change of attitude in the General. He had turned cold and stern to his former acquaintances, especially to those in the Central Government. He purposely avoided them and surrounded himself instead with a new group of people who called themselves 'Democrats.' He seemed to consider this 'Third Force' to be representative of the people of China.

"There could be two reasons for his behavior. First, he was extremely disappointed in the Generalissimo's leadership and the corruption of the

Nationalist Government. Second, he was influenced by the recent change of American policy toward China, namely, the notion to 'Let them stew in their own juices.' I once thought that Wedemeyer was truly the one person who had sincerely attempted to help the Generalissimo by suggesting reforms in building a new China. When by chance I come upon his proposal in Nanking, I was elated and thought it to be the exact medicine China had needed. However, the foolish Chinese had looked upon his opinions as inconsequential, not worthy of consideration.

"Nevertheless, Wedemeyer was wrong in thinking that all people in the government were rotten and disgraceful. As rotten as the top tiers were, there still remained patriotic underlings. I regretted that he did not take into account the fact of the eight-year heroic war the Chinese had fought in WWII alongside the allies. How could China have resisted for so long, and done so well, if the entire government were corrupt? Wedemeyer's attitude was an insult to the 'good people' in the lot. He had misjudged the pulse of the nation and had made a dangerous move by insulating himself with members of the Third Force. In doing so he had created an opportunity for the Communists, and the outcome would be like piling rocks on his own feet."

At the end of that day's diary, Yi wrote:

"I related my disappointment with Wedemeyer to the personal secretary of Ambassador Stuart, who in turn relayed my mood to the Ambassador and the General. On that very evening, I received a visit from the secretary, who conveyed to me Wedemeyer's sincere apology. He further added that, if time permitted, the General would like very much to have another meeting with me. The secretary made further excuses for Wedemeyer, saying that the General had had a distressful morning with the communist leaders; that he was unhappy to have wasted my time; that his curtness stemmed from his own annoyances; that he asked for my forgiveness."

In a later diary entry, Yi wrote:

"We [Yi and Wedemeyer] never had another meeting, but saw each other briefly on the morning of his departure. I was there as the Head of the City. He left Nanking on the 24th of August, 1947. He had issued the following words [given here in a translation from the Chinese]: *'The Chinese people are united in a fervent hope for peace. If the Chinese*

Communists were patriotic they would abandon their military aggression against the government. The government, on the other hand, should unashamedly cut away the corrupt officials. They must realize that a mighty army is no contest to a Communist doctrine.' I took his medicinal words as sincere sentiments coming from the bitter lips of a grandmother's heart ('ku-co puo-shin'). Wedemeyer[7] was a faithful friend after all."

Yi further noted that,

"The attitude of the United States was made evident by their cutting off all aid to Nationalist China, a unilateral withdrawal of an earlier U.S. loan earmarked for $500 million plus a promised assistance, made in September 1946, for the 'Eight and One-Third Air Group Program[8].' America had clearly deserted her old comrade-in-arms and was earnestly courting a new alliance with the Chinese Communists, whom they believed to be agrarian reformers not taking orders from Moscow."

Sorrowfully, my husband ended the day's diary by writing:

"It surely is another vital blow to China, almost as hard as the Yalta Agreement, and the United States would again be making a grievous mistake affecting the world."

U.S. Ambassador John Leighton Stuart. His countenance was cold and serious, but Ambassador Stuart's heart was warm and full of enthusiasm. His voice was low, but his words were determined and energetic. He had been considered a foreigner in China, though he himself was born in China, in Hangchow with the bewitching scenery of its Hsi Hu [West Lake], the beautiful city where I was born. He had devoted almost his entire life to educating the younger generations of Chinese students [Stuart, 1954], though I doubt that many of his pupils would still remember this kindly old gentleman—Dr. John Leighton Stuart—the last American Ambassador to the Nationalist Government on the mainland and a great friend to my country, my husband, and me.

"We are little fellow-villagers ('shao tung-shian')."

He would say, when introducing me to others. Dr. Stuart and I had shared the same birthplace, Hangchow, and he spoke Mandarin with our local accent, "*co-yin.*" Seemingly tired of the ceaseless formalities to which we were continually subjected, he said to me one day,

"Wouldn't it be a nice change if we could have some hometown dishes ('*jia-shian tsia*') and a few friends with whom we could talk freely?"

I promised him that I, myself, would cook some of his favorite Hangchow delicacies at home and we would then all enjoy a relaxing evening. To my regret, this promise was never fulfilled. Precipitously, the political situation in China had turned into turmoil and confusion. Dr. Stuart had been fully occupied in attempting to make peace between the Nationalists and the Communists. He failed. But, then, we all failed!

At this same time, Yi had been inundated by waves of crises of price control, currency reform[1] and the so-called "rice mob" [*Chapter 10*], forced on the people by the Central Government ("*Zhon-yang Tzen-fu*"). Each man had been occupied in his own undertakings, heading-off in separate directions but all for the mission of peace. Yi and I had not seen Dr. Stuart for six months. Then, the great storm came upon us like a hurricane. All efforts had been fruitless. All hopes for peace had evaporated into the distant dim gray skies. Separately, we and our good friend Dr. Stuart had bided our time as the coming history descended like the face of doom. The capital was in a semi-dead state. The rich, the well-to-do families of high officials, had fled at top speed. To say the least, the mood was terribly glum.

One chilly evening in December 1948, K.P. Fu, the adopted son of Ambassador Stuart, came to call. The entire city had been in a state of triple darkness—darkness of winter, darkness of the nation, and darkness of the city's nonfunctioning electrical supply. As my husband and I sat silently by a quivering candle, Mr. Fu came unannounced, like a ghost that jolted our solitude. In a secretive gesture, he whispered the words that good news was forthcoming, that our good friend "*Szetu Leideng*" (a Mandarin version of "Stuart, Leighton") had worked out a solution. This message came like fresh rain after a long draught! We could not contain our excitement.

We waited, waited, and waited for the good news from Embassador

Stuart. But, finally, we were disappointed. The dear man, our dear, dear friend, had tried hard to the very end, but even he could not avert the bitter tragedy. On the 23rd of April 1949, the capital was lost to the Communists, as wave after wave of Communist troops advanced on Nanking. After a short confinement of three to four months under the new Red regime, *Szetu Leideng*, with a weary body and a broken heart, set sail for home [Stuart, 1954].

Footnotes:

[1]Currency reform (August 19th, 1948; *Chapter 10*), under the pressure of hyperinflation, was initiated by the Chiang regime. Once established, one of the oldest of all con games unfolded, when new banknotes, "backed" by gold—the so-called gold-notes ("*Jin-yuan Juan*") were officially issued (Seagrave, 1985). The common people ("*Lao bai-shin*") were told to turn in all their personal holdings of the old legal notes ("*Fa-pi*") and silver and gold savings encouraged by the government earlier (*Chapter 10*), in exchange for the newly minted currency.

The urgency of the currency exchange was captured by the lens of the French photographer Henri Cartier-Bresson who shows crowds of people pushing, pulling and even bobbing above a three- to four-deep queue to exchange "*Fa-pi*" for the new "*Jin-yuan Juan*"; the caption of the photo reads: "Sale of gold in the last days of the Kuomintang, Shanghai, China, 1949" (*Los Angeles Times*, 2004).

Inside information of the exact date of currency exchange, ostensibly known only to Prime Minister T.V. Soong, led to a "gold rush" of withdrawal of funds from Chinese banks (Seagrave, 1985). As a result, President Chiang finally lost all trust in Soong, fired him from his job, and placed him under investigation (see *footnote*[4], below).

President Chiang then appointed General Chiang Ching-kuo (Chiang's son) to enforce the now-failed reform and to remove all elements of corruption from the government. This, too, soon failed, brought to defeat by well-heeled crime syndicates (such as the Shanghai Green Gang) and aided, ironically, by Chiang Ching-kuo's own cousin-by-marriage, David Kung, a nephew of Chiang Kai-shek's wife (Seagrave, 1985), and the Generalissimo's brother- and sister-in law, H.H. Kung and Soong Eiling.

[2]Geologist Dr. Wong Wen-hao was twice elected President of the Chinese Society of Engineers, 1942 and 1943, a position also held by the

author's husband, Shen Yi, in 1949 and again in 1962 (China Society of Engineers Archive, 2002). With the defeat of the Nationalists, Wong elected to remain on the mainland rather than retreating to Taiwan, and his Nanjing home at *Wutai San* (*Chapter 10*) was ultimately appropriated by Mao's new government.

Because of the appropriation of Wong's property by the government, Premier Chou En-lai later arranged for Wong to be reimbursed for his house. Upon Wong's death, he bequeathed all of his assets, exactly equaling the funds he had received from the sale of his house, to the Communist Government (Qian, 1998).

[3]Wong Jin-wei, "puppet-president" during the Japanese occupation of WWII, was a brilliant strategist and, earlier in his career, a rival of Chiang Kai-shek for leadership of the Kuomintang (Melby, 1971).

[4]In March 1948, during the first constitutional session of the National Assembly, pressure both from within China (by political liberals) and from without (backed by the U.S. government) led to a revolt among the Kuomintang (Melby, 1971). By Chiang Kai-shek's order, the much respected philosopher-academic Dr. Hu Shih (Plate 1) was to be elected President. But to maintain his control of the party, Chiang, himself, would be elected Premier. In the final outcome, however (on May 20th, 1948), Chiang found that he, rather than Hu had been elected President (Plate 6) and, much to his dismay, that the leader of the rival Kwangsi clique, General Li Teng-jen, had been elected Vice President (Plate 6). Wong Wen-hao, a patriot and a man of integrity, was appointed Prime Minister (*footnote*[2], above; *Chapter 10*).

Despite the reforms by the Nationalists, President Chiang maintained a strong hold on governmental affairs that for the most part rendered the other elected officials powerless, a dominance referred to as the "same wine, same bottle" status quo (Melby, 1971). Five months later, in August 1948, came the currency reform, which failed (as did its associated governmental house-cleaning; *footnote*[1] above), but by this time the loot acquired by the *Soongs* and *Kungs* had already been moved offshore (Seagrave, 1985).

[5]Gen. Pai Ch'ung-hsi was among the few chief Nationalist officials who were regarded as being free of corruption (Melby, 1971). Pai was a leader of the Kwangsi clique and, before Chiang Kai-shek, a prominent member of the Kuomintang.

[6]Shen Yi, Chairman of the Public Works Committee of the Supreme National Economic Council of the Nationalist Government from 1946 to

1948, was intimately involved in formulating a response to Wedemeyer's plan of public works (Boorman and Cheng, 1970).

[7]On his return to the U.S., Wedemeyer submitted a report recommending support of the Nationalist Government: "a bold program of military and economic support, lasting at least 5 years, contingent upon Chiang's promise to initiate sweeping political and social reforms." His suggestion was rejected by the U.S. administration (Hsü, 1975).

[8]According to Johnson (1983), between 1945 and 1949 the Nationalist Government had been scheduled to receive a $500 million economic stabilization loan and a total of $2 billion in aid from the U.S. government.

CHAPTER 9
NEW-LIFE MOVEMENT: NANKING WOMEN WORK COMMITTEE

Background ----------

Upon his ascension to head the Nationalist government, Chairman Chiang Kai-shek in 1933 introduced the regimen of the New-Life Movement, "Xin Sen-huo Yun-dong." This program represented a concerted effort to reestablish national spirit and Chiang's own popularity—a political move he may have thought necessary after he had sternly admonished the Chinese people about the evil of smoking opium [Tuchman, 1972] and other practices of which he did not approve [e.g., public dancing, Chapter 1; Wakeman, 1995].

The New-Life Movement was led by Chiang himself, and was prominently promoted by his wife, Mme. Chiang, as a "New Deal" for China [Seagrave, 1985]. Intended to define proper human conduct, the Movement was based on the Confucian philosophy of the "Four Boundaries of Men" ("Ren-zi Si-wei"), propriety, justice, integrity, and conscience ("Li, Yi, Lian, Chi") [see, Hahn, 1941]. To these, Chairman Chiang added codes of dressing, eating, housing, and self-carriage ("yi, ser, zhu, xing"), the four qualities he regarded as necessary for proper daily living. In their family lives, citizens were encouraged to aspire to the four goals of neatness, cleanliness, simplicity, and modesty [Lin, 2000].

Chairman Chiang himself seemed to follow his own rules for daily living, but many of his relatives and close associates did not [Seagrave, 1985; see Chapter 5]. Since home responsibilities fell on the women of the households, Mme. Chiang became Director of the Movement's Women Committee, in which capacity she enthusiastically occupied herself with meetings, writings, speeches, and travel. The result, however, termed "big thunder, little rain" [Lin, 2000], was less than successful.

Nevertheless, and despite the pitifully meager resources it was afforded, the Nanking Women Work Committee, under the leadership of the author, made a valiant effort and achieved small but substantial progress toward improving the lot of the needy people of Nanjing.

In 1933, shortly after Generalissimo Chiang Kai-shek had proclaimed the New-Life Movement ("*Shin Sen'whoa Yuen'dong*"), a Women Advisory Committee was established with its principal to provide social welfare for needy women and children. Nominally headed by Gimo himself, its real chief was Mme. Chiang Kai-shek. Under its umbrella, regional subcommittees were established in the cities and provinces. By a clever ploy intended to ensure the involvement of civic leaders, these local subcommittees were to be headed by the wife of the leader of each region, regardless of her qualifications or willingness to serve, and to be financed by the local government. Thus, because of my husband Yi's position, I was drafted to head the Nanking Women Work Committee. Despite my inexperience, I would not be permitted to resign as long as my husband remained mayor.

Accepting this fate of an "appointment without consent," my first act was to advertise for an Executive Secretary to help me with the task. Within a short time, a Miss Wu Wan-tzen had been signed on. Miss Wu [Plate 10], a well-educated woman, had acquired much experience during her earlier service at the Movement's National Headquarters. Because of this, on May15, 1947, I delegated Miss Wu to stand in for me at the formal inauguration ceremony of our new Nanking Branch, held at the Headquarters' central office.

Upon assuming my chairmanship, I was surprised to be informed that, prior to my appointment the Nanking Women Work Committee had incurred a large debt of 18,000 Yuan [~$900 U.S.; see *Chapter 10*]. Because of this deficit, the former Chairman, Mrs. Mah (wife of the interim mayor), was more than anxious to discharge her duties so that she could transfer the Committee's deficit to my hands. This was unsettling. I was not pleased. Moreover, I had been told that the building that housed the committee offices was spacious. But, when the building was finally handed over to our new group, I found that the original space had dwindled to one-third of its former size—with the servants of Mrs. Mah occupying the remainder of the space! I was angry.

And though my Executive Secretary, Miss Wu, was insistent that the entire Nanking Branch building should be reclaimed by the Women Committee, I was in no mood to do battle with the wife of the former interim mayor, Mah Chao-jun [Rabe, 1998]. With the backing of her husband, and his powerful military support, she had the magic of pulling wool over the eyes of the public.

The only assets that remained to my Nanking Branch were a few pieces of worn and broken furniture and a few sheets of battered stationary. Nevertheless, I was convinced that our task was important, notwithstanding the looming debit on our ledger. But I was at a loss as to how to begin the needed work. Under these nearly impossible circumstances—yet being deeply affected by the poverty I had witnessed during my journey from Shanghai to Nanking [*Chapter 1*]—I was called by a sense of duty to try to do the best I could.

My first order of business at the Committee was to find a way to pay off the huge debt. For this, I made countless visits and urgent pleas to various sectors of the city government. Fortunately, this was successful. We soon received the needed assistance.

I formally arrived on duty at the Nanking Women Work Committee on May 24, 1947. Together with Miss Wu, we surveyed the grounds. The building was situated in a run-down slum district of the city [Plate 10]. The building itself was large, but the space left to our Branch consisted of only a single large room, divided into three smaller sections, fronting onto a narrow mostly unpaved dusty street. The rear of the office opened onto a large courtyard that adjoined the part of the building that because of Mrs. Mah's people was now off-limits. A weathered plaque hung on the front entrance had the Committee's name, Nanking Women Work Committee ("*Nanking Fu'nu Gong'tso Wei'yuan Hue,*" [Plate 10]). I was greatly dismayed by the dilapidated condition of the building and its lack of furnishings. We had neither a suitable desk for our work or even a proper chair to sit on. Presented with these circumstances, I was forced to call on the various branches of the city government. Once again, I had become a common beggar.

My staff of the Nanking Branch consisted of eleven people, including one worker carried over from my predecessor. Besides Miss

Wu and me, the rest of the crew was all young women, freshly out of school. I was proud, indeed, of this first-rate staff—with a zealous attitude toward our worthy cause, they were not discouraged by the tattered looks of our shabby office. I called the group together and seated them closely on two large benches, the only functional furniture we had inherited. I did not give a lengthy lecture. Instead, after words of welcome, I gave them a pep talk.

"Everyone of us should look upon our work at the Nanking Women Work Committee as a duty to our society."

"We should hope to bring good to those who are helpless and less fortunate than ourselves."

"Our first job is to make a survey of the neighborhood, and to come up with a tally of how many families are qualified for relief assistance."

To boost the staff's spirits at the Committee, I told them that we had been promised that we would soon be moving to a wonderfully nice new office at Lotus Hall in the scenic Hsuan-wu Lake Park [*Chapter 2*], and that the new building would also provide dormitory living space for all of them. Their eyes lit up as they heard the news.

According to formal directives, the Nanking Committee was required to establish an Advisory Board consisting of 12 to 16 members. This soon was done. But it was pure bureaucratic nonsense, mere window-dressing. The board often was more interfering than helpful, and its membership consisted solely of the wives of high government officials. Their function was minimal, their help virtually non-existent.

One month after our small Committee Office first opened its door, we established a Children's Health Station [Plate 10]. Most of the powdered milk and vitamin pills available to us for distribution had been allotted by the UNRRA[1] (United Nations Rehabilitation and Relief Administration). At first we could handle just 50 to 60 youngsters, having enough milk to be distributed to the early arrivals that made up our "morning group." With much effort, we later increased the care to nearly 200. Although our staff was enthusiastic and hard working, the shortage of space limited us from caring for hundreds more. I counted the days until our new office building would finally be ready so that we could expand.

Two months later, In the middle of July, the Nanking Women Committee moved into its new quarters. The building was located on the west side of Hsuan-wu Lake park near Hsuan-wu Gate [Xuanwu Gate, *Frontispiece*], facing eastward onto a lake full of lotus. It was a rather small old house of traditional Chinese design [Plate 10] surrounded by large trees. In reality, the building itself was plain and simple, but because of the beautiful surroundings and the recent remodeling, the place had become splendid. Compared to our old office, it was a breath of brisk fresh air. Altogether, we had six large rooms in the main structure, with a long corridor at the rear leading to four small dormitory bungalows.

My girls at the Committee were ecstatic. I, too, was much heartened. Nevertheless, I knew all too well that we had been slow in making headway toward meeting our goals, much like a tiny bird building a nest with patience and painstaking labour, twig by twig. But, thanks to the city government, our financial status had greatly improved. Under the spirit of Confucius' *Four Boundaries of Men*, I worked with a deep sense of commitment. I was the only one in the office who received no salary or any other tangible reward. Seeing the happy faces of the women and children we helped was satisfaction enough for me to carry on. And, in any case, for Yi's sake, this had become my wifely duty!

All told, the Committee was remarkably successful in our undertakings. We had still maintained our old office space in the city slums, which by now had become fully occupied by the Children's Health Station. Through the help of the Nanking Bureau of Public Health, the decrepit rooms of the building had now been renovated and the Bureau further provided us, free of charge, a doctor and two nurses each morning [Plate 10]. But, still, we could reach only a relatively few children, far fewer than the vast number that were in dire need.

When I returned home from work each day, I would tell my husband my troubles, hoping that he might give me a few good ideas. But Yi, of course, was burdened with his city affairs. Except for listening in sympathy to each other's woes, neither of us could do much to help the other. We shared the opinion that our country's widespread poverty and run-away inflation[2] would one day lead China into immense peril. Clearly, in the long run these problems could be even more disastrous than the menace of communism which through its wild promises had already taken hold of the innumerable poor and undermined the Nationalist Government.

As an aftermath of the war with Japan, poverty had raised its nasty head throughout the country, yet Chiang's government seemed oblivious, unable or unwilling to provide solutions. To the contrary, many high government officials padded their own pockets and robbed people of the huge amounts of relief aid coming from the United States and the United Nations [*Chapter 5*]. The sole concern of those in power was war, civil war, which they deemed to be the only way to counter the communist threat—and if they were to fail and the Communists were to win their power would be no more.

Our leaders had forgotten, or perhaps had never fully realized, that as long as poverty spread over the land, Communism could never be contained. Poverty had become the breeding ground for the Communist doctrine.

I well remembered what Yi had once told me about his visit to a refugee camp with the Generalissimo. The Chairman had planned to bring food as a gesture of good will, and though such food would no doubt have been welcome, Yi advised him that such a gesture would do little to solve the fundamental problem. These refugees had once been productive farmers in northern Jiangsu Province. But because their rich farm fields had now become a giant battleground, they had drifted and became homeless. Those who ended up in the capital were just a drop in the bucket. There were many more. What these people had wanted from the government was work and the self-respect it carries, not empty gestures, not temporary and superficial handouts. They would have taken *any* job just to earn their way and keep starvation at bay.

The Generalissimo took Yi's suggestion to heart. For the need of jobs of the displaced people Gimo immediately sent orders to increase work places for the refugees ("*nan-ming*"). Within a short time, 80,000 refugees were relocated from Nanking to other parts of the country where jobs could be provided. The problem was solved very rapidly, because the UNRRA had just recently instituted numerous rehabilitation centers where workers were needed. The old saying held true that "when a thing is done right, there can be success most bright." I have long maintained that if there is a job to be done it must be done properly, effectively and thoroughly. I tried mightily to follow this rule in my own work with the Nanking Women New Life Movement.

Pitifully, our Branch's minuscule budget could never be expected to bring about full-scale relief to the multitudes of Nanking's needy. Further, we were constantly plagued by being undercut by the Movement's National Headquarters (directed by Mme. Chiang Kai-shek), the "powers-that-be" that had the option of taking for themselves our portion of the relief goods allotted by the National Relief Administration. Our position was untenable. It was virtually impossible for us to carry out relief work—we had good intentions but woefully empty hands!

The Nanking Committee appealed many times to the Chinese National Rehabilitation and Relief Administration (CNRRA[3]), fashioned after the UNRRA. Though sympathetic, the officials there deferred decisions to our Headquarters. And the Headquarters, as it turned out, consistently used a "double-dip" approach, each time giving us less and less but demanding more and more.

To seek financial help from the community, I established at the Branch a Board of Finance composed of local bankers and other people of means. By a stroke of luck, I had on my Board a member by the name of Tao Gue-lin, a self-made architect/contractor who generously and unconditionally donated fifty-thousand Yuan.

Additionally, through the generosity of the Nanking Park Administration, the Nanking Branch was given a piece of land adjoining our office building by the lotus lake. Using these donations, a library was soon designed by the city architect, Mr. Tung Da-yo. But because inflation was rampant[2], it was important for us to spend the money as quickly as it came into our hands. Our library was completed within three months. This welcome new structure, nestled in a thicket of trees, soon became the one and only children's library in all of Nanking. Its completion pleased me beyond my wildest dreams.

Before the library was built the Branch had just one reading room that could accommodate only one hundred children a day. The new library was much larger and furnished with built-in furniture. During the course of construction, we had solicited books from publishers. However, to my dismay and deep disappointment, the only donation, a large number of books, came from the Tsong-hwa Publishing Company; no other publisher in the nation had responded to our pleas. Nevertheless, with this start, together with books donated by us, my own staff, our library had become quite adequate.

By consent of the Nanking Park Administration, the Committee then was given another piece of land, at one side of the new library, surrounded by a natural fence of wintergreens. This area we soon converted to a playground, thanks to a donation from the Nanking Bureau of Public Welfare which installed a fine set of playground equipment.

Early in the following spring, both the library and the playground were opened to the public at the building of the Nanking Women Committee. It was heartening to see needy children reading and playing all around. Why should these innocent children be left behind, forsaken and uneducated, while children of the well-to-do had everything? I felt deeply about this human injustice. My earnest wish was to be able to improve and educate all the children, poor or rich, in our neighbourhood.

By another stroke of luck, the Work Committee had received six sewing machines from the UNRRA and two more from Headquarters. As old and battered as these blessed machines were, they were nevertheless fully functional. We set up sewing classes in the former reading room, and an instructor was hired to teach needy young mothers this new skill so they could earn a living. As news spread about our sewing classes, women and girls came in droves. We had more heart than room to accommodate them all.

The winter of 1948 was unusually severe in Nanking. We, at the Work Committee, were faced with an urgent and necessary task that tested our ingenuity. On my personal guarantee, I had obtained an interest-free loan of twenty-thousand Yuan from the Municipal Bank. I did this without my husband's knowledge. I did not wish to bother him. He never knew about it. At this point, I was too desperate to be concerned about how I would later get the money to repay this colossal debt.

Once again, due to unrelenting inflation, the Committee had to purchase quickly the necessary material for winter garments. My entire staff, my close friends, and the students from our sewing classes were mobilized to concentrate on making the relief garments for the poor.

And to begin to counter the huge debt, I brought together the Committee's Advisory Board for a fund drive. I presented plans for our winter relief project and solicited their ideas for approval and support. Though I had anticipated that I would encounter a barrage of arguments, the endless and largely mindless speeches by the society matrons on the Board thundered me into speechlessness. What could I say? Still, by this time it came as no surprise to me that it had become fashionable for women of stature to voice inconsequential opinions.

Miss Wu, my Executive Secretary at the Work Committee, forewarned me that if such nonsense were to happen we should first listen, quietly and politely, but then ultimately push for the passage of our plan. In the eyes of the group, our plan was considered to be too modest, too humble. But I remained insistent. I had long before learned that to do something substantial with a small plan would be far better than to have nothing accomplished in one grand stroke. A compromise was reached; both plans, the Board's grandiose notions and our more modest proposal, would be tested.

(The Board's unspoken agenda was to shirk responsibility, especially when it came to charity from their own pockets. Nevertheless, in spite of their reluctance, their vanity would not permit them to refuse to accept the subscription booklets for a fund drive. So, although this drive was urged upon them, rather than having been voluntary, I still managed to get their help—for which I and the entire Committee were deeply grateful.)

Within a short while, the Committee's modest plan had been

accomplished. Privately, I counted my blessings, for I was now able to repay the loan from the Municipal Bank!

The Committee's staff first made a survey of the local families in dire need of warm clothing, taking their names, ages, and sex. We next compiled a list of the five hundred neediest living in our immediate neighborhood (a tiny drop in the bucket of the Nanking poor[4]). Using this list, we issued each person a voucher to be exchanged for a garment on a specific day. Then, as luck was with us, happily if unexpectedly, a few days before the beginning of distribution, Headquarters dispatched to us bundles of cotton quilts (*"mien'bay"*), a much needed item for the winter.

Near the end of December 1948, on a bright sunny day after a huge snowstorm, a multitude of needy people, men, women and children, gathered in the courtyard outside our Work Committee office. Their faces were ecstatic as they clutched the packages we gave them, bundles of physical and spiritual warmth [Plate 10]. Each person received a quilt, a quilted cotton suit, and a woolen vest, garments all made by our own hands, and each was given a small bag of flour or rice. Wrinkles deepened on the faces of the elders as their lips spread into broad smiles, and the youngsters jumped with joy and laughter, feeling new warmth under their little arms. I sighed deeply as I realized how easily they had been satisfied with so little, so late, for so few.

My stint of nineteen months at the Nanking Women Work Committee flew by like a flash. If it had not been for the able assistance of my Executive Secretary, Miss Wu Wan-tzen, the selfless efforts of my staff, and great help from the Nanking City Government (no doubt urged-on by the Mayor's Office), we could never have achieved so much, so well, and in so short a time. Our winter relief plan was a great success. But, this would be the Nanking Branch's last hurrah. Our government was besieged with defeats in its two great wars, the war with the Communists and the war with poverty.

Like the plaintive songs of swans (*"si'mien tzu'ger"*), news of defeat came from all fronts. We anticipated that Nanking would fall to the Communists at any moment. And though many noted families had fled, not a single one of my staff had quit. When the war with the

Communists had reached its tumultuous peak, when the Nation's capital was finally under siege and in imminent danger, my husband's mayoral post was transferred to a military man by decree of President Chiang Kai-shek—sadly, thus ended a fervent ambition that Yi had harboured for the reconstruction of the nation's capital into a New Nanking.

It was understood at Yi's appointment of mayor that my responsibility as Head of the Nanking Women Work Committee would cease when Yi left his post. Yet no word came from the Headquarters. I was puzzled and annoyed, for Yi and I had planned to leave for Shanghai on New Year's Eve, 1948. I certainly did not wish to stay in Nanking alone, without Yi and without my children. Unbeknownst to me, the leader of our New Life Movement, Mme. Chiang Kai-shek, had by that time already departed for the United States[5], leaving our country as soon as the Hsuchow area, the southwestern bastion fronting Nanking, had fallen to the Communists.

My good and thoughtful Executive Secretary, Miss Wu, understood my difficulty and gallantly offered to take charge of the Nanking Branch until word could be received from the Movement's Headquarters. She also promised to represent me in the ceremony of transference. Miss Wu was not only of able assistance in deed, but she was also a friend in need. Within a day, we brought the affairs of the Nanking Women Work Committee to a satisfactory conclusion.

By this time at the year end I was so frantic to close our home on Peiping Lu that I did not have a spare moment to express my gratitude, nor even to bid a proper farewell to Ms. Wu and my staff at the Nanking Work Committee. This, I have always regretted. These hard-working "comrades-in-humanness" [Plate 10], with whom I shared a common goal and shouldered common burdens for two difficult but productive years, had become a part of me. I felt, in the deep of me, that I had been terribly remiss.

Three days before my departure from Nanking, I paid a courtesy visit to the wife of the new mayor. I also wanted to brief her about the activities of the Committee. Our meeting was odd—one might even say ridiculous. The following are my memories of that encounter, as

I concluded my duties as Chairman of the Nanking Women Work Committee of the New Life Movement.

It was on the very cold morning of December 26, 1948, when I called on Mrs. Teng, the wife of the soon-to-be inaugurated new mayor. My husband's Personal Assistant, Mr. Shen Yufu, made the appointment and accompanied me. The gate to the Teng's newly built house was immediately opened upon the approach of our car.

In the courtyard of the mayor's-to-be house, I was startled by the large contingent of uniformed soldiers. Mr. Shen, sitting in the front seat, looked back and, noticing my puzzlement, explained that they were guards and servants of the newly appointed mayor, Teng Chieh [see, *Chapter 11*], who had just been recalled from the battlefront at Hsuchow. In spite of this explanation, I remained bewildered. "Why on earth should a military officer enjoy the privilege of having such a large number of enlisted men as his own personal guards and servants?" I asked. To my mind, these soldiers should be serving their country, not simply waiting on the whims of one man and his family! My perplexity was interrupted as I was shown into a dark hallway where an expressionless woman in her thirties stood motionless by the door.

Notwithstanding the dimness of the hall in the Teng's house, I was dazzled by the combination of brilliant colors, of red, black, and white, distributed across the woman's face. Her face was a powdery and pasty white, accented by heavily drawn jet-black eyebrows and eye shadow, and her cheeks and lips were painted a bright red. In truth, she had the appearance of a character from a Peking opera. Yet, instead of a normal Chinese gown, she wore a silk smock of fancy colors, short and quilted, a pair of western slacks, and exceedingly high-heeled shoes that gave the impression that she might trip and tumble at any moment. I did not know what to make of this rather oddly dressed woman, but assuming her to be someone of no consequence I did not even hesitate a quick nod.

Fortunately, Mr. Shen promptly stopped me and introduced the brilliantly decorated women as the wife of the mayor-to-be, the mistress of the house, the very person on whom I had come to call. I was greatly embarrassed. But I told myself not to make the matter worse by apologising. I quickly reached out my hand to her. To my surprise, she did not extend hers but instead tipped her body into a low and slow bow (a stage-like performance suggesting to me that Mrs. Teng needed education on new etiquette from the woman officials of our city [see *Chapter 5*]). Faced with this situation, I returned her bow. She uttered not a word, not even a reply to my greetings.

Soon after the mute encounter, the lady of the house stepped backward and made a hand gesture, ushering us in. We three seated ourselves in a small room, an entryway of some sort that had a few sofas and tiny tables scattered here and there. A big earthen pot, filled with glowing embers, stood in the middle of the room where an old woman sat next to the pot having her two bound-feet[6] ("*shao jao*") propped on top of the warm pot. Her feet, tiny, thin and deformed, were a rare sight, foot-binding being a vestige of China's past. She wore a short black quilted satin smock, a pair of black satin trousers, and a black silk turban with a hair knot perched high above her neck. To me, her hairstyle brought to mind a bouncing Venetian gondola. Her pants were loose and bulky, and each leg was bound tightly near the ankle with a black silk wrap.

Though the elderly woman seemed to pay no attention to our intrusion into her sitting room, as soon as I took a seat behind her she turned and intently stared me up and down. I tried not to appear bothered, but the hostess sensed my discomfort. She walked toward the rather oddly attired elderly woman and they exchanged a few quiet words. Abruptly, the old woman rose and ambled out of the room. Although I could not hear what they had said, the word "mama" was distinctly audible. Mr. Shen glanced at me with an understanding smile.

The three of us, Mr. Shen, the mistress of the house and I, sat in silence. Three people sitting face to face in a deep and long muteness was almost too uncomfortable to bear. The hostess with her downcast eyes sat motionless like a female Buddha. Mr. Shen, a near-sighted man, sat on a sofa opposite her, keeping himself as still as the hostess, occasionally adjusting his eyeglasses. I had to restrain myself from crying aloud ("*tee'shao jie'fei*") at being placed in the midst of this mum show. Finally, I broke the silence by commenting on the cold weather.

Perhaps Mrs. Teng hadn't noticed. The silence persisted. From time to time she smiled, and nodded, but offered nothing.

Confronted with this most strange situation in the room, I told myself that I need not exchange pleasantries or details of my mission with Mrs. Teng except to say that I was leaving the Nanking Women Work Committee's affairs in the hands of my Executive Secretary, Miss Wu Wan-tzen, who would act on my behalf. I concluded by adding,

"The office of Nanking Committee had a humble beginning during my term but our financial problems seem over."

"The Committee is now well endowed, and we even have a surplus."

I had no clue that this statement would elicit any response, so I was surprised when the hostess broke her silence and excitedly rejoined.

"Please, bring me a list of those surpluses, as soon as possible."

Attempting to ignore her rudeness and obvious greed[7], I grew serious.

"I must beg your pardon, Mme. Teng, but I have no authority to hand over to you those items at this time."

"These are not my personal property; they are not mine for giving or taking."

"Moreover, I have not yet formally discharged my duties as Chairman."

"As soon as the order comes from Headquarters that I am relieved of my post and you are appointed my successor, I would be more than pleased to transfer the entire office to your charge."

Hearing this, the hostess immediately resumed her silence, once again. I knew my response was a bit harsh, but at that moment, under those circumstances, I could not help myself of my disgust. Instinctively, I rose from my chair and, with the best smile I could muster, I wished Mrs. Teng well in her future work with the Nanking Women Work Committee.

The visit was over. We all once again bowed, in silence, and Mr. Shen and I took our leave.

Footnotes:

[1]Between 1945 and 1947, the UNRRA (United Nations Rehabilitation and Relief Administration) shipped more than $685 million U.S. of goods, food, clothing, and equipment to China (Seagrave, 1985). Although T.V. Soong, Minister of Finance, had emphasized that the Chinese people would reap the full benefit of all foreign aid, the funds were actually under the control of Soong himself, who went on to become one of the richest men in the world (see, *Chapter 5*; Seagrave, 1985). If the foreign aid had been equitably distributed among the Chinese people, as Soong had originally promised, it could have greatly relieved the poverty pervasive in Nanking.

[2]"If there was any one factor that destroyed the KMT [Kuomintang, the Nationalists], it was inflation" (Johnson, 1983).

During a ten-day period in November 1948, commodity prices on the whole rose some twenty-fold (Bodde, 1967). For example, at noon on November 8, the price of a 133-pound bag of rice leaped from 300 Gold Yuan ("*Jin-yuan Juan*") to GY1000, an increase of more than three-fold, and by nightfall it had again nearly doubled, to GY1800 (Johnson, 1983). At the U.S. Navy Y.M.C.A., a plate of pork chops that cost GY7 at 11 o'clock in the morning had raised to GY24 three hours later, a nearly four-fold jump (Bodde, 1967). In *Chapter 4*, the author encountered the doubling of prices of watermelon, a welcome treat for the dog-days of summer.

[3]CNRRA, the Chinese National Rehabilitation and Relief Administration that had been fashioned after the UNRRA of the United Nations, was established by Minister of Finance T.V. Soong to serve as a direct conduit of UNRRA's relief goods and aid to China (Seagrave, 1985). The deal struck by Soong was that after arrival of goods from the United Nations, Soong's men would take full guardianship and control (Seagrave, 1985). Like letting a raccoon into a chicken coop "this was a situation ready-made for abuse" (Seagrave, 1985).

[4]The population of Nanking at the time was about 1.2 million (Topping, 1999), at least one in ten of whom was jobless and in poverty.

[5]Dovoan (1982) wrote, "Generalissimo Chiang Kai-shek [in late 1948, before retreating from the mainland], played what had once been an ace sending his wife [Mme. Chiang] to the United States to plead for a large

new aid program [see, *Chapter 5*]. But Truman and Marshall spurned her requests."

[6]Beginning in China as early as the 10th century, foot-binding of women was regarded as bestowing a mark of beauty, an asset that made them especially marriageable (Chu, 2002). To achieve this "beauty" (that of the "Golden Lotus," a bound foot in the shape of a dazzling small lotus bud), binding or wrapping of a girl's feet began at the age of five or six. "The bandages would fold down the four small toes toward the sole of the foot and force the heel inward, exaggerating the arch ... [and the] cloth [was] wound tight enough to break the bones, bend the foot and stunt growth ... The process was excruciating. Flesh would rot. Girls wept in agony" (Chu, 2002).

To Chinese and Western men alike, tiny feet were as sexually attractive as the most private parts of a woman's body (Harrison, 2000), and an especially erotic foot would be minute and pointed, three to four inches long, the tip of the foot being no more than a stunted big toe (Plate 9). The most desirable women were those having a pair of Three-inch Golden Lotuses ("*San-cun Jin Lian*").

Foot binding is a practice that is an embarrassment to today's Chinese society. The companies making shoes for such foot-binders (Plate 9) are predicted to disappear in the next decade or so (Chu, 2002). "Mama," nursemaid of the Author's children (Plate 9), had bound feet, and the Author's mother (Plate 4) and godmother (*Gan-niang, Chapter 4*) both had such Golden Lotuses.

[7]The excitement of the in-coming mayor's wife over the "surplus-in-the-pot" is reminiscent of the greed-and-grab approach of the new Nanking mayor, Teng Chieh (*Chapter 11*). According to the Managing Editor of the *New York Times,* Seymore Topping (1999), on April 22nd, 1949, two days before Nanking fell to the Communists, the new mayor Teng attempted to abscond with some 300 million Yuan (gold notes) that he had looted from the City Treasury. He was caught and beaten by his own chauffeur and bodyguards.

CHAPTER 10
OUR VERY OWN!

It was the first time in our life that we built from scratch a home of our very own. We named it *"Villa Sheaffer"*—after the Sheaffer fountain pen[1], well known in the United States and Europe—without doubt, a strange name for a house. Yet had I not had in hand a set of Sheaffer pens, this dream house of ours might never have come to be. As I now look back on the years of World War II, a time painful for me to recall, I shudder to think what a difficult life we Chinese had and find it odd to realize that ownership of such a seemingly common Western name-brand item as a Sheaffer pen-set was a great extravagance. Such, however, was the way it was, and during those hard war years, I was one so blessed.

During the four years of the war with Japan, our family had the great fortune to live in the hinterland, in the tranquil rural city of Lanchow where we were more or less immune from the ravages of the horrendous conflict [see *About the Author, Chapter 6*]. One day in 1945, before the unconditional surrender of the Japanese, my husband Yi returned from the wartime capital of Chunking and presented me a Sheaffer gift-set given to him by his brother-in-law, Chien Tsang-chao, the husband of his younger sister, Xing-yuan [Plate 2; see *Chapter 2*]. Chien, in turn, had been given this set of pens by the Nationalist Minister of Finance, T.V. Soong [*Chapter 5*]. To own such a splendid Sheaffer set at that time and place was a wondrous luxury.

I was overjoyed by this beautiful gift from Yi, a gorgeous set of light-gray pens decorated with tiny bright white stars. I very much needed a new pen at that time, for my old one had become scratchy and almost impossible to ink. However, as I excitedly examined the lovely gift-set, I discovered that the pens were made for men, not for women. They had a large, almost cigar-sized girth—a good fit for a man's hand, but too bulky for me to use without wrapping my hand around the fountain pen in a tight fist. Still, I was delighted, and not wishing to hurt my husband's feelings, I kept quiet. A few days later, with my children huddled all around me, we together fondled and enjoyed the gift for quite awhile. I then cleaned off our handprints and returned these precious treasures to their original box. I tucked them away in a chest with the rest of my most-prized possessions. I never used them, never opened the box again.

Some weeks later, a visiting friend asked if I had Parker pens. This seemed an odd question, coming out of the blue, but I answered truthfully,

"No, I don't." Yi, who had overheard our conversation, then jokingly remarked,

"Though she doesn't have Parkers, she might have something better."

My friend, wanting to know more, immediately turned serious and surprisingly earnest. In a most solicitous manner, she excitedly began to poke and prod about the availability of whatever fountain pens I might have. When I became impatient with her relentless jabber, she finally disclosed her mission—a high-ranking officer of the Military First Division, an intimate friend of hers, needed to find a pen as a gift for his boss. Her officer-friend was leaving the next day for Dihua. The officer was willing to pay whatever it cost, but he needed the pens right away, before he headed off to the outlying province of Shinjiang. My friend insisted on seeing for herself my precious pen-set. I was more than a little hesitant, but Yi thought that there would be no harm in showing them to her, regardless of whether they were for sale. I hesitantly agreed.

When I fetched the pen box from my chest, she abruptly grabbed it and, clutching it firmly in her hand, insisted that I give her a price. Right away, without giving it any thought, I blurted out:

"Oh ... I would never part with these pens for less than twenty thousand dollars."

In truth, I was totally at sea about the real value of twenty thousand Chinese dollars, but it sounded monumental at the time and my goal was to staunch her queries and bring this nonsense to a stop. My friend, however, was not only not deterred by this colossal price, but she cheerfully suggested that she would show the pen-set to her friend and get back to me in a couple of hours.

Less than an hour later, she rang saying that her military man would buy the pens if I would be willing to cut the price by ten percent. With no hesitation I told her "No," and went on to explain that I was really in no mind at all to part with Yi's lovely present.

Overhearing this exchange, another friend who was visiting at the time piped up:

"Shen *Tai-tai* (Mrs. Shen), don't be foolish. Why not sell them to him? Eighteen thousand dollars can fetch nine ounces of gold, some $900 U.S. Why not agree to the deal?"

Yi, sitting opposite my desk, nodded in agreement. I was reluctant, but I grudgingly consented. I would trade my cherished treasure for a treasure of another sort. The deal was struck.

I received the eighteen thousand dollars the following day. Adding to it all that I had saved-up over the years, another two thousand dollars, I rang my friend, Mr. Hsu, and asked him to purchase for me ten ounces of gold. He gladly agreed, but said that the gold would be delivered in six-month's time. The gold was to come from the government's recently announced so-called "gold savings program," the centerpiece of a campaign to encourage Chinese citizens to save their earnings in gold, with the promise of high yield as the value of gold increased, rather than in Chinese currency.

I am very much of a "wood head" (*moo-tou*, dense) when it comes to investment and finance. Yi is no better. We had very little money and no special skill in its management. But soon after our twenty-thousand-dollar investment, the price of gold did indeed rise. Pleased with this success, I became keen to follow it up with more gold savings. To obtain spare cash to invest, I rummaged through my treasure chest for sellable items and visited pawnshops from time to time. Whenever I had accumulated enough funds from selling or pawning various valuables, I would contact Mr. Hsu and have him buy another ounce of gold[2] (one gold bar). I felt happy and very rich when my gold savings, including that from the pen-set, had grown to fifteen ounces. Yi was unaware of my pawning runs. I was waiting for an opportune time to give him the splendid surprise.

The victory of WWII, with the unconditional surrender of the Japanese, came in September 1945. The whole nation rejoiced in celebration. Though our family had been wonderfully fortunate to spend the four years of the war in peaceful Lanchow, as only temporary residents of the hinterland ("*hou-fang jen*"), we were excited about our forthcoming return to our roots in Shanghai. Nine months before the children and I left Lanchow, Yi had assumed the post of Deputy Minister of Communications in the war capital of Chunking. During his nine-month absence, I had a free hand to extend my gold venture.

The long-sought end to WWII was a welcome huge relief, but for us, it was also bittersweet. In the spring of 1946, when we finally returned to Shanghai and the Civic Center built under Yi's guiding hand, we found that our *Jiang-wan* house had been destroyed by Allied bombing [Plate 9]. We had no choice but to live as a "grant-of-favor" with Yi's relatives.

After only a short while, however, our luck changed and we had the good fortune to be assigned a rental apartment, a property previously under Japanese occupation. It was a nicely furnished place with one good-sized bedroom, a fully functioning bath, and a living room with a dining area and kitchen, located in the former French Concession on San-tsong Lu (Road). Ideal as this accommodation might seem, for a family of seven plus two servants it was terrifically congested. We had just one bed. All the elder children and their nursemaid, Mama [Plate 9], slept on the floor in the living room.

One morning, the doorbell rang while the children were still sprawled across the living room sound asleep, exhausted from playing late with their daddy who had just returned from Manchuria. Eldest daughter Hwa-hwa dragged herself out from under the covers, opened the door just a crack, and sleepily whispered,

"Oh …, Wong *Bai-bai* (Uncle Wong), "*dui bu-chi*" (sorry), but I cannot let you in just now."

"My sisters and I have not yet put away our bedding on the floor."

The caller was Yi's friend Wong Wen-hao[3] who much enjoyed relating this story to our many common friends as a sort of sorry comedy.

The apartment, however, looked quite presentable in the daytime. No one would have imagined that this residence of an official in the Nationalist government would become transformed into a refugee shelter each night. Yi had to travel quite a lot in those days, shuttling between Shanghai and Manchuria as he waited to assume the position of mayor of the Manchurian port city of Darien, scheduled to be turned over to the Nationalist government following its occupation by the Japanese and then the Soviets [Plate 6; *Chapter 6*]. During one of Yi's visit home, when he saw the children sleeping on the floor, he sighed with regret and sadly noted,

"It's a real shame that after twenty years of working as a public servant ('*gong-wu yuan*'), I still cannot provide adequate housing for my family."

A hopeless optimist, Yi is always satisfied with what he has. He never complains, no matter what the hardship. In fact, this was the very first time in our nearly twenty years of marriage that I had ever heard him bemoan our meager living conditions. For the most part, I, too, like to look on the bright side. Whenever things seemed bleak, as they sometimes truly did, I would try to cheer us up by saying,

"Don't forget, we own a big bar of gold[2]. Actually, we are quite rich! We could even have a house of our own."

In November 1946, when our government was unsuccessful in reclaiming Manchuria, including Darien, from the Russians, Yi was appointed mayor of Nanking, the nation's new capital-of-return ("*hui-du*"). Because of this new posting, early in the following year our household moved again, this time from our apartment in Shanghai to the city-allotted official mayor's residence, the "White House," in Nanking [*Chapter 3*]. Our family had moved, and "re-moved," and now had moved once more. Over all this time, I kept recalling a well-fitting proverb: "The best of the best way-shelters for a passerby can be enjoyed only for just a little while." I had never stopped plotting a way for us to have a house of our very own.

One summer afternoon in Nanking, when all our children had gone off swimming, Yi and I had some rare moment to be alone. We were in the backyard, walking and talking and airing our souls in the radiance of Nature. As we strolled and quietly chatted, I saw the chance to raise the question that had long been in my heart. Seizing the opportunity, I became serious.

"Jun-yi, wouldn't it be nice if we had a house of our own?" Quickly responding, Yi punched his index finger in the air and mused,

"Absolutely. It's never far from my mind, but we don't have the resources to do it."

"What if we first buy a piece of land?" I asked.

Yi cocked his head. "That's a fine idea, if only we were able."

"Suppose I could find a way."

"You mean by borrowing money?" Yi asked quizzically, not very pleased with the prospect.

"Not for buying the land. But owning a lot would be a first step to building a house," I confidently suggested.

"Then, you think you have enough money to buy a piece of property?"

"Why, have you forgotten the big gold bar? Now is the time we could use it."

"Oh, Yeening, my dear wife ("*wode tai-tai*"), you are so wonderfully innocent. One big bar of gold is hardly enough for a plot." He burst out laughing.

"But what if I had more?" (The time was ripe for me to reveal my stash, my splendid surprise.)

"Where did you get them from?" Yi was puzzled.

"Well, I managed to add a bit more from pawning a few things in Lanchow, while you were away in Chunking."

"How much more do you have?"

"A full five more ounces, fifteen total."

Yi laughed again and said, "I still don't think it's enough. How large a property do you have in mind?"

"I want at least three moo⁴," I said, firmly asserting my best hope.

"What a big appetite!" Yi shook his head, repeatedly, and with a short sigh he said, almost too softly for me to hear,

"Well, let's give it a try."

"Don't be discouraged, Jun-yi," I excitedly blurted, "I still have more things I can sell!"

"What else is left?" asked Yi, becoming even more perplexed.

"I have antique jade and pearl jewelry, the '*so-she*' Mother prepared for my '*jar-tweng*' (dowry)."

Yi now became serious. "I won't hear of it! How can you part with the keepsakes from "*Unn-niang*⁵?"

Knowing that I had already parted with some of these items, while Yi was away from Lanchow, I blushed. I was deeply ashamed. After some silence, I awkwardly continued: "I'm sure you're right. It would be terrible to sell the family heirlooms. But I do have the mink coat you bought me while we were in Moscow years ago" [*About the Author*].

I reached out for his hand. This time he did not argue. He smiled and lovingly patted me on the shoulder as though I were a child.

During this whole conversation, we had walked aimlessly around the backyard, ending up at a little stone table behind the pond where we sat on the nearby stools and rested [*Chapter 3*]. But given the headway I had already made toward getting the go-ahead to pursue my dream, I was anxious to resolve the matter. So I pressed him again:

"Jun-yi, if you give me the full liberty of figuring out how to get a piece of land—and if somehow I manage to find something suitable— will you be willing to take up your part and build a house on it?"

Yi said nothing. He cupped my face in his hands, nodded and sweetly smiled. I felt his warmth.

Unfortunately for my great dream, there was actually very little hope that we would find a piece of land, since there was no way that we could search for one publicly. Because of Yi's position, it would have been out of the question to give inquiring newsmen any such excuse to pry into our private lives. Though I then spent a fair amount of time looking on my own for a proper home-site, a half-year soon passed with no promise of a plot in sight. The asking prices were all too high to fit our limited resources. And, to tell the truth, Yi was not at all enthusiastic. After awhile, even my interest began to wane. I almost gave up the plan of having a house of our own.

Then, unexpectedly, a promising prospect came our way! It was toward the end of 1947, a few days before Christmas. I was in good spirits, happily decorating our Christmas tree with lights and beautiful tinsels and trinkets on-loan from Duan [Plate 3], my younger sister in Shanghai. While I was in the midst of dressing the tree, a British-trained architect and recent acquaintance of our family, Mr. Chen, came to call.

During our conversation, Chen mentioned a good piece of land in a residential neighbourhood that he knew was up for sale, owned jointly by Chairman Chiang Kai-shek's two sons and a nephew. The nephew, Mr. Chu, an air force pilot, was Chen's good friend. The pilot was to be dispatched to the front within the next few days and he wished to sell his part of the property, just short of three moo at a firm price of fifteen ounces of gold. What a wonderful opportunity—the cost of the land fit our budget and this was about the size of the plot I had been looking for! I immediately rang up Yi and asked him if he could find a free moment to take a look at the property with Mr. Chen.

Late in the afternoon of that very day, I accompanied Yi and Chen to see the lot. Located in a quiet neighbourhood adjacent to the Ginling University Forestry Experimental Station [see *Frontispiece*, Nanking University], the parcel of land was at the top of a hill near the residence of Mr. Douglas Copland, the Minister of Australia [*Chapter 7*]. The British Embassy was a little way down the hill to the west, on a main thoroughfare. The surroundings were ideal, but the plot was peppered with the huts of squatters who might prove difficult to evict. Mr. Chen assured us that through prior discussions these uninvited occupants had agreed to leave if a house were to be built on the property.

Our decision to buy the plot was set. By four o'clock on Christmas Eve, the papers of land-transfer were signed by both parties. My stash of fifteen ounces of gold had been instantly transformed into the paper deed that I held in my hands. This was the happiest Christmas Eve of my life!

Full of enthusiasm and glee, the kitchen staff and I prepared a sumptuous Christmas Eve dinner to be served in our grand dining room. Sitting around the long dining table, Papa (my father), *Ganniang* (my godmother), relatives and friends joined our family to share that festive evening, enveloped by gentle candlelight sparkling from the tall Christmas tree. Amidst our happy chatting, drinking, eating, laughing and singing, we were visited by a group of cheery carolers, Hwa-hwa's classmates from the nearby Ginling Girls School. I invited them in from the darkness and the falling snow. In a dreamy hush, the sweet angelic voices of these lovely innocent girls filled the softly glowing dining room woven around the majestic twinkling tree. It was magical!!! Before bidding them farewell, the youngsters were treated to cakes and hot coco prepared by our ever-resourceful chef, Ben-yao. Our daughters, in high spirits, danced and swirled across the huge dining room floor until late into the night. This was a Christmas Eve that we will all forever cherish!

In the following February, a house design incorporating our ideas was produced by our eminent architect-friends, Misters Foong and Tung [see *Chapters 3, 9*]. The stage was now set for Yi to act on his promise to take charge of building the house, his part of our joint effort (*"fung-gong heh-zuo"*). Despite having been less than enthusiastic about this project, Yi now became masterfully involved. By his signature alone, without collateral for security, he obtained a bank loan of thirty-thousand dollars. (Although I have never known the details, it is my guess that this unusually generous arrangement was helped along by certain of his distinguished and notable friends.)

Even with these monies in hand, however, things did not go smoothly. Right from the start, we had trouble with the squatters on our newly purchased property, almost all of whom turned out to be families of military men associated with the Generalissimo's sons, the owners of the unsold part of the parcel. Despite our offer to pay their moving expenses, these unwelcome intruders refused to budge. They were firm, they were defiant, and they were full of threats. To us, this was a great problem!

In truth, however, the squatters on our land had no place to go. During this period, a slump in the value of Chinese currency, coupled with a rapid rise in the rate of inflation, created havoc for the people. Afraid of the currency devaluation and the unending inflation, the well-to-do had put their money into real estate and new buildings. So, new houses and buildings were springing up like bamboo shoots after a spring rain all across Nanking. But this was of little help to the "*lao bai-shin*" (common people), since the Nanking landlords had found they could make huge sums by leasing their property to foreign tenants who could pay hundreds of times higher rent than the local Chinese. The shortage of housing in the city had become a hugely serious problem.

Yi and I found ourselves in a distressingly suffocating situation, holding a thirty-thousand-dollar loan that was losing its value day-by-day, week after week. Caught up in this problem by our ignorance of financial matters, the colossal loan had created a colossal dilemma—on the one hand, we needed the money to build the house, yet on the other hand, the rapidly devaluating loan still needed regular monthly interest payments. To offset the rampant inflation, good and knowledgeable friends advised us to purchase building materials as fast as we could [see *Chapter 9*]. I, however, thought the best plan would be to put the house construction on hold and return the loan to the bank. Because it had been difficult for us to meet the interest payments, we had so far borrowed the funds from a friend. As best I could tell, we were digging ourselves into a deeper and deeper hole.

Yi disagreed. He held the firm view that no matter how burdensome this venture might seem, we should not and could not abandon the task in mid-stream. I relented. We pressed on. Some of the building materials were quickly purchased (though in hindsight, this was a ridiculous way to proceed since we still had not let bids for the project or even found a builder).

A month or so later, in May of 1948, Yi's brother-in-law, Tao Moon-ho [*Chapter 7, footnote*[16]], informed us that he was looking for a buyer for a piece of his personal property on *Wutai San*, Nanking's Holy May Hills, that had a commanding view of the city [see *Frontispiece*]. He told Yi that if we could find a buyer for half of his property, he would be willing to exchange the other half for the squatter-occupied hilltop plot that had been giving us such problems.

Within a short time, half of brother-in-law Tao's land was sold at a good price and the other half (a little less than three moo) was exchanged for our troubled plot. The new lot, on *Wutai San*, neighboured a house of our friend Wong Wen-hao and was close to the home of Yi's schoolmate and good friend Tann bai-yu [see *Chapter 7, footnote*[1]]. With this unexpected transaction having given us the chance to move into a neighbourhood of close friends—for which we were very grateful—we were finally ready to build our own home.

At long last my dream was to come to pass, but it did not take long before I came to realize what an overwhelming struggle it is to build a private house. After all this time, I could now understand Yi's lack of full-blown enthusiasm for the venture, wisdom he no doubt gained from his 10-year-stint as Chief of the Bureau of Public Works in Shanghai [*About the Author*].

When bids were finally tendered, we found that all the estimates were more or less the same, totaling around a minimum of twenty-eight gold bars—an abominable sum and much more than we could muster! Where would we ever find the funds needed to meet this sum? Though I had a secret backup plan, the monies it might bring were dwarfed by the huge bids. Yi had cautioned me that we could not spend beyond the means provided by the now-dwindling thirty-thousand-dollar loan. We should build a house to satisfy our family needs, but only that and nothing more.

My idea, however, was to construct something a bit more special, a thoroughly pleasant home that would provide a solid foundation for our family so that Yi would no longer have to worry about our well-being. Because of this, I took it upon myself to set out with earnest to help our family achieve a better financial base, one that could then free

Yi to pursue his deep commitment to public service. Further, it seemed to me that the better the quality of the house we built, the easier it would be to lease it out, if that ever became necessary, when it would then fetch a good income. Though I found these notions encouraging, they were also unsettling for I knew that if they actually came to pass I would be viewed as having shamelessly merged with the profit-seeking landlords.

All this while, I had pinned my financial hopes on an apartment in Shanghai, on Sha-fei Lu, which had been given to Yi by the government. I easily recall Yi's reaction at the time he received this unexpected reward from on high, when he happily proclaimed *"chung-jen tian boa-yu"* (Heaven protects the poor). He was delighted, humbled, and thankful for his very good fortune. My secret backup plan was to raise income from the leasing of this apartment.

Since our move to Nanking, the Shanghai apartment had been occupied by my sister Duan's family. My friends suggested that the leasing of it would fetch a sizeable amount of so-called "key money," an arrangement common at that time in Shanghai, a sum of extra funds that could be used for the building of the house on *Wutai San*. I chose not to bother Yi about my plan. He would have prevented me from carrying it out, for, after the war, he had the unhappy experience in Shanghai of not being able to come up with the required key money and, because of this, had been turned down in his attempt to provide a house for our family.

In search of funds, I traveled to Shanghai alone to discuss the problem with my sister and brother [Plate 3]. Sister Duan, knowing well my urgent need for money, approached me with a proposal. Her rather well-to-do husband, Jen-ming, liked our apartment and wanted to continue to live in it in exchange for six bars of gold, half of the key money that such an apartment could usually fetch, while the property would remain registered in our names. Since this transaction would not involve a transferal of title, I felt fairly sure that Yi would approve. We settled the matter then and there. But this addition would not be enough. I needed to find still more resources for the construction on *Wutai San*.

During our stay in Shanghai in 1946, while Yi was shuttling to and from Manchuria as he awaited his posting to Darien, my brother Huai-san [Plate 3] had handled an investment for me that by now had increased in value to some eighteen hundred U.S. dollars. With these funds and a loan of two more gold bars from my brother, I now had some twenty bars in hand. Regretfully, as I soon learned from Jean Koo (Mrs. Thomas Lea), a dear friend from my days at the McTyeire Girls School in Shanghai [*About the Author*], even this sum was still not enough to begin building a house. Jean's family, the Leas, had just started a house in Nanking themselves, and though it was smaller than our family would need, it cost much more than all the bars I had so far amassed.

I was at my wits ends. I had run out of ideas and had not the least notion of where I could find more money. Upon my return to Nanking, our architects advised me that we could cut costs by doing away with the steel-framed doors and windows I had planned for the house, but though these were probably the most expensive items of all the building materials, they were also my very favorite. I lost sleep for a whole night as I tried to scheme-up a plan to achieve my goal. In a flash, I suddenly remembered the steel-framed doors and windows we had in our bombed-out house at 91 Min-fu Lu in *Jiang-wan* in the Shanghai Civic Center [Plate 9; *Chapter 3*]. Though this property was now very much devalued, it was all paid for. If the door- and window-frames had survived the bombing, we could use them for the house on *Wutai San*. I was overjoyed to have recalled this blessed ruin.

The very next day I again traveled to Shanghai, this time to pay a visit to our *Jiang-wan* house, a home in which our family had spent a pleasant and rewarding two years but that now had been reduced to nothing more than a stark skeleton [Plate 9]. Happily, the steel frames of doors and windows of the bombed-out structure were still intact[6]. To buy these same materials at this time, according to the architects, would have cost about ten bars of gold. I was delighted. Triumphantly tallying my collection of gold bars—six from sister Duan, two borrowed from brother Huai-san, and some fifteen from my Shanghai investment—plus the salvaged steel doors and windows from *Jiang-wan*, I reached a sum that might be just enough to start building our house and paying down the bank loan and interest.

With my mission now accomplished, I returned to Nanking and related my success to Yi. He was pleased with my good work, especially because none of my arrangements had gone against his principles. Nevertheless, and to our mutual sad surprise, when the final bid came in it had increased six bars from what was originally tendered. I had no more resources, no more backup plans. I was defeated! It would now be up to Yi to make up the six-gold-bar deficit. I knew then that the only way out would be for him to borrow the needed funds from someone, somewhere. Ever resourceful, he managed this task. (But I did not know at the time that the benefactor was his brother-in-law, the very person who had exchanged the lot in the first place for our squatter-occupied hilltop parcel. Yi repaid this loan a year later, from the very first paycheck he received after his appointment to the United Nations ECAFE [*Chapter 7, footnote*[16]]).

On a fine day in mid-August 1948, the construction of our house on *Wutai San* happily began. The contractor promised to finish it within 100 sunny days, with a penalty to be levied for each day of delay. Supervisors for the architects and contractor would be assigned to oversee the construction so that Yi and I need not be bothered.

Though this arrangement was quite sensible, for much of my life I had been keen on architecture and construction [see Plate 7; *About the Author*]. So, I soon became the self-appointed (and uninvited) overseer of the project, monitoring progress at the construction site day by day. As I made my rounds, I noticed many mistakes, overlooked or neglected by the supervisors, which needed to be corrected to bring the work to a proper state. By and large, my observations and adjustments brought excellent improvement. Though the supervisors were sometimes displeased with my "meddling" in their affairs, they tolerated and many times seemed to appreciate my efforts. I followed the progress of the construction with great enthusiasm, going to the site even on rainy days, and I was overjoyed to eventually see the red roof-tiles glisten beautifully in the sun.

For a good many weeks, work on the house went smoothly with

the entire outer shell having been rapidly completed. Then, suddenly, disaster struck. On one day in December, the work ground to a halt as our house-builders went on strike. The problem was citywide. The combined high cost and low supply of food staples, the so-called "rice mob," had brought Nanking to a standstill [*Chapter 4*]. Unable to afford or even to obtain the staples for their daily meals, all labourers in the city halted their work. The city's granaries closed, for fear of rioting and violence. The city's businesses were paralyzed. The universal workers' slogan proclaimed, "*No rice, no work!*" Yi, as Nanking's mayor, was confronted with the task of handling, and then trying to remedy, this citywide calamity.

The cause of the uprising was runaway inflation, the cost of almost all goods rapidly rising higher and higher [*Chapter 9, footnote²*]. Salaried employees found that day by day the value of their income was eroding away. The chaotic situation enveloped the whole nation. Our government seemed not to understand the seriousness of the problem. Its solution was to institute price controls, especially on the cost of rice. As a result, grain merchants were forced to sell what rice they had at a much-reduced price, and since they could no longer make a profit from its sale, they refused to stock more rice. At the same time, the hardworking farmers, toiling all year round, became unwilling to sell their grain at the government's new low price—so they kept their harvest off the market, snuggly stored on the farms. In actuality, the rice shortage was not brought on by an insufficient supply, but by the government-imposed price control. On top of this great problem was a government-mandated reformation of currency, begun on August 19, 1948, that caused even more havoc in the marketplace [*Chapter 8, footnote¹*]. Over time, the situation worsened further still.

Fortunately for us, the construction of the *Wutai San* house was funded by gold, a commodity more or less immune from devaluation. But we had no way to urge resumption of construction, since the builders could not work on empty stomachs. Even for those who had enough money, there was no rice to be bought [*Chapter 4*]. I was terribly unhappy to see our building project slow to a halt. Yi, in the meantime, hoping to find a resolution to the crisis, was occupied day and night in meetings with the people involved. Given the now countrywide-span of the chaos, he had difficulty coming up with a satisfactory solution. This was too great a problem to be solved by one man, one lone voice and two empty hands.

Because Nanking is not located in a food-producing area, for a great many years the capital had been supplied with staples by the neighbouring provinces. And because past experience had shown that there had always been a sufficiency of food for the Nanking people, the local government had never worried about the city's food supply. Well before the onset of the rice mob crisis, as prices rose and food started to become scarce, the need for staples had been offset by a large rice ration provided each month by the China Relief Mission of the United States to China's five largest cities—Nanking, Shanghai, Peiping, Tiensin and Canton. Because of this largesse, Nanking had been adequately supplied. Nevertheless (and unbeknownst to Yi), unscrupulous cliques within the Nanking City Council had used their privileged position to set up schemes by which to buy this rationed rice at cheap prices and then resell it for profits.

When Yi finally got wind of these goings-on he was outraged, and demanded that these illegal dealings immediately cease. The City Council members involved, many long antagonistic toward the mayor, now held him in even deeper disdain. Then, with no warning, the higher-ups of the U.S. China Relief Mission suddenly declared that the city of Nanking would no longer receive its rice ration, since in their view the mayor had done a poor job in handling its distribution to needy citizens. To compound this slap in the face, the chief of the Mission, Mr. Kilpatrick, without knowing the facts, issued a shocking news release denigrating the Mayor of Nanking for major mismanagement of the rice ration. After some time, and a number of earnest and sometimes heated conversations, Kilpatrick saw the light. Rice was again issued from the Mission to the city of Nanking. But Mr. Kilpatrick never apologized to Yi for the Mission's ill-informed action nor did he ever retract the needlessly mean-spirited news release.

Regardless of all the many blows rained down on Yi by his detractors, he was not depressed. As always, he continued to cherish facts and hard work, and he had not the slightest inclination to play personal politics. His hard-and-fast "standing platform" (*li-chang*) was that he was concerned about the masses and their needs, not his personal glory or the blame that had been showered on him. Unlike too many others in the Nationalist government, his goal was to accomplish something worthwhile rather than to rise higher in the ranks.

The rice mob turmoil began first in Shanghai and then rippled outward, surging into Nanking on December 9, 1948. There was enormous pressure on Yi to resolve the problem, and he held meeting after meeting in an attempt to reach a solution. On the third day of the crisis, Yi returned home for lunch, his voice hoarse and his face lined with exhaustion, yet he was in remarkably bright spirits. In a happy tone, he declared with great relief,

"Rice is coming, all the granaries are stocked. The mob is over!"

Beaming still, he fluttered his two up-held hands and smiling said, "Don't you think I am a magician?"

My face showed my astonishment—I could not believe that the crisis could go away in just three days. "How can this be?" I asked. "It can't be possible for rice to come so quickly from the farms into the city."

"But it is already here, in the city, now!"

Yi then abruptly changed the subject. "What nice dishes have you prepared for lunch today? I'm starved."

"I won't tell you more until I have my food." He was clearly in a very good mood. I became cheery, too.

As it turned out, Yi's team, after a rapid study of the situation, found that in fact there was still a goodly stock of rice in the city shops, but because the owners were afraid of the price-cut, one after another had stashed away his supply. As Yi was sympathetic with the dilemma facing these grain merchants, he was loath to put further pressure on them. Instead, he showed his understanding of their plight by telling them that if they helped him resolve the crisis by bringing their rice onto the market, he, in turn, would guarantee that the government would provide them a reasonable profit. As soon as word of this agreement had gotten out, tall heaps of white grains sprang up at storefronts all across Nanking. I was pleased and proud of Jun-yi's thoughtful ingenuity!

Happily, our house construction resumed once again, now at top speed, but I deeply lamented the fate of the Nationalist Government as it lurched toward total collapse. Deep in my mind, I harboured the notion that having experienced the zigzag history of our land dealings, our house-building venture might be prone to the same disastrous fate that our country was now suffering. My growing sorrows deepened day by day as turmoil grew across the capital and the bad news from the battlefront seemed to never end. Throughout all this, I had the fearful recurring thought that *when the history of this tumultuous time is finally written, this very era would seen by all as the time of China's Great Tragedy!*

Still, and despite all my worries, our new home, built from scratch and our very own, was eventually completed. A plan on paper—affordable for us only through the selling and pawning of my personal treasures, the salvaging of remnants from a bombed-out house, intricate financial arrangements with my relatives and friends, and Yi's dealings with his brother-in-law and with kindly bankers—was ultimately transformed into a fine new house. From the thoroughfare below, I could see *Villa Sheaffer* gloriously perching high above on *Wutai San*, Holy May Hills [Plate 9].

It was our great expectation that when Yi had retired from his position as mayor, this house would provide a sweet home for our family and a warm nest for the two of us "tired birds." Though all loans and construction costs had been paid and the land and house deeds had been properly registered[7], at the end of the day this dream of ours never came to pass. With the fall of Nanking and our departure from the capital on New Year's Eve of 1948, we were never to see this house again.

On the day when the Sheaffer pens were sold, everyone congratulated me on my good fortune. Yes, this good luck pen-set had indeed brought us happiness—but for only a very brief while.

Footnotes:

[1]Sheaffer has its beginning in 1912 when Walter A. Sheaffer pioneered the fountain pen business in Fort Madison, Iowa. The United Nations Charter was signed with a Sheaffer pen on June 26, 1945 (Lover, 2008).

[2]One ounce of gold, amounting to one gold bar, was at the time equivalent to about 2,000 Chinese dollars or $100 U.S.; a *large* gold bar, ten ounces of gold, was costing 20,000 Chinese dollars ($1,000 U.S.).

[3]Two years later, in 1948, Wong Wen-hao, a geologist, patriot, and Yi's close friend, was elected Prime Minister of the Nationalist Government (see *Chapter 8, footnotes*[2, 4]).

[4]A moo is a unit of area equal to about one-third of an acre.

[5]*Unn-niang* is the name used by the author and her husband to address the author's mother in her native Hangchow dialect.

[6]In 1978, soon after the successful episode of "pin-pong diplomacy" between U.S. President Richard M. Nixon and China's Chairman Mao Tse-tung, a ten-member delegation of American botanists was invited by the Chinese Science and Technology Association for a month-long tour of China's scientific institutions. Both the editor and her husband, representing different areas of botanical expertise, were selected to be members of the delegation. Author Inyeening Shen and her husband Yi, the parents of the editor, hovered about her as she readied for this historic journey, urging her repeatedly to take note of their Nanking house on *Wutai San* (Holy May Hills) and mentioning specifically the steel-framed doors and windows that had been transferred from their bombed-out *Jiang-wan* home in Shanghai (Plate 9). Because of their departure from Nanking as the Communist army surged toward the city (*Chapter 11*), the author and her husband never had the opportunity to see in its entirety the finally completed *Villa Sheaffer*. During the editor's 1978 trip it did not prove possible to visit the site. On subsequent occasions, however, most recently in 2005, with sad nostalgia she returned to her parents' "heart-and-blood-spent" (*fei-jin xin-xue*) house at 4 *Bai-bu Po* on *Wutai San* (*Chapter 7, footnote*[15]). The steel-framed doors and windows salvaged from the family's bombed-out home in the Shanghai Civic Center are still in use (Plate 9).

[7]To protect their privacy from inquisitive reporters, Mayor and Mrs. Shen Yi chose to register the deed of the property on *Wutai San* (Holy May Hills) under the name of their eldest daughter, Hwa-hwa, Shen Yu-hwa (Mrs. Ting-li Cho; see *Chapter 7, footnote*[12]).

CHAPTER 11
FAREWELL NANKING, FARE WELL!

December of 1948 was my last month in Nanking. It was a momentous time. Yet of all that happened during that final month, an event that occurred on the evening of December 7th stands out as being especially unsettling. My husband, Yi, and I were at the home of an American couple, Mr. and Mrs. Trone, who had invited us to dinner.

There were no other dinner guests at the Trone's house. They had wanted to share news with us. After exchanging pleasantries, we sat together in friendly conversation. It was not long, however, until I was shocked out of my wits—with obvious enthusiasm, our host opined that Mao's communism was the salvation of China and that he was absolutely certain the Communists would like to have my husband on their side! Mr. Trone urged Yi not to relinquish his mayoral post but, instead, pressed him to smooth the way for the arrival of the new regime. He also advised Yi to safeguard the municipal water and electricity supplies, lest they become destroyed during the take-over.

I was astounded. How dare Mr. Trone to have spoken such treason to the Mayor of the Nationalist capital! In a mysterious manner, he then lowered his voice and uttered an odd and seemingly nonsensical phrase.

"Be patient in your cradle—your kind mother will be with you soon."

As we listened, Yi did not respond. He chose not to express an opinion. Deeply annoyed (and inwardly furious), I was impatient to take leave. The Trones called several times thereafter, but we wished to have nothing to do with them again.

(My husband later told me that Mr. Trone's words were not without reason, for Yi had on several occasions openly expressed dissatisfaction with the Nationalist Government and its policies in our war-torn country. Nevertheless, Trone had been unbelievably mistaken to even imagine that Yi would ever betray his own country.)

It was near midnight on December 10, 1948 when we returned from a dinner given by British Ambassador and Lady Stevenson [*Chapter 7*]. Upon our arrival, a crowd of people, including the municipal census-takers and a few reporters, streamed into our house. Yi and I, still in our formal attire, gathered with our entire household in the dining parlour. As the census officials then instructed, each of us placed our citizen-identification papers in a pile in the middle of our long dining table. The officials proceeded to examine the documents, calling out each name. When they came to the papers of our six children—but found no children to be present—they were less than pleased. Yi immediately explained that, for the children's safety, we had sent all six to Shanghai with Mama[1] [Plate 9]. Smiling derisively, the census-takers said nothing.

While the census taking was in progress, the newsmen snapped photo after photo and they then badgered my husband for his comments on many public issues. The next day's papers reported the scenes from the city census, highlighting the events in the mayor's home. They described every detail of those parts of the White House they had seen—down to the lamps, the vases, and even the buttons on the servants' uniforms (no doubt re-used from Yi's old clothes and sewed in place by my godmother)—and they went out of their way to note the absence of our children. To someone else, their news reports might have been hurtful—but they did not bother me; I felt that my children's safety came first.

I left for Shanghai the following day after the census, to pay a visit to Mama and the children. On December 12th my husband phoned me in Shanghai to tell me that President Chiang Kai-shek had officially accepted Yi's resignation and that the Generalissimo had inquired as to whether Yi had a new job in mind. Yi's reply was that if there were a job that could use his talents he would gladly serve the country, at any time and under any circumstance [see, *About the Author*]. I was much relieved by President Chiang's acceptance of Yi's resignation. My spirits soared.

I returned to Nanking on December 17th. When my train approached Nanking's Heh-ping Mung [the Gate of Peace], one stop ahead of the main city station, I heard a knock on my window. I was surprised—and wonderfully pleased—to see Yi standing on the platform.

"How very kind of you, Mr. Mayor, to come to meet my train."

Jokingly I said as I disembarked. This was the first, and was to be the last time that this mayor would come to meet his wife at the Nanking station. I was excited to see him and excited to know what our future held, so I blurted out:

"Well, what news do you have?"

He nodded, said nothing, and hurried me into his car. I prodded again, this time more gently, and seeing that I could wait no longer he told me the good news that he had been paid visit a few hours earlier by the Minister of Water Conservancy who had asked permission to place Yi's name in nomination for the post of Chief of the United Nations Bureau of Flood Control and Water Resources Development of ECAFE, the U.N.'s Economic Commission for Asia and the Far East[2].

Yi felt that his experience in hydraulic engineering could benefit the entire region, not just China (where the Communist regime would be loathe to take his advice), and that it would be a great honour to represent his country in this capacity. After proper consideration, Yi gladly agreed to the placement of his name in nomination to the United Nations ECAFE.

By late December 1948, the winter was in full force as a three-day snowstorm blanketed the city. Nanking was painted white, bleak, and tranquil. On the 23rd of December Jean Lamb, wife of Sir Lionel Henry Lamb, British Minister to the Republic of China, had invited me to tea. As my driver and I neared her home, my car slipped and slid into a high mound of snow that flanked the icy street. As I huddled in the car, my chauffeur managed to dig us out and we finally got to the home of the British Minister.

As soon as I entered the room where Mrs. Lamb was waiting, she took my cold hands and led me to a warm fire. We were silent for a long while until a servant brought tea. I then began to tell her of my regret for being unable to continue our normal routine of giving each other Chinese and English lessons [*Chapter 7*].

"Then you are leaving Nanking soon?" She asked, with evident disappointment.

"Yes, perhaps you haven't heard, but my husband's resignation has been approved."

"We plan to leave at the end of the year." She was surprised.

"I am sorry; I will miss you both." Jean Lamb bowed her head looking down trodden.

Because of her husband's position, the Lambs were expected to remain in Nanking, even should the city fall to the Communists. The reason she had invited me to tea was simply to let me know that she would give me help in any way she could. And when I told her that I was leaving soon, by the end of the month, she drew her chair even closer and with great sincerity she softly said,

"I don't mean that you will not stay in Nanking."

"But if you have trouble in safeguarding your valuables, I would like to help." She was earnest. I understood her meaning.

"You are a dear friend."

"Thank you, so very much, Mrs. Lamb." I was grateful for her concern.

"But I want to be frank." I cleared my throat.

"You must not think of us as being like those rich government officials who have brought such shame to the country."

"We have no valuables of worth."

"Actually, rather than being wealthy, we have accumulated quite a debt in building our house on *Wutai San* [see, *Chapters 7, 10*]."

"And though we *do* have a lot of rather nice old furniture, accumulated over the years that we've used in the mayor's residence, I don't think your house is large enough to keep them all."

We both laughed. Arm-in-arm we walked to the terrace. As she told me about her plans for raising flowers in the spring, I became nostalgic for my own Nanking springs. Yet noting her fondness for plants I became pleased, and I told her warmly,

"I am so happy to hear that you like plants, as do I."

"In fact, I have cultivated with my own hands a large variety of potted plants in my warm-house (*'nwen-fung'*)."

"I have been worried that they would be neglected when I leave."

"Perhaps I could place them in your care."

She was delighted. So was I. Her parting words were,

"I will take good care of them, and will return them when you are again back in Nanking."

I have never seen her since, but Lady Lamb's thank-you note for the plants I arranged to have delivered to the home remained tucked in my desk drawer for many years.

Contrary to the happy and beautiful Christmas Eve my family cherished in 1947 [*Chapter 10*], this one in 1948 was a glum scene of good-byes. Yi gave a dinner at our home for some forty of his colleagues from the City Government. Although "farewell" is itself not a sad word, it had by now become weighted-down with a deep sense of gloom. Everyone was filled with the sorrow of parting. Yi stood and said a few words, concluding with,

"A bond of spirit can never be broken by separation."

A heavy silence followed. Unexpectedly, a timid voice from a young man broke the still. With a soft Soochow accent, the young worker from Yi's office shyly related his admiration for Yi's words and his deeds for the city. In appreciation and friendship, Yi walked over to his table and shook his hand. In spite of being merely a low-ranking typist, this young man had been privy to all the confidential documents that passed through the mayor's office. (Quite surprisingly, we later learned, shortly after the capital had fallen to the communists that this shy young fellow had advanced to become a fairly important figure in the

Red Regime. All the while, as he worked for Yi and the city, he had been a communist sympathizer[3]!)

The ceremony of Nanking mayoral transference took place on December 27. My husband had sent his car and chauffeur to fetch the newly appointed mayor, Teng Chieh. I was startled when Yi's chauffeur, Wong "*Siji*" ["master engineer," i.e., engine operator], with a pale expression and a trembling voice, barged into my study declaring:

"I am here to borrow your car, '*Tai'tai*' [Mistress]."

"The mayor needs it."

"Wong *Siji*, is something wrong with the mayor's car?"

"No," he loudly answered.

"We no longer have his car; it has been taken [confiscated] by the new mayor's men, very rude, most barbaric!" I tried to calm him down.

"But Wong *Siji*, you must understand, it is a government car, we must give it to them."

"After all, '*Shen-sen*' [*Master*, meaning the mayor] will soon relinquish his mayoral post." Wong's rejoinder was full of fury.

"But do you know, *Tai'tai*, they took it even before the seal of mayor had been placed in the new man's hands?"

"Rude! No manners ('*Mayo gwei'ju, Mayo li'mao*')!"

He was terribly upset. To put him right, I called on my inner strength.

"Get hold of yourself '*Lao Wong*' [Old Wong]. I am moved by your loyalty, but you must continue your good work for the new master." He calmed, but just a bit.

"Oh, *Tai'tai*, don't worry about *Lao* Wong."

"*Lao* Wong is a good *siji*."

"*Lao* Wong will not starve."

"But, *Lao* Wong would rather starve than become the driver for that '*shao'tze*' [little son]!"

I stopped him from saying more. I told him to take my car. He did. (Later, I was informed that when Yi had sent his car to fetch Teng Chieh to the inaugural ceremony, the new mayor's men had recognized the car and had immediately substituted their own driver in place of Wong *Siji* and had absconded with the car.)

Soon after Lao Wong had left, Mr. Shen Yu-fu, Yi's Personal Assistant arrived. With a deep sigh he delivered a message from my husband, telling me that Yi and his staff would be coming to our home for lunch. The City Hall at *Futze Miao* had now become a military camp, and it had become too chaotic for the food hall ("*fang-tang*") to prepare meals.

After delivering his message, Mr. Shen pulled out a large box containing a stack of shiny satin banners that had been presented to Yi during the ceremony that morning, banners that came from the many communities of Nanking. Over and over, again and again he told me,

"It was the most impressive scene I have ever witnessed!"

When I returned from the kitchen to alert my cook about the unexpected lunch guests, I saw that all the banners had been hung on a wall in the dining room. I knew that my husband would not like this display. But I left them up since I did not wish to hurt Mr. Shen or to insult what I knew to be his good intentions.

Later, when Mr. Shen and I retreated to my study for tea, I asked him what he had meant by the "impressive" scene. Now in a somber mood, Shen replied:

"What was most impressive, deeply moving, was that just before the ceremony of mayoral transference, banners were offered to Mayor Shen from the communities."

"The last group, the Union of Water Works, was led by its Chief, Mr. Chi, who with a marching band proceeded all the way to the front of the Mayor's Office Building."

"Holding a banner embroidered with four characters, "*Ming Ai*

Yuon Tzuen" (Love Forever from the People), and standing very straight and tall in the middle of the grounds, "Mr. Chi, with tears streaming down his cheeks, shouted out at the top of his lungs: 'We love you Mayor Shen! We want you to return, Mayor Shen!"

"Not only that, but Chi was scheduled to give a speech following this presentation from his Union."

"He was so overcome with emotion that he could not continue. There were tears in everyone's eyes, and the crowd grew silent."

"Amidst this hush, the voice of the master of ceremonies called out: 'Offer up the banner to the Mayor!"

"And though the band struck once again, Chi and all the bystanders remained quiet and sorrowful." Mr. Shen took a long deep breath.

"Was this not impressive?"

After some time, Shen's mood became lighter, and toward the end of our conversation he related a comical scene that occurred near the close of the ceremonies.

At the City Hall ceremony, when the band struck up a song of farewell to Yi, a bombastic symphony of firecrackers was let-loose and a procession of drab-colored army cars appeared. An entourage of military personnel accompanying the mayor-to-be had entered the grounds. The first person to step out of his car was the mayor-designate himself, Teng Chieh, who had mistakenly imagined the band's salute to be for him. He took off his hat, and nodded again and again to the crowd. At that display, the band abruptly ceased playing and the crowd dispersed. As he finished the story, Mr. Shen Yu-fu[4] roared with satisfaction.

A few days later, after more farewell gatherings, I returned, for the last time, to the White House, our home for the last two years. Alone, before my husband had returned to take me to the train station for our departure, I took one final stroll around the pond, so that I could have a last private moment with my garden and my many plants.

The pond at the White House was now covered with snow and empty of lotus. The fish were silent. Only the evergreens stood tall and brilliant. Remembrances of the glorious scenes of spring, summer, and autumn filled my heart. Daffodils now peeped in the cold-frame, ushering hopes of a new season, and all of my best potted-plants had been transferred to Lady Lamb. I had done the best I could to care for this place, but I still could not let go.

"Be hardy and *fare well*, my lovely garden!" I murmured, wistfully.

When the clock struck three in the afternoon of December 31, 1948, Mr. Hsu, our Accounting Officer, announced that it was time for us to be on our way. My heart beat rapidly. I had wanted another moment—and another, and another—but the throng of good-wishers would not allow it. With a forced smile, my husband rose to the occasion and tried to cheer up our friends.

"It is New Year's Eve my friends—instead of saying goodbye let us greet each other for a Happy New Season!"

We parted our home sadly—but with hope, for ourselves and for our country—amidst forced but cheerful farewells. As our car drove out of the front gate, I turned and looked with both pride and sorrow at the White House, a place of my creation, the home I had made for my husband and my children, a place for which I had a deep and heartfelt attachment. I was swept up with emotion as our car slowly turned away from 38 Peiping Lu for the very last time [Plate 3].

A short while later, as Nanking's Shah-guan train station came into view our car was slowed to a standstill. High above the station hung a huge broad banner of red that glittered with gold characters reading: "*Farewell Mayor Shen.*" When our car came to a stop, firecrackers erupted all around and a band struck up a triumphal tune that followed us to the platform. On the platform were long lines of people from the Nanking communities and schools, each group flying their own banner. A thunderous roar began:

"We love our Mayor, we await your return!"

This sad yet joyous out-pouring of emotion was followed once more by a ceremony of flag presentations, festivities that lasted more than an hour. Yi, with eyes glistening, stood on the steps of the train waved to the crowd, telling them for the last time:

155

"I thank everyone. Thank you, I treasure our friendship!"

As our train pulled slowly out of the station, the band struck up yet one last time. We moved into the falling snow as *Tze Jin San* [Zijin Mt., *Frontispiece*], Purple Gold Mountain, became misty and distant. Farewell, Nanking, *fare well!*

To the City of Nan-King⁵

[Translation by Cranmer-Byng (1928), in *"Lotus and Chrysanthemum"*]

Thou that hast seen six kingdoms pass away,
Accept my song and these three cups I drain!
There may be fairer gardens light the plain;
Thine are the dim blue hills more fair than they.

Here Kings of Wu were crowned and overthrown,
Where peaceful grass along the ruin wins;
Here—was it yesterday?—the Royal Tsins
Called down the dreams of sunset into stone.

One end awaits for all that mortal be;
Pride and despair shall find a common grave:
The Yang-tze-kiang renders wave and wave
To mingle with the abysms of the sea.

Li Bai⁶ (706-765 A.D.)

Footnotes:

¹"Mama" (Mrs. Zhou Feng-shan; Plate 9), the wet nurse for the eldest daughter of the family, Hwa-hwa, came from the countryside of Yangzhou where she had a daughter at home of about Hwa-hwa's age. She remained with the Shen family throughout her life giving care to even the youngest children, and all of the family regarded her as one of their own (*"zi-ji ren"*). Mama died of a heart attack in Bangkok in 1959.

²The United Nations, conceived before the death of President Roosevelt, was founded formally on June 24, 1945, immediately following the end of World War II. The Republic of China (the Nationalist Government) was

one of the five initial members of the U.N. Security Council (Tuchman, 1972; Miller, 1974; Donovan, 1982). The United Nation's Economic Commission for Asia and the Far East (ECAFE), to which the Author's husband, Shen Yi, devoted 11 years of service, was one of three regional economic commissions (for Africa, Asia, and Europe) established under the auspices of the Security Council (U.N. Regional Commissions, 2008). Dr. Shen served as Head of ECAFE's Bureau of Flood Control and Water Resources Development, the formation of which was proposed by the U.N. Chinese Delegation in 1948 (Shen-Y, 1985; Dag Hammarskjöld Library, 2008).

[3]Many sympathizers and liberal intellectuals who supported the Communists and their aims suffered tragic fates. Journalist Seymour Topping of the *Associated Press* (1999) recalled that his assistant, J.C. Jao, was one such enthusiast. In 1951, the Chinese Communists (like the Soviet Communists, before them) mounted a purge, reported to have led to the execution of as many as three million people thought to be associated with the Nationalist cause. Jao was among the first to be shot.

[4]Shen Yu-fu was a trusted assistant and friend of Mayor Shen Yi. Nevertheless, as recently as 2002 and using the slightly disguised name of "Shen *Yi*-fu," this former assistant authored an article in a U.S. Chinese newspaper (*Hua-sheng*, the "Chinese Community News") about Mayor Shen Yi that was less than truthful. Shen Yu-fu may have harbored ill feelings toward the mayor, who chose not to invite him to serve as his personal assistant at the United Nations (presumably because of Shen Yu-fu's lack of familiarity with the English language).

[5]Archeological remains show that Nan-King (known also as Nanking or Nanjing, meaning Southern Capital) has been inhabited since 4000 B.C. Emperor Qin Shi Huang-di, credited with linking older walls together to form the Great Wall of China in 221 B.C., used this city as his command-post. Nanking enjoyed its stature of high honor for six dynasties over a period of several hundred years (Summerfield, 1992) and was an important cultural center during the prosperous Tang Dynasty (A.D. 618-907).

[6]Li Bai (706-765), perhaps the most famous scholar in all classic Chinese literature, was born in Sichuan Province during the Tang Dynasty, the "Golden Age of Chinese Poetry" (see *Transliterations, footnotes*[1, 2]), a period famous for its professional poets whom the emperors delighted to honor. Li Bai "lived for the moment, and the moment is often wine-flushed, like the rosy glow of dawn, or gray and wan, as the twilight of a hopeless day" (Cranmer-Byng, 1928).

TRANSLITERATIONS

<u>Note</u>: *English transliterations given below in italics for Chinese terms and phrases in the text of the three front sections of the volume—the "Prologue," "About the Author," and "Historic Foreword"—are primarily from new pinyin, following the conventions of the Xin Hua Dictionary (1982), with the English meaning enclosed by parentheses. References are enclosed by brackets ("[…]"). Some old pinyin transliterations are enclosed by italicized brackets ("[...]").*

CONTENTS

Great effort, *"jiu-niu er-hu:"* *jiu* (nine), *niu* (ox), *er* (two), *hu* (tiger); using the combined effort of nine ox and two tigers; p. x

PROLOGUE

Common people, *"lao bai-xing:"* *lao* (old), *bai* (hundred), *xing [shin]* (surnames); a usage that dates from the Tang Dynasty, 618-907 [*Ci Hai*, 1976]; p. xiv

Corruption, *"jia(jie)-gong ji-si:"* *jia* (feign; or *jie*, borrow from), *gong* (public), *ji* (help, subsidize), *si* (ownself, private); as in *Biography of Heroes of Sons and Daughters*, *"Er-nu Ying-xiong Zhuan,"* *er* (son), *nu* (daughter), *ying-xiong* (hero), *zhuan* (biography) [*Chenyu* Story, 1980; Zhang, 2000]; p. xiv-xv

Death, *"jian bei*, or, *"mu jian bei:"* *mu* (mother), *jian* (sees, meets), *bei* (back); meaning that mother died, as in the volume *Jing Shu*, the Biography of Li Mi, Tang Dynasty, 618-907 [*Ci Hai*, 1976]; p. xvi

Dictionary, *"Zidian:"* *Zi* (word), *dian* (standard, book); as in *"Xin Hua Zidian,"* *Xin* (new), *Hua* (China), *Zidian* (word standard); the Chinese title of the *New China Dictionary* [1982]; p. xix

Encyclopedia of Phrases, *"Ci Hai:"* *ci* (phrase), *hai*, (sea, ocean); a two-volume encyclopedia of definitions and origins of phrases [16th edition, 1976] collected from the classic *Book of Jing Shu* and *Shi Ji* from the Song through the Qing Dynasties, 960-1911; p. xviii

Husband, "*hua-mei ren:*" *hua* (paint, painter), *mei* (brow), *ren* (man); literally, "painter of the brow"; p. xvi

Old brother, "*lao Xiong:*" *lao* (old), *xiong* (elder brother); a respectful and affectionate salutation coined during the Song Dynasty (960-1279) by poet Ouyang Xiu [*Ci Hai*, 1976]; p. xx

Plain talk, "*bai-hua:*" *bai* (clear), *hua* (talk, speak); a simplified form of Chinese language popularized by the distinguished scholar Dr. Hu Shih (Plate 1) in the early 1900s; p. xvi

Proverbial, ready-made sayings, "*chenyu:*" *chen* (ready, ready-made), *yu* (sayings); phrases of historical, poetical, proverbial, or provincial origin [Smith, 1965; Zhang, 2000; cf., *Chenyu* Story, 1980]; p. xvii

ABOUT THE AUTHOR

300 Poems of Tang, "*Tang-si San-bai Shou:*" *Tang* (Tang Dynasty), *si* (poem), *san* (three), *bai* (hundred), *shou* (verses); a classic volume of poems of the Tang period[2]; p. xxxv

Ability, "*ben-ling:*" *ben* (self), *ling* (leadership); p. xxii

Able hands, "*qiao shou:*" *qiao* (able), *shou* (hands); p. xxx

Author's name, "*[Inyeening]:*" *In* (echo), *yee* (virtuous), *ning* (crystallinity), *Echos-of-Virtuous-Crystallinity*; **Plate** 2, p. xxiii

Beauty, "*mei-nu*": *mei* (beautiful), *nu* (woman, female); p. xxiv

Biographical Literature, "*Zhuanji Wenxue:*" *zhuanji* (biographical), *wenxue* (literature), p. xxii

Choice, "*Xiong-zhang ho yu-chi:*" *xiong* (bear), *zhang* (paw), *huo* (or), *yu* (fish), *chi* (fins, viz., shark fins); the making of a difficult decision, from the classic *Diary of Lao Cán's Travel* by Qing author Liu È [*Ci Hai*, 1976]; p. xxxiv

Congratulations, "*gong-xi, gong-xi:*" *gong* (solemn), *xi*, (celebration);

greetings used at traditional celebrations, e.g., of birthdays, weddings, and the New Year; p. xxvi

Double-eyed Well, "*Shuang-yan Jing:*" *shuang* (double), *yan* (eye), *jing* (well); the local name of a water-well at the Hangzhou homestead of the author's grandfather, Ying Bao- shi; p. xlii

Dragon Gate Academy, "*Longmen Su-yuan:*" *long* (dragon), *men* (gate), *su-yuan* (academy); a school for the poor established in Shanghai by the author's grandfather; p. xlii

Educated Family, "*su-xian ren-jia:*" su (book), *xian* (fragrance), *ren-jia*, (people's family); a household replete with books, from the classic poem of Lin Jinxi [*Chenyu* Story, 1980]; p. xxiv

Elder brother, "*xiong:*" opposite *di* (younger brother); p. xxi

Exalted Scholar (a title), "*Ju-ren:*" *ju* (exalted), *ren* (man, person); an honorary title awarded during the Qing Dynasty (1644-1911) to scholars who had passed regional government examinations [*Ci Hai*, 1976; Fu, 1984]. Both the author's grandfather (Ying Bao-shi) and the author husband Shen Yi's father (Shen Bing-jun) earned the title of *Ju-ren*. This title, a higher accolade than that of "*jin-shi*," ranked below only the very highest scholars ("*Zhuang-yuan*"). During the Qing Dynasty, Nanjing's *Fuzi [Futze] Miao* (pp. xlvii, 31, 100) where the Nanjing City Hall was situated when this memoir was written, was the site of such examinations [Zhu, 2002]; p. xl

"*Expectant Doves*," "*Chico:*" *chi* (belated, awaited, expectant), *[co]* (dove); awaiting peace, "belated peace," being the author's name for their home in Taipei, Chico Villa on Grass Mountain (or Yang-ming San); "*chi*" comes from the *Book of Late Han, Memoir of Emperor Zhang Di* (25-220 AD) [*Ci Hai*, 1976]; **Plate** 7, p. xxx

Fleeting moment (precious moment), "*tan-hua yi xian:*" *tan hua* (cactus flower), *yi* (one), *xian* (appearance); from *Fa-hua Jin* [*Chenyu* Story, 1980], referring to the short-living blooms of the night-flowering cactus, *Cereus* (*Selenicereus grandiflorus*); p. xliii

Free Dialogue, "*Zi-you Tan:*" *zi-you* (free), *tan* (dialogue); p. xxii

Garden of Tranquility, "*Shi Yuan:*" *shi* (tranquil), *yuan* (garden);

name of the Hangzhou homestead of the author's grandfather, Ying Bao-shi; p. xxxvii

Girl from good family, *"da-jia gui-xiu:"* *da* (great), *jia* (family), *gui xiu* (unmarried young woman of high status); from the classic *Books of Jing* [*Chenyu* Story, 1980]; p. xxiv

Go-between, *"mei-ren:"* *mei* (liaison), *ren* (person); marriage broker; p. xxv

In happiness, *"tao-zui:"* tao (happily), *zui* (inebriated); p. xxii

Journey in a Netted-Cage, *"Sha-Long Xing:"* *sha* (netted), *long* (cage), *xing* (journey); title of the author's *Auto-Bio-Poetry* which she composed in her breezy studio, enclosed on three sides by screens (the "netted cage;" **Plate** 4), built for her by her husband in Bangkok; p. xxxvi

Local produce, *"tu-chan:"* *tu* (local, earth, soil), *chan* (produce); p. xxxi

Love-mate, *"dui-xiang:"* *dui* (opposite), x*iang* (image); a term used in courtship; p. xxv

Maiden, *"gu-niang:"* *gu* (sisterhood), *niang* (womanhood); a young unmarried woman; p. xxiv

Mutual reliance, *"xiang-yi wei-ming:"* *xiang* (mutual), *yi* (reliance), *wei* (for), *ming* (life); from the writings of the Tang scholar Su Zhe [Zhang, 2000]; p. xliii

Patriotism, *"guo-jia xing-wang, pifu you-ze:"* *guo-jia* (nation), *xing* (prosperity), *wang* (demise, fate), *pifu* (individual), *you* (has), *ze* (responsibility); a phrase meaning that a nation's prosperity is the responsibility of each of its citizens, from the classic prose of Gu Yanwu [*Chenyu* Story, 1980; Zhang, 2000]; p. xxix

Prescious daughter, *"shou-shang ming zhu:"* *shou* (palm), *shang* (on, upon), *ming* (lustrous), *zu* (pearl); from classic poems of the Tang Dynasty (618-907) poets Du Fu[1] and Bai Juyi [Zhang, 2000]; p. xliii

Prosperous family, *"san-yang kai-tai:"* *san,* (three), *yang* (sheep), *kai* (open, usher), *tai* (peace, prosperity); *"yang,"* sheep, refers to a zodiacal sign in the Chinese lunar calendar, a family having three "sheep" said to be particularly prosperous. The use of "yang" in this phrase is something of a pun since it has the same sound as the word for sun in the traditional New Year's greeting "*Many sunny days* (not, many 'sheepy' days) *of spring*" [Zhang, 2000]; p. xxxiv

Unit of distance (Chinese unit), "*li:*" closely equivalent to half a kilometer; p. xxxi

Wife, "*nei ren:*" *nei* (inner), *ren* (person); a title first used by court officials in Late Han (25-220 AD); this title later became a literate term a man addressing his wife to new aquintances [*Ci Hai*, 1976]; p. xxi

Women without ability are women of virtue, "*nu-zi wu-cai bian-shi de:*" *nu-zi* (women), *wu* (without), *cai* (scholarship), *bian-shi* (is therefore), *de* (virtuous); a phrase expressing a traditional view in feudal China [*Chenyu* Story, 1980]; p. xxiv

World, "*tian-di:*" *tian* (Heaven), *di* (earth); p. xxii

Yangtze River, "*Zhang Jiang:*" *Zhang* (long), *Jiang* (river); dating from the Sui Dynasty (589-618), *Yangtze* was used for the names of towns, villages, and bridges near the mouth of *Zhang Jiang*, the major river that enters the Yellow Sea (*Huang Hai*) in Jiangsu Province, leading Westerners to adopt the name for this river [*Ci Hai*, 1976]. In earlier times, when China was more isolated from the Western world, school children were taught that the *Zhang Jiang* (*Yangtze*) was the longest river in the world. *Zhang Jiang* (long river) is the name commonly used in China for this river; p. xxvi

Youth, "*qing-chun:*" *qing* (green), *chun* (spring); originated from Southern-Northern Dynasty (420-589) *Emperor Liang-Yuan Di's Collection* [*Ci Hai*, 1976]; p. xliii

HISTORIC FOREWORD

Beijing University, "*[Peita]:*" *pei* (north), *[ta]* (big); a nickname for *[Peijing]* BeijingUniversity (*ta-xue*); p. xlix

Capital-of-Return, "*hui-du:*" *hui* (return), *du*, (capital); at the end of WW-II, the Nationalists moved the seat of government to Nanjing

(*Hui-du;* see *Chapter 10*) from their former wartime "accompanying capital" (*pei-du*), Chongqing *[Chunking]*; p. lvi

China, "*Zhong Guo:*" *zhong* (middle), *guo* (kingdom); a name originally used by many Chinese for their country that denoted its central status in the world, it is still used today; p. xlvii

Emperor Qin, "*Qin-shi Huang-di:*" *Qin* (Qin Dynasty), *shi* (beginning), *Huang-di* (emperor); honorable inaugural emperor of the Qin Dynasty, 221-206 BC [*Ci Hai*, 1976]; p. xlvii

Foreign devil, "*yang gui-zi:*" *yang* (foreign), *gui* (devil), *zi* (son); son of a foreign devil; p. xlvii

Marco Polo Bridge Incident, "*Qi-qi Lugou Qiao Shi-bian:*" *Qi-qi* (seven-seven, July 7, 1937), *lu* (reed), *gou* (ditch), *qiao* (bridge), *shi-bian* (incident); like many place-names in China (Nanking, Peking, etc.), the name "Marco Polo" applied to this ancient Beijing bridge was a British invention, having no relation to *Lougou* (see *[Loo-gou Chiao])*; p. *l*

May Fourth Movement, "*Wu Si Yundong:*" *wu* (five), *si* (four), *Yundong* (movement); the student movement against Japanese expansionism that erupted on May 4th, 1919; p. xlix

Military Alliance of Eight Nations, "*Ba-guo Lian-jun:*" *ba* (eight), *gou* (nation), *lian* (alliance), *jun* (army); the invading Western forces that defeated the Qing Dynasty in 1901; p. xlvii

Mukden Incident, "*Jiu-Yi-Ba:*" *Jiu* (nine), *Yi* (one), *Ba* (eight); the event occurring on Nine-One-Eight (September 18th, 1931) in Shenyang, Liaoning Province, that set the stage for the Sino-Japanese war; p. *l*

Patriotism, "*re xue:*" *re* (hot), *xue* (blood); from the classic Song Dynasty poem "*Zan Cheng Nanshi*" [*Ci Hai*, 1976]; p. xlix

Strict observance of order, "*yan shou ci-xu:*" *yan* (strict), *shou* (observance), *ci-xu* (order); with reference to an attempt by the student organizers to promote a orderly non-violent demonstration of the *Wu Si Yundong* (May Fourth Movement); p. xlix

Young People's Society of China, "*Shao-nian Zhong-guo Xue-hui:*" *shao* (young), *nian* (age), *Zhong-guo* (China), *xue-hui* (learned society); founded in 1919, a forerunner of China's "New Cultural Movement"; p. xlix

<u>Note</u>: *Transliterations given below for Chinese terms in the text of Chapters 1-11 are mostly old pinyin, the form in use in 1947-1954 when this memoir was written.*

CHAPTER 1   SHANGHAI TO NANKING

Cradle, "*yao-lan:*" *yao* (rocking), *lan* (basket); p. 1

Eyes on broad views, hands in little niches, "*da-zu zoa-yen, shao-zu zoa-sou:*" *da-zu* (broad area), *zoa* (apply), *yen* (eyes), *shao-zu* (small places), *sou* (hands); p. 4

For Heaven's sake, "*tian shao-de:*" *tian* (sky), *shao-de* (knows); p. 5

Ginling Girls School, "*Gin Nu-da Fu-zhong:*" *Gin* or *Ginling* (another name for Nanjing), *nu-da* (short for women's college), *fu* (subsidiary), *zhong* (middle, short for middle school, "*zhong xue*"); p. 6

Happiness, "*man-mien tzuen-fung:*" *man* (full), *mien* (face), *tsuen* (spring), *fung* (breeze); from the Tang poet Dufu[2] [*Chenyu* Story, 1980]; p. 5

Little (small), "*Shao:*" a diminutive used to address a child or young person, as in *Shao* Lan, "little Lan," the author's young daughter Lan-Lan; p. 2

Little treasure (an endearment), "*shao bao-bei:*" *shao* (little), *bao* (treasure), *bei* (sea shell); during the Sui Period (589-618), the shell ("*bei*") of a clam (*Cyraea tigris*) was presented to Emperor Wen Di as a treasured ("*bao*") offering [*Ci Hai*, 1976]; p. 5

Madame (Mme.), "*Fu-ren:*" *Fu* (husband's), *ren* (person); used since the Han Dynasty (206 BC-220 AD) to refer to the wife of an important official [*Ci Hai*, 1976]; p. 1

Minute, "*shao, shao:*" literally, "little, little"; p. 4

Nanking-Shanghai Railway, "*Jin-Hu Tia'lu:*" *Jin* (a name for Nanjing), *Hu* (a name for Shanghai), *Tia* (Iron), *Lu* (Road); p. 1

New People's Daily, "*Shin-min Rer Pao:*" *shin* (new), *min* (people), *rer* (daily), *pao* (newspaper); p. 4

Purple Golden Mountain, "*Tze Jin San:*" *tze* (purple), *jin* (gold), *san* (mountain), see *Frontispiece*; the signature mountain of Nanjing, which for this reason was historically known as the "City of Purple and Gold;" p. 3

Satisfaction, "*zou-mah sun-ren:*" *zou* (walk), *mah* (horse), *sun* (to), *ren,* (work); p. 5

Thatched huts, "*mao-wu:*" *mao* (hairy), *wu* (hut); p. 1

CHAPTER 2   A DAY ON HSUAN-WU LAKE

Body guard (personal attendant), "*Fu-guan:*" *fu* (deputy), *guan,* (officer); p. 10

Eldest, "*lao-da:*" *lao* (old), *da* (big); p. 7

Hsuan-wu Lake: *hsuan-wu* (north; [*Ci Hai*, 1976]); the lake was so named because of its location in the northeastern corner of the city; it is transliterated in new pinyin as "Xuanwu" Lake (*Frontispiece*); p. 7

Last-moment appeal, "*linzhen bao fo-jiao:*" *linzhen* (before a battle), *bao* (embrace), *fo* (Buddha), *jiao* (feet), a last-moment prayer; p. 11

Yellow River, "*Huang He:*" *Huang* (yellow), *He* (river); the "River of Sorrow," historically and to the present, this river has been filled with yellow silt [*Ci Hai*, 1976]; pp. xxvi, 10

CHAPTER 3   "WHITE HOUSE" OF NANKING

Artificial hill, "*gia-san:*" *gia,* (artificial, false), *san* (hill); man-made hills that occur commonly in Chinese landscaping; p. 19

Civic Center, "*Shi Zhong-xin:*" *shi* (city), *zhong-xin* (central-heart); an area in Shanghai composed of three districts (Jiang-wan, Nan-shi, and Zha-bei), each including residential and office buildings, that was developed and built under the supervision of the author's husband, Shen Yi, from 1927 to 1937, when Shen was Chief of the Bureau of Public Works; p. 17

Corruption, *"tian-sha wu-ya yee-ban hay:"* *tian-sha* (under the sky), *wu-ya* (black crow), *yee-ban* (uniformly), *hay* (black); p. 15

French concession, *"Fa Zu-jai:"* *fa* (French), *zu* (lease), *jai* (district); a region of Shanghai conceded to the French by the Qing Dynasty in 1901 at the close of the "War of Eight Nations;" p. 17

Gatehouse, *"mung-fang:"* *mung* (gate), *fang* (house); p. 16

Grade D: *"ting:"* a low grade; in the grading system followed in Chinese schools, *jia,* is the highest grade, equivalent to an "A"; *yi,* to "B"; *bing,* "C;" and *ting,* "D;" p. 17

Incorruptible, *"tzen-jin boo-pah whoa:"* *tzen* (pure), *jin* (gold), *boo* (not), *pah* (afraid of), *whoa* (fire); high integrity; p. 15

Peiping: *Pei* (northern), *ping* (peace); former name for *Peking* (northern capital), now Beijing; pp. 16, 22

River bend, *"Jiang-wan:"* *jiang* (river), *wan* (bend); a particular area of Shanghai's Civic Center region; see *Chapter 10*; p. 17

Road, *"Lu;"* p. 16

CHAPTER 4 MAYOR'S HOUSEHOLD

Bamboo wraps (food), *"zong-zi:"* bamboo packets that contain sticky rice, meats or sweets, traditional food for the celebration of the Midsummer (lunar May 5th) festival in remembrance of the poet and patriot Qu Yuan; p. 37

Celebration of birth, *"tso yue-tze:"* *tso* (celebrate, do), *yue-tze* (month-let); also, *"man-yue"* (full month of birth); a traditional celebration held one month after the birth of a child; p. 25

Confucius Temple, *"Futze Miao:"* *Futze* (highly respected person), *miao* (temple); *"Futze"* from *Annals of Spring & Autumn,* 770-476 BC [*Ci Hai,* 1976], a respectful term transliterated in new pinyin as *"Fuzi,"* is used here to refer specifically to the scholar philosopher Confucius (551-479 BC; *Kong Fuzi,* new pinyin; formal name *Kong Qiu*); p. 31

500 grams, "catty:" a *catty,* also known as a *jin,* is a unit of weight; 100 catties is equivalent to 1 *dan;* pp. 32, 35, 37

Godmother, "Gan-niang:" *gan* (dry), *niang* (mother); literally, one who without giving birth but provides a mother's care; the term "*gan,*" meaning 'lack of,' is said to have originated from the Qing official Zeng Guo-fan [*Ci Hai,* 1976], a friend of author's grandfather, Ying Bao-shi; p. 23

Gold-yuan Notes (GY), "*jin-yuan juan:*" *jin* (gold), *yuan* (dollar), *juan* (certificate); a form of currency issued by the Nationalist government in late 1948 during the monetary reform executed by Finance Minister T.V. Soong; p. 35

Little-thing (endearment), "***shao tung-shi:***" *shao* (little), *tung* (east), *shi* (west); "*tung-shi*" used together means "thing"; p. 28

Midsummer Festival, "Duan-wu Jie:" *duan* (beginning), *wu* (May), *jie* (festival); the celebration held on May 5th (in the mid-summer of the Chinese lunar calendar) in memory of poet patriot Qu Yuan, festivities that feature boat races and eating traditional "***zong-zi***" (see bamboo wrap above) [*Ci Hai,* 1976; *Xin Hua Dictionary,* 1982]; p. 28

Muddled accounting (a curse), "***wan chang:***" *wan* (murky, unclear), *chang* (accounting); p. 29

Save face, "***yao mian-zi:***" *yao* (want), *mian-zi* (face); avoidance of being humiliated, the opposite of "losing face," "***diu lian,***" *diu* (lose, throw away), *lian* (face); p. 27

Smart, "ti-mian:" *ti* (wholesome), *mian* (face, front); originated from the late Yuan Dynasty (1279-1368), *Shui-hu Zhuan,* Chapter 41, authored by Luo Guan-zhong [*Ci Hai,* 1976]; p. 31

Sound (of falling rock), "***calon-tung;***" p. 34

Sound (of foot-paddled sewing-machine), "***gedong, gedong, gedong;***" p. 25

CHAPTER 5   AUDIENCE WITH THE FIRST LADY

Lady official, "*neu-guan:*" *neu* (female, woman), *guan* (official); p. 45

Sun Yat-sen styled uniform, "*Tzong-sen tzuan:*" *Tzong-sen* (a name of Sun Yat-sen), *tzuan* (uniform); p. 47

Three People's Principles, "*San Min Zhu Yi:*" *san* (three), *min* (people), *zhu yi* (principle); Sun Yat-sen's doctrine of people's rights, people's governance, people's livelihood; pp. *l*, 44

CHAPTER 6   EVENTS LEADING TO MY BAPTISM

Central Government, "*Zhong-yang Tzen-fu:*" *zhong-yang* (central), *tzen* (administrative), *fu* (office); in reference to the Nationalist Government; p. 72

Elder Sister, "*jie:*" opposite of "*mei*" (younger sister); p. 69

Great hinterland, "*da hou-fang:*" *da* (great, big), *hou* (hinter), *fang* (area); locales (such as Lanzhou, Chongqing, etc.) far removed from the battle lines with Japan during WWII; pp. 71, 130

Perfect match (in marriage), "*mung-dang hu-dui:*" *mung-dang* (gate-to-gate), *hu-dui* (house-to-house); perfect accordance; from *Literature on Historic Records, Shi-ji Wen-xue* [*Chenyu* Story, 1980; Zhang, 2000]; p. 66

Prince Edward Road, "*Tai-zi Tao:*" *tai-zi* (prince, royal-son), *tao*, (road, Boulevard); p. 69

Public berth, "*tung tzang:*" *tung* (open), *tzang* (berth); accommodations of the lowest of the various ranked classes on ocean liners; p. 70

Trouble doesn't travel singly, "*huo-boo dan-shing:*" *huo* (trouble), *boo* (not), *dan* (single), *shing*, (travel, walk); from the classic volume *Xuan Deng Lu* [*Chenyu* Story, 1980]; p. 69

West Lake dyke, "*Sue-tee:*" *Sue* (named after poet Su Dong-po), *tee* (dyke); transliterated "*Sudi*" new pinyin; a beautiful dyke built at

Hangzhou's West Lake during the Song Dynasty (960-1279); **Plate** 9, pp. 61, 67

CHAPTER 7 FRIENDS OF "WINE AND MEAT"

Bad motives, "*hay-shin'yen:*" *hay* (*black*), *shin* (heart), *yen* (eye); literally, "eyes of a black heart"; p. 86

Deaf ear, "*er-bian fung:*" *er* (ear), *bian* (side), *fung* (breeze, wind); "a breeze passing by the ear," from a classic Tang poem of Wang Anshi [Zhang, 2000]; p. 80

Destiny of hard work, "*lao'lo ming:*" *lao lo* (hard-working), *ming* (destiny); p. 84

Fair weather friends, "*jo'rou peng'yoo:*" *jo* (wine), *rou* (meat), *peng'yoo* (friend); literally, "friends of wine and meat" [Zhang, 2000]; pp. xv, 92

Gold bars, "*jin tiao:*" *jin* (gold), *tiao* (bar, strand); pp. 89, 145

Holy May Hills, "*Wutai San:*" *wu* (May, five), *tai* (platforms, as for worship), san (hill); see *Frontispiece, Chapter 10*; pp. 89, 137, 145

Hot stove (boiler), "*huo-lu:*" *huo* (fire), *lu* (stove); with reference to Nanjing, Wuhan, and Chongqing, the three cities in China said to have the hottest summers; p. 94

Inexperience, "*Shin'zu mao'lu:*" *shin* (newly), *zu* (out of), *mao* (hairy), *lu* (hut); literally, equivalent to the English phrase "wet behind the ears," from the classic poem "*Chu Shi Biao, Battle Call*" by the innovative general Zhu Geliang, 220-263 AD [Zhang, 2000]; p. 87

Slope of Hundred Steps (Nanking street name), "*Bai-bu Po:*" *bai* (hundred), *bu* (step), *po* (slope, incline); the street of the author's home on *Wutai San* (Holy May Hills); pp. 95, 145

Top Desk (official title of Qing Dynasty), "*Toe'tai:*" *toe* (head), *tai* (desk); a Qing Dynasty high official title (higher than that of a present-day city mayor), an title held by the author's grandfather, Ying Bao-shi, in Shanghai in 1865-1869; p. 82

CHAPTER 8 ENVOYS FROM THE UNITED STATES

Accent, "*co-yin:*" *co* (lips), *yin* (sound); p. 107

Fellow villager, "*shao tung-shian:*" *shao* (little), *tung* (common), *shian* (village); p. 106

Fence sitter, "*chi-chian pye:*" *chi* (sitter, rider), *chian* (fence), *pye* (faction); p. 104

Government notes, "*fa-pi:*" *fa* (legal), *pi* (currency); currency issued by the Nationalist Government before the monetary reform of 1948; p. 108

Home dishes, "*jia-shian tsia:*" *jia* (home), *shian* (village), *tsai* (dish); p. 107

Leighton Stuart, "*Szetu, Leideng:*" *Szetu* (from Stuart, literally "master step" [*Ci Hai*, 1976]), *Leideng* (Leighton); newsmen's transliteration of the Chinese name for U.S. Ambassador John Leighton Stuart; pp. 107, 108

Sincere sentiment, "*ku-co puo shin:*" *ku* (bitter), *co* (lips), *puo* (grandmother), *shin* (heart); "stern words from a loving heart," from the classic *Shi Ji, Historical Records* [Zhang, 2000]; p. 106

CHAPTER 9 NEW-LIFE MOVEMENT: NANKING WOMEN WORK COMMITTEE

Bound foot, "*bao juo* or **shao juo:*" *bao* (bound), *juo* (foot), or *shao juo* (small foot); feet as small as lotus buds, a mark of beauty in feudal China [Harrison, 2000; Zhang, 2000]; pp. 123, 126; also, "*san-cun jin lian:*" *san* (three), *cun* (inch), *jin* (golden), *lian* (lotus); a poetic term for bound feet [Smith, 1965]; pp. 123, 126

Cotton quilt, "*mien'bay:*" *mein* (cotton), *bay* (quilt); p. 120

Embarrassment, "*tee-shao jie-fei:*" *tee* (holler), *shao* (laugh), *jie* (both), *fei* (impossible); perplexed; from the classic poem *Princess Le Chang* [*Chenyu* Story, 1980; Zhang, 2000]; p. 123

Four Boundaries of Men (teachings of Confucius), "*Ren-zi Si-wei:*" *ren-zi* (people's), *si* (four), *wei* (boundary); the four boundaries are

"Li" (propriety), *"Yi"* (justice), *"Lia"* (integrity) and *"Chi"* (shame, conscience); p. 111

Mottos of daily living (Chairman Chiang Kai-shek's New-Life Movement), *"yi, ser, zhu, xing:"* *yi* (clothes), *ser* (food), *zhu* (living), *xing* (behavior), terms equated to neatness, cleanliness, simplicity and modesty; p. 111

New-Life Movement, *"Xin Sen-huo Yun-dong:"* *xin* (new), *sen-huo* (life), *yun-dong* (movement), a phrase in new pinyin equivalent to the old pinyin, *"Shin Sen 'whoa Yuen 'dong,"* a program formulated by Chairman Chiang Kai-shek in 1933 during the Sino-Japanese war; p. 111

Refugees, *"nan-ming:"* *nan* (suffering), *ming* (people); p. 116

Swan songs, *"si mien tzu'ger:"* *si* (four), *mien* (direction, front), *tzu* (sorrowful), *ger* (song); "songs of defeat from all fronts," in an historical tale of the late Han Dynasty, ~220 AD [*Chenyu* Story, 1980)]; p. 120

Women Work Committee, *"Fu'neu Gong'tso Wei'yuan Hue:"* *fu'neu* (women), *gong'tso* (work), *wei'yuan hue* (Committee, association); the committee for the Nanking relief effort headed by the author; p. 113

CHAPTER 10   OUR VERY OWN!

Collaboration, *"fung-gong heh-zuo:"* *fung-gong* (divided work), *heh-zuo* (combined task); p. 135

Dense, *"moo-tou:"* *moo* (wood), *tou* (head); p. 129

Dowry, *"jar-tweng:"* *jar* (given away, as in marriage), *tweng* (apparel); p. 133

Hardwork, *"fei-jin xin-xue:"* *fei-jin* (spent, used up), *xin-xue* (heart and blood); p. 145

Heaven protects the poor, *"chung-jen tian bo-yu:"* *chung-jen* (poor people), *tian* (Heaven), *bo-yu* (protects); p. 138

Jewelry, *"soo-she:"* *soo* (hand), *she* (decorated item); p. 133

Mother (in Hangchow dialect), "***unn-niang***:" *unn* (endearment), *niang* (mother); p. 133

My wife (my lady), "***wode tai-tai***:" *wode* (my), *tai-tai* (wife, Mrs.); also see *Chapter 11*; p. 132

Public Servant, "***gong-wu yuan***:" *gong-wu* (public work), *yuan* (person); p. 131

Residents of hinterland, "***hou-fang jen***:" *hou-fang* (hinterland), *jen* (residents); p. 130

Sorry, "***dui bu-chi***:" *dui* (facing with), *bu-chi* (regrets); p. 130

Standpoint, "***li-chang***:" *li* (standing), *chang* (platform); p. 142

Uncle, "***bai-bai***;" used by children to address parents' close friend; p. 130

CHAPTER 11   FAREWELL NANKING, FARE WELL!

Cafeteria, "***fang-tang***:" *fang* (food,), *tang* (hall); p. 153

Chauffeur, "***siji***:" *si* (operator), *ji* (engine); p. 152

Hothouse (greenhouse), "***nwen-fang***:" *nwen* (warm), *fang* (house); p. 151

Intimate person, "***zi-ji ren***:" *zi-ji* (intimate) *ren* (person); referring to a close friend who is not a blood relative; p. 156

Little son (curse word), "***shao'tze***:" *shao* (little), *tze* (son); a nasty term of derision; p. 153

Love Forever from the People, "*Min Ai Yuon Tzuen*:" *min* (people's), *ai* (love), *yuon* (forever), *tzuen* (lasting); pp. 153, 154

Master (Mr.), "*Shen'sen*:" *shen* (early), *sen* (born); a respectful salutation, dating from the Han Dynasty (206 BC-220 AD) [*Ci Hai*, 1976], used to address one's employer or teacher, or used following a surname to address an acquaintance; p. 152

Mistress (Mrs.), "*Tai'tai*:" a respectful salutation for one's female employer, also a polite term for a wife of an acquaintance; compare this with the more formal term, "***Fu-ren***" (Mme.), also see *Chapter 10;* p. 152

Nan-king (Nanking, Nanjing): *nan* (southern), *king* (capital); Nanjing, the capital city of many dynasties; p. 156

Old, "*lao:*" (old), a term used before the surname of an acquaintance to show familiarity; a form of endearment, as in "*Lao Xiong,*" old elder brother [*Prologue*]; p. 152

Rude, "***mayo gwei'ju, mayo li'mao:***" *mayo* (do not have), *gwei ju* (order), *li mao* (civility, politeness); no manners; p. 152

Footnotes:
[1]Du Fu (712-770), a friend and contemporary of the great Chinese poet Li Bai (see, p. 157), was acclaimed by his countrymen as the Lord of Verse who "seeks after simplicity ... as a diver seeks for gold" (Cranmer-Byng, 1927). Du Fu was renowned not only for his verse, but also for his painting.

[2]The Tang Dynasty (618-906 AD) is considered to have been China's "Golden Ages of Poetry." In 1707, a mammoth collection of 48,900 Tang poems was published in a set of 30 volumes (Giles, 1927). Of these, the "*Three-Hundred Poems of Tang*" contains popular selected entries (see p. xxxv).

REFERENCES

Associated Press (1995) Six in WWII Japanese army group describe atrocities, *Los Angeles Times* (Feb 12).

Associated Press (2002) Saburo Ienaga, 89, fought censorship, *Los Angeles Times*, Obituaries (Dec 2).

Asuma, S (1999) *Diary of Shiro Asuma* (English translation), Jiangsu Edu. Publ., Nanjing, China, 505 pp.

Barton, S (1994) Taming the river wild, *Time Magazine*, pp. 62-64 (Dec 19).

Beijing Daily (2000) Water of the Yellow River will come clear in 50 years (Aug 20).

Bengelsdorf, IS (1992) China caught between progress and preservation, *Blade-Citizen,* CA, p. B6 (Jul 16).

Bodde, D (1967) *Peking Diary: 1948-1949, A Year of Revolution,* Fawcett World Library, NY, 288 pp.

Boorman, HL, Cheng, JKH, eds (1970) *Biographical Dictionary of Republican of China,* Columbia Univ. Press, NY, pp. 115-116.

Boorman, HL, Howard, RC, eds (1967) *Biographical Dictionary of Republican of China,* Columbia Univ. Press, NY, pp. 47-52, 109-111, 319-338.

Brazil, J (1995) Truth emerging on ailing POWs, Japan germ unit, *Los Angeles Times*, pp. A1, A18 (Mar 20).

Bryant, A (1959) *Triumph in the West – A history of the War Years Based on the Diaries of Field-Marshall Lord Alan Brooke, Chief of the Imperial General Staff,* Greenwood Press, Westport, CT.

Bullitt, WC (1946) A report to the American people on China, *Life Magazine* (Oct. 13).

Bullitt, WC (1947) How we won the war and lost the peace, *Life Magazine* (Dec. 22).

Butler, L (2004) *Yangtze Remembered, the River beneath the Lake,* Stanford Univ. Press, Palo Alto, CA, 194 pp.

CCTV9 (2005) Repatriation of WWII Japanese military immigrants from Manchuria, Los Angeles *Adelphia Channel 180*, China international documentary (Jan 16).

Chang, I (1997) *The Rape of Nanking, the Forgotten Holocaust of World War II,* Penguin Books, NY, 290 pp.

Chenyu Story (1980) *Historical Stories of Ready-Made Sayings* (*Chenyu*), Siyi Book Store, Tainan, Taiwan, 366 pp (in Chinese).

China Science & Technology Newsletter (2004) Special Issues: China's top ten S & T Developments in 2003, no. 354, p. 2 (Jan 10).

Chinese Society of Engineers (2002) Past Presidents, Archives of the Chinese Society of Engineers, Taipei, Taiwan (in Chinese).

Chu, H (1999) Yellow River giving China sorrow, *Los Angeles Times*, pp. A1, A11 (Feb 18).

Chu, H (2002) The shoes fit, but feet grow rare, *Los Angeles Times*, pp. A1, A4 (Apr 4).

Ci Hai (1976) *Encyclopedia of Phrases* (vols. I, II; 16th edition), Zhong Hua Publ, Taipei, Taiwan, 3398 pp (in Chinese).

Cranmer-Byng, L (1928) To the City of Nan-King, a poem by Li Bai (English translation), In: JL French, ed, *Lotus and Chrysanthemum, An Anthology of Chinese and Japanese Poetry*, Horace Liveright Publ., NY, p. 75.

Dag Hammarkjöld Library (2008) UN ECAFE Bureau of Flood Control and Water Resources Development, UNBISnet, 3pp.

Donovan, RJ (1982) *Tumultuous Years: The Presidency of Harry S. Truman 1949 to 1953*, WW Norton, NY, 444 pp.

Duke, JA (2002) *Handbook of Medical Herbs*, 2nd edition, CRC Press, Boca Raton, LA, 870 pp.

Durdin, T (1946) China tells Soviet she wants Darien, *NY Times*, p.12 (Jun 26).

Efron, S (1994) Japan's high court rules against rewriting history, *Los Angeles Times*, pp. A1, A14 (Jul 15).

Efron, S (1999) War again is raging over Japan's role in 'Nanking massacre', *Los Angeles Times*, p. A32 (Jun 6).

Elman, BA (2001) *From Philosophy to Philology, Intellectual and Social Aspects of Change in Late Imperial China*, 2nd edition, UCLA Asian Pacific Monograph Series, Univ. California., Los Angeles, 346 pp.

Fairbank, JK (1983) *The United States and China*, 4th edition, Harvard Univ. Press, Cambridge, MA, 632 pp.

Fang, YG (2004) De Gaulle's Invitation to Shen Yi, *Qiao News*: Historical Events, U.S. Publ. p. C2 (in Chinese).

Farley, M (2005) Annan has a plan to revitalize U.N., *Los Angeles Times*, pp. A1, A10 (Mar 19).

Fleming, R (1946) Damming the Yangtze Gorge, *Popular Mechanics*, vol. 85, pp. 100-103.

Fu, LC (1984) *Chinese History* (vols. I, II), Great China Textbook Publ., Taipei, Taiwan, 793 pp (in Chinese).

Giles, HA (1924) A History of Chinese Literature (Appleton), In: JL French, ed, *Lotus and Chrysanthemum, An Anthology of Chinese and Japanese Poetry* (1928), Horace Liveright Publ., NY, pp. 221-222.

Hahn, E (1941) *The Soong Sisters*, Doubleday, Doran, NY, 349 pp.

Harney, A (2004) Distrust of Japan lives on in hearts of young Chinese, *Financial Times*, p. 4 (Mar 27-28).

Harrison, K (2000) *The Binding Chair*, Clays Ltd., St. Ives Plc, England, 312 pp.

Hillel, D (1991) Lash of the dragon -- A millennia of struggles to subdue it, China's mighty Yellow River remains untamed, *Natural History* (Aug), pp. 29-37.

Holley, D (1992) Huge Yangtze River Dam "Okd" by China's parliament, *Los Angeles Times*, pp. A1, A8.

Hori, H (2000) *The Mekong: Environment and Development*, U.N. Univ. Press, Tokyo, 398 pp.

Hsü, ICY (1975) *The Rise of Modern China*, Oxford Univ. Press, NY, 1002 pp.

Hu, S (1962) *Selected Writings of Hu Shih*, Far Eastern Library Publ., Taipei, Taiwan, 373 pp (in Chinese).

Hu, S (1967) China in Stalin's Grand Strategy [an address to the United Nations, Sept 26, 1957], Zhong-hua Publ, Taipei, Taiwan, 76 pp (in Chinese and English).

Hu, S (1969) *History of Bai-hua*, Hu Shih Memorial Museum, Taipei, Taiwan, 407 pp (in Chinese).

Hu, S (1971) *On the Lake* (poem) 1920, In: *Collections of Pursuits [Ch'ang-shi ji]*, Mei Ya Publ., Taipei, Taiwan, pp. 207-208, (in Chinese).

In, Y (1935, 1st edition; 1938, 2nd edition) *Diary from Europe*, Zhong-hua Publ., Shanghai, China (in Chinese).

In, Y (1971) *Journey of Seventy Days* (vols. I, II), Biographical Literary Publ. [Zhuanji Wenxue], Taipei, Taiwan, 327 pp (in Chinese).

Jameson, S (1992) Japan admits sexual slavery in WWII, express remorse, *Los Angeles Times,* pp. A1, A14 (Jul 7).

Jameson, S (1994) Japan plans a fund as amends of sex slaves, *Los Angeles Times,* pp. A1, A21 (Aug 30).

Jenkins, D (1968) The lower Mekong scheme, In: *Asian Survey,* Univ. Calif. Press, Oakland, pp. 456-464.

Johnson, P (1983) *Modern Times – The World from the Twenties to the Eighties,* Harper Perennial, Harper-Collins, NY, 817 pp.

Kahn EK, Jr. (1976) *The China Hands – America's Foreign Service Officers and What Befell Them,* Penguin Books, NY, 337 pp.

Kang, C (1995) Breaking silence, *Los Angeles Times,* pp. B1, B3 (Aug 12).

Kempster, N (1995) U.S. to block aid for China dam-project, *Los Angeles Times,* p. A10 (Oct 15).

Kristof, L. (1993) China breaks grounds for world's largest dam, *New York Times,* pp. B5, B6 (Jun 22).

Life Magazine (1949) The looting of Nanking, photographs by Henri Cartier-Bresson, pp. 35-39 (May 9).

Lin, BW (2000) *Soong MayLing, The Cross-Century First Lady,* Shi-pao Cultural Publ., Taipei, Taiwan, 556 pp (in Chinese).

Lin, GZ, Hsu XH, Yang XY, Hsu HY (1998) Engineering of China's Yangtze Jiang Three Gorges Dam (1946-47): 1997 Anniversary of the Dam's initial design group, Yuan Mung Group Publ., Cerritos, CA, 149 pp (in Chinese).

Los Angeles Times (1994) A royal denunciation of horrors, p. B7 (Jul 9).

Los Angeles Times (2003) UC Berkeley Professor Tung Yen Ling, Obituaries (Oct).

Los Angeles Times (2004) French photographer Henri Catier-Bresson (1908-2004), Obituaries (Aug 3).

Lover, B (2008) History behind Sheaffer pens, *Google,* blog on Fountain Pens, 2 pp.

Lower Mekong River Commission, MRC, http:www.mrcunkong.org/ start1999/05/07.

Magnier, M (2003) Yayori Matsui, 68, Japanese journalist became noted women's rights activist, *Los Angeles Times*, Obituaries, p. B10 (Jan 8).

Magnier, M (2005) Taiwanese denounce anti-secession plan, *Los Angeles Times*, p. A3 (Mar 7).

Marshall, T, Magnier, M (2004) Taiwan's Chen defends move on referendum, *Los Angeles Times*, pp. A1, A5 (Feb 8).

Meisler, S (1995) In Washington a WWII icon dazzles dignitaries once more, *Los Angeles Times*, p. A5 (Jul 27).

Melby, JF (1971) *The Mandate of Heaven – Record of a Civil War, China 1945-49*, Anchor Books, Doubleday, Garden City, NY, 378 pp.

Miller, M (1984) *Plain Speaking: An Oral Biography of Harry S. Truman,* Berkeley Publ. Grp., NY, 480 pp.

Mills, H (1999) The living Buddha, *Los Angeles Times*, Book Reviews, pp. 8-9 (Jul 25).

Moffet, S, Hamilton, D (1994) Protest and praise greet royal visitors, *Los Angeles Times*, pp. B1, B3 (Jun 22).

MRC (Mekong River Commission) Annual Report (2003), http:www.Google.com.

MRC (Mekong River Commission) Annual Report (2006), http:www.Google.com.

Murphy, DE (1994) Germany asks for Poland's forgiveness, Europe: Apology issued on the 50th Anniversary of the Warsaw Uprising, *Los Angeles Times*, pp. A1, A6 (Aug 2).

Ni, CC (2005) China Environmental Agency takes on giant dam corporation, *Los Angeles Times*, p. A3 (Feb 3).

Parade Magazine (2004) A vision of greatness: Eddie Adams (1933-2004), p. 12 (Dec 26).

Qian CZ (1998) *Memoir of Qian Changzhao*, China Historical Publ., Beijing, China, 204 pp (in Chinese).

Rabe, J (1998) *The Good Man of Nanking*, Vintage Books, N.Y., 294 pp.

Reuters (2002) Yangtze blockage complete, *Los Angeles Times*, p. A5 (Nov 7).

Rhodes, BD (1989) From Cooksville to Chungking: The dam-designing career of John L. Savage, *Wisconsin Magazine of History*, vol. 72, pp. 243-272.

Roberts, JAG (1999) *A Concise History of China*, Harvard Univ. Press, Cambridge, MA, 341 pp.

Salonga, R (2001) Japanese journalist speaks about tribunal: slavery – Matsui talks on punishing war crimes in "comfort women" system, *Daily Bruin*, Univ. Calif., Los Angeles (Feb 7).

Seagrave, S (1985) *The Soong Dynasty*, Harper and Row, NY, 532 pp.

See, L (2003) Waters of Three Gorges Dam will wash over world culture, *Los Angeles Times* (Jul 8).

Sempa, FP (2003) *William C. Bullitt, Diplomat and Prophet*, 15 pp (Feb), http:www.AmericanDiplomacy.org

Service, JS (1975) *Lost Chance in China: the World War II Dispatches of John S. Service*, JW Esherick, ed, First Vintage Books, Random House, NY, 411 pp.

Shen, I (1985) *Shen Inyeening: Autobiography*, Biographical Literary Publ. Co. [Zhuanji Wenxue], Taipei, Taiwan, 373 pp (in Chinese).

Shen, Y (1970) Ten Years in the Shanghai Municipal Bureau of Public Works, Literary Publ. Co. [Zhuanji Wenxue], Taipei, Taiwan, vol. 2, pp. 11-18 (in Chinese).

Shen, Y (1974) *The Huang He [Yellow River] Problem, a Discussion*, Sung-wu Publ. Co., Taipei, Taiwan, 410 pp (in Chinese).

Shen, Y (1985) *Shen Yi: An Autobiography*, Biographical Literary Publ. Co. [Zhuanji Wenxue], Taipei, Taiwan, 311 pp (in Chinese).

Shen, YF (2002) Shen Yi in Nanjing, *Chinese Community News - Hwa Sheng*, U.S. Publ., p. 14 (Oct 10) (in Chinese).

Smith, AH (1965) *Proverbs and Common Sayings from the Chinese*, Paragon Reprints, Dover, NY, 374 pp.

Stuart, JL (1954) *Fifty Years in China: the Memoir of John Leighton Stuart, Missionary and Ambassador*, Random House, NY.

Sullivan, M (1999) Daring experiments in styles, *Chronicle of Higher Education*, p. B20 (Oct. 29).

Summerfield, J (1992) Fodor's China, a Complete Guide, Fodor's Travel Publ., NY, 593 pp.

Sun, YF (1992) *From Venice to Osaka: A voyage into Ancient Chinese Civilization, UNESCO Retraces the Maritime Silk Route,* Pictorial Publ. House, Beijing, China, 264 pp.

Tempest, R (1995) Deng's failing health gives boost to huge dam project, *Los Angeles Times,* pp. A1, A9 (Feb 6).

Time Magazine (1946) Earthquake Man [Dr. Wong Wen-hao], (June 07), Google.com.

Time Magazine (1946) Honest and Able, 2 pp (Dec. 02), http:www. time.com/time/magazine/article/09171,887262,00.html.

Timeline China 1929-1995, 1931 Flood on the Huang He River, http:www.google.com.

Timeline China 1929-1995; China's Mekong River (Lancang), http:www.google.com.

Times Wire Services (2005) Premier vows China will never let Taiwan secede, *Los Angeles Times,* p. A4 (Mar 6).

Topping, S (1999) A reporter recalls tumultuous days of revolution in Nanjing, *International Herald Tribune,* p. 6 (Oct 2-3).

Trounson, R (2001) Sheldon Harris, historian detailed Japan's germ warfare, *Los Angeles Times,* Obituaries (Sept 6).

Truman, M (1993) *Harry S. Truman,* Avon Books, NY, 602 pp.

Tuchman, BW (1972) *Stillwell and the American Experience in China, 1911-45,* Bantam, NY, 794 pp.

UN Regional Commissions (2008) http:www.un.org/issues/reg-comm.html

Verhovek, SA (2003) A reservoir of pride, dread, *Los Angeles Times,* pp. A1, A6 (Jun 2).

Wakeman, F, Jr (1995) Licensing Leisure: The Chinese Nationalists' attempt to regulate Shanghai, 1927-49, *J. Asian Study,* vol. 54, pp. 12-42.

Wallace, B (2004) Japan marks WWII surrender with mixed sentiments, *Los Angeles Times,* p. A3 (Aug 15).

Wallace, B (2006) Corporate giants pressure Japan's politicians to stop visiting war shrine, *Los Angeles Times,* p. A32 (May 28).

Wallace, B (2007) WWII sex slavery issue revived, *Los Angeles Times,* p. A3 (Mar 02).

Wallace, B, Ueno, H (2008) Japanese cinemas bow out of showing film on war shrine, *Los Angeles Times,* p. A3 (Apr 2).

Watanabe, T (1994) Hirohito's brother assailed Japan's WWII aggression, *Los Angeles Times,* pp. A1, A13 (Jul 7).

Watanabe, T, Walsh, MW (1995) Facing the demons of war guilt, *Los Angeles Times,* pp. A1, A12-13.

Welkos, RW (2008) Remembering Nanking, *Los Angeles Times,* p. E4 (Jan. 11).

Wightman, D (1963) *Toward Economic Cooperation in Asia: The United Nations Economic Commission for Asia and the Far East,* Yale Univ. Press, New Haven, CT, 400 pp.

Woo, E (2003) Charismatic, feared emissary of China's Nationalist Regime, *Los Angeles Times,* pp. A1, A10-11 (Oct 25).

Xinhua China Daily (2004) Let the dead be remembered, Beijing (Apr 3, 4) (in Chinese).

Xin Hua Dictionary (Zidian) (1982) New Chinese Dictionary, Chinese-English Pinyin Dictionary, Shang-wu Publ., Beijing, 636 pp (in Chinese).

Xu, ZG (1987) *Massacre of Nanking: A 50th Anniversary Remembrance of the World War against Japan and the Fascists,* Jiangsu Literary Publ., Jiangsu, China, 331 pp (in Chinese).

Yang, CQ (2004) Construction of the Three Gorges Dam, Ten Unexpected Woes, *U.S. Wei News* p. A6 (Jun 24) (in Chinese).

Zhang, ZY (2000) *Dictionary of Chenyu,* Ziyang Publ., Taiwan, 714 pp (in Chinese).

Zhu, CS, ed. (2002) *The Picture Collection of Nanjing Massacre and International Rescue,* Jiangsu Ancient Book Publ. House, Nanjing, China, 205 pp (in Chinese and English).

AUTHOR BIOGRAPHY

Author Inyeening Shen (1907-99), an acclaimed writer, essayist, poet and artist, was a graduate of the Shanghai Muer-tang Women's Academy (1923). She received an honorary Ph.D. degree from the Chinese Institute of Culture, Taiwan (1976), where she was Professor of Chinese Literature.

Editor, J. Shen-Miller Schopf, daughter of the author, received advanced degrees from Michigan State University. She has held positions at the Argonne National Laboratory, Illinois, the U.S. National Science Foundation, Washington, D.C., and the University of California, Los Angeles. An internationally known plant biologist, she has germinated seeds of sacred lotus (*Nelumbo nucifera*) 1300 years old, among the longest living seeds known to science. Her current studies focus on understanding the biochemical and genetic bases of such exceptional longevity.

"*NANKING*" is a deeply moving personal account by the First Lady of the Nationalist Capital of China during a pivotal time in the emergence of the Peoples Republic of China. Inyeening Shen began to write this book in 1947 in Nanking, where her husband, Dr. Shen Yi (1901-80), was Mayor of the last capital of the Nationalist Government on the China mainland. After the fall of Chiang Kai-shek's Nationalists in 1949, she continued her work in Bangkok, Thailand, where she and her family had taken up residence. Although the manuscript was finished in 1954, she held off publication fearing that her criticism of corruption and incompetence would offend the Nationalist Government.

This is the Inyeening Shen's sole work in English, a skill she learned in missionary schools where her Buddhist parents had placed her only because they thought such western Christian schooling would be of little consequence, occupying their daughter's time but not taxing her mind. The Chinese feudal attitude was that for a proper wife, having a "mindless" demeanor was something of a virtue. Inyeening Shen was a mother of seven. But given a choice, she would certainly have preferred not to raise a family. She was the product of an earlier time— when woman's ambition was suppressed by tradition—an entrenched culture that molded her being and constrained the course of her life. Throughout it all she maintained a fierce determination to achieve. Not only a writer, she was also an accomplished artist—a prize student of China's grandmaster Chang Ta-ch'ien who admiringly inscribed her "*White Sacred Lotus*" painting (included in this book, Plate 2).

With her nation beset by corruption and inflation, her reminiscences of Nanking in 1946-48 vividly chronicle the struggles she encountered in maintaining the mayoral household, hosting visiting dignitaries, forging friendships with the "high and mighty" and those well beneath her station, overseeing the construction of her very own home, interacting with Chairman Chiang Kai-shek's imperious wife, Mme. Soong Mayling, and organizing an impressive relief effort for Nanking's refugees.

Given encouragement of the Chinese educator/philosopher/diplomat Dr. Hu Shih, she later published her autobiography. Included here is a translation of her "*Auto-Bio-Poetry*," a poem that recounts the first half of her life including her time in Nanjing. In her waning years, she entrusted the manuscript of this book to her daughter who has edited it for publication. With the help of Jean Stone, editor and wife of the American biographical novelist Irving Stone, and the Author's award-winning author/editor son-in-law, UCLA Professor J. William Schopf, Inyeening Shen's deeply moving personal story is now ready for the world.

This book is written for a general autobiographical audience in addition to those having historical and scholarly interests.

INDEX

187